Beautiful C++

Beautiful C++

30 Core Guidelines for Writing Clean, Safe, and Fast Code

J. Guy Davidson
Kate Gregory

Addison-Wesley

Boston • Columbus • New York • San Francisco • Amsterdam • Cape Town
Dubai • London • Madrid • Milan • Munich • Paris • Montreal • Toronto • Delhi • Mexico City
São Paulo • Sydney • Hong Kong • Seoul • Singapore • Taipei • Tokyo

Many of the designations used by manufacturers and sellers to distinguish their products are claimed as trademarks. Where those designations appear in this book, and the publisher was aware of a trademark claim, the designations have been printed with initial capital letters or in all capitals.

The authors and publisher have taken care in the preparation of this book, but make no expressed or implied warranty of any kind and assume no responsibility for errors or omissions. No liability is assumed for incidental or consequential damages in connection with or arising out of the use of the information or programs contained herein.

For information about buying this title in bulk quantities, or for special sales opportunities (which may include electronic versions; custom cover designs; and content particular to your business, training goals, marketing focus, or branding interests), please contact our corporate sales department at corpsales@pearsoned.com or (800) 382-3419.

For government sales inquiries, please contact governmentsales@pearsoned.com.

For questions about sales outside the U.S., please contact intlcs@pearson.com.

Visit us on the Web: informit.com/aw.

Library of Congress Control Number: 2021947544

Copyright © 2022 Pearson Education, Inc.

Cover image: IROOM STOCK/Shutterstock

All rights reserved. This publication is protected by copyright, and permission must be obtained from the publisher prior to any prohibited reproduction, storage in a retrieval system, or transmission in any form or by any means, electronic, mechanical, photocopying, recording, or likewise. For information regarding permissions, request forms and the appropriate contacts within the Pearson Education Global Rights & Permissions Department, please visit www.pearson.com/permissions.

ISBN-13: 978-0-13-764784-2
ISBN-10: 0-13-764784-0

1 2021

Pearson's Commitment to Diversity, Equity, and Inclusion

Pearson is dedicated to creating bias-free content that reflects the diversity of all learners. We embrace the many dimensions of diversity, including but not limited to race, ethnicity, gender, socioeconomic status, ability, age, sexual orientation, and religious or political beliefs.

Education is a powerful force for equity and change in our world. It has the potential to deliver opportunities that improve lives and enable economic mobility. As we work with authors to create content for every product and service, we acknowledge our responsibility to demonstrate inclusivity and incorporate diverse scholarship so that everyone can achieve their potential through learning. As the world's leading learning company, we have a duty to help drive change and live up to our purpose to help more people create a better life for themselves and to create a better world.

Our ambition is to purposefully contribute to a world where:

- Everyone has an equitable and lifelong opportunity to succeed through learning.
- Our educational products and services are inclusive and represent the rich diversity of learners.
- Our educational content accurately reflects the histories and experiences of the learners we serve.
- Our educational content prompts deeper discussions with learners and motivates them to expand their own learning (and worldview).

While we work hard to present unbiased content, we want to hear from you about any concerns or needs with this Pearson product so that we can investigate and address them.

- Please contact us with concerns about any potential bias at https://www.pearson.com/report-bias.html.

To Bryn

To Sinead

To Rory and Lois

C.47: Much love, JGD

To Jim Allison, though he is unlikely to see it. Research works. And to Chloe and Aisha who have not been at the front of books before, KMG

Contents

Selected C++ Core Guidelines

P.2: Write in ISO Standard C++ (*Chapter 1.1*)
https://isocpp.github.io/CppCoreGuidelines/CppCoreGuidelines#Rp-Cplusplus

P.4: Ideally, a program should be statically type safe (*Chapter 5.1*)
https://isocpp.github.io/CppCoreGuidelines/CppCoreGuidelines#Rp-typesafe

P.10: Prefer immutable data to mutable data (*Chapter 5.2*)
https://isocpp.github.io/CppCoreGuidelines/CppCoreGuidelines#Rp-mutable

P.11: Encapsulate messy constructs, rather than spreading through the code (*Chapter 2.1*)
https://isocpp.github.io/CppCoreGuidelines/CppCoreGuidelines#Rp-library

I.3: Avoid singletons (*Chapter 3.2*)
https://isocpp.github.io/CppCoreGuidelines/CppCoreGuidelines#Ri-singleton

I.11: Never transfer ownership by a raw pointer (T*) or reference (T&) (*Chapter 3.1*)
https://isocpp.github.io/CppCoreGuidelines/CppCoreGuidelines#Ri-raw

I.23: Keep the number of function arguments low (*Chapter 2.2*)
https://isocpp.github.io/CppCoreGuidelines/CppCoreGuidelines#Ri-nargs

I.26: If you want a cross-compiler ABI, use a C-style subset (*Chapter 2.3*)
https://isocpp.github.io/CppCoreGuidelines/CppCoreGuidelines#Ri-abi

I.30: Encapsulate rule violations (*Chapter 5.3*)
https://isocpp.github.io/CppCoreGuidelines/CppCoreGuidelines#Ri-encapsulate

F.21: To return multiple "out" values, prefer returning a struct or tuple (*Chapter 4.1*)
https://isocpp.github.io/CppCoreGuidelines/CppCoreGuidelines#Rf-out-multi

F.51: Where there is a choice, prefer default arguments over overloading (*Chapter 1.2*)
https://isocpp.github.io/CppCoreGuidelines/CppCoreGuidelines#Rf-default-args

C.45: Don't define a default constructor that only initializes data members; use in-class member initializers instead (*Chapter 1.3*)
https://isocpp.github.io/CppCoreGuidelines/CppCoreGuidelines#Rc-default

C.47: Define and initialize member variables in the order of member declaration (*Chapter 2.4*)
https://isocpp.github.io/CppCoreGuidelines/CppCoreGuidelines#Rc-order

C.90: Rely on constructors and assignment operators, not memset and memcpy (*Chapter 3.3*)
https://isocpp.github.io/CppCoreGuidelines/CppCoreGuidelines#Rc-memset

C.131: Avoid trivial getters and setters (*Chapter 1.4*)
https://isocpp.github.io/CppCoreGuidelines/CppCoreGuidelines#Rf-default-args

Enum.3: Prefer class enums over "plain" enums (*Chapter 4.2*)
https://isocpp.github.io/CppCoreGuidelines/CppCoreGuidelines#Renum-class

ES.5: Keep scopes small (*Chapter 4.3*)
https://isocpp.github.io/CppCoreGuidelines/CppCoreGuidelines#Res-scope

ES.10: Declare one name (only) per declaration (*Chapter 1.5*)
https://isocpp.github.io/CppCoreGuidelines/CppCoreGuidelines#Rconc-task

ES.22: Don't declare a variable until you have a value to initialize it with (*Chapter 5.4*)
https://isocpp.github.io/CppCoreGuidelines/CppCoreGuidelines#Rp-typesafe

ES.50: Don't cast away const (*Chapter 3.4*)
https://isocpp.github.io/CppCoreGuidelines/CppCoreGuidelines#Res-casts-const

Per.7: Design to enable optimization (*Chapter 5.5*)
https://isocpp.github.io/CppCoreGuidelines/CppCoreGuidelines#Rper-efficiency

CP.3: Minimize explicit sharing of writable data (*Chapter 2.5*)
https://isocpp.github.io/CppCoreGuidelines/CppCoreGuidelines#Rconc-data

E.6: Use RAII to prevent leaks (*Chapter 5.6*)
https://isocpp.github.io/CppCoreGuidelines/CppCoreGuidelines#Re-raii

E.28: Avoid error handling based on global state (e.g. errno) (*Chapter 3.5*)
https://isocpp.github.io/CppCoreGuidelines/CppCoreGuidelines#Re-no-throw

Con.5: Use constexpr for values that can be computed at compile time (*Chapter 4.4*)
https://isocpp.github.io/CppCoreGuidelines/CppCoreGuidelines#Rconst-constexpr

T.1: Use templates to raise the level of abstraction of code (*Chapter 4.5*)
https://isocpp.github.io/CppCoreGuidelines/CppCoreGuidelines#Rt-raise

T.10: Specify concepts for all template arguments (*Chapter 4.6*)
https://isocpp.github.io/CppCoreGuidelines/CppCoreGuidelines#Rt-concepts

T.120: Use template metaprogramming only when you really need to (*Chapter 2.6*)
https://isocpp.github.io/CppCoreGuidelines/CppCoreGuidelines#Rt-metameta

SF.7: Don't write using namespace at global scope in a header file (*Chapter 3.6*)
https://isocpp.github.io/CppCoreGuidelines/CppCoreGuidelines#Rs-using-directive

NR.2: Don't insist to have only a single return-statement in a function (*Chapter 1.6*)
https://isocpp.github.io/CppCoreGuidelines/CppCoreGuidelines#Rnr-single-return

Foreword

I enjoyed reading this book. I enjoyed it especially because it presents the C++ Core Guidelines (CG) very differently from how the CG itself does it. The CG presents its rules relatively tersely in a fixed format. The CG rules are often expressed in language-technical terms with an emphasis on enforcement through static analysis. This book tells stories, many coming from the games industry based on the evolution of code and techniques over decades. It presents the rules from a developer's point of view with an emphasis on what benefits can be obtained from following the rules and what nightmares can result from ignoring them. There are more extensive discussions of the motivation for rules than the CG themselves can offer.

The CG aims for a degree of completeness. Naturally, a set of rules for writing good code in general cannot be complete, but the necessary degree of completeness implies that the CG are not meant for a systematic read. I recommend the introduction and the philosophy section to get an impression of the aims of the CG and its conceptual framework. However, for a selective tour of the CG guided by taste, perspective, and experience, read the book. For true geeks, it is an easy and entertaining read. For most software developers, it offers something new and useful.

—Bjarne Stroustrup
June 2021

Preface

The complexity of writing C++ is diminishing with each new standard and each new piece of teaching literature. Conferences, blogs, and books abound, and this is a good thing. The world does not have enough engineers of sufficient quality to solve the very real problems we face.

Despite the continuing simplification of the language, there is still much to learn about how to write good C++. Bjarne Stroustrup, the inventor of C++, and Herb Sutter, the convenor of the standards body that maintains C++, have devoted considerable resources to creating teaching materials for both learning C++ and writing better C++. These volumes include *The C++ Programming Language*[1] and *A Tour of C++*,[2] as well as *Exceptional C++*[3] and *C++ Coding Standards*.[4]

The problem with books, even this modest volume, is that they represent a snapshot in time of the state of affairs, yet C++ is a continuously evolving language. What was good advice in 1998 may no longer be such a smart idea. An evolving language needs an evolving guide.

An online resource, C++ Core Guidelines,[5] was launched at the CppCon Conference in 2015 by Bjarne Stroustrup and Herb Sutter during their two[6] keynote[7] talks. The guidelines provide excellent, simple advice for improving your C++ style such that you can write correct, performant, and efficient code at your first attempt. It is the evolving guide that C++ practitioners need, and the authors will be delighted to review pull requests with corrections and improvements. Everyone, from beginners to veterans, should be able to follow its advisories.

1. Stroustrup, B, 2013. *The C++ Programming Language, Fourth Edition*. Boston: Addison-Wesley.
2. Stroustrup, B, 2018. *A Tour of C++, Second Edition*. Boston: Addison-Wesley.
3. Sutter, H, 1999. *Exceptional C++*. Reading, MA: Addison-Wesley.
4. Sutter, H, and Alexandrescu, A, 2004. *C++ Coding Standards*. Boston: Addison-Wesley.
5. Isocpp.github.io. 2021. C++ Core Guidelines. Copyright © Standard C++ Foundation and its contributors. Available at: https://isocpp.github.io/CppCoreGuidelines/CppCoreGuidelines Accessed 16 July 2021.
6. Youtube.com. 2021. CppCon 2015: Bjarne Stroustrup "Writing Good C++14". Available at: https://www.youtube.com/watch?v=1OEu9C51K2A Accessed 16 July 2021.
7. Youtube.com. 2021. CppCon 2015: Herb Sutter "Writing Good C++14... By Default." Available at: https://www.youtube.com/watch?v=hEx5DNLWGgA Accessed 16 July 2021.

The guidelines provide excellent, simple advice for improving your C++ style such that you can write correct, performant, and efficient code at your first attempt.

At the end of February 2020, on the #include discord,[8] Kate Gregory canvassed interest in producing a book about the Core Guidelines and I cautiously jumped at the chance. Kate gave a talk at CppCon 2017[9] where she looked at just 10 of the Core Guidelines. I share her enthusiasm for promoting better programming. I am the Head of Engineering Practice at Creative Assembly, Britain's oldest and largest game development studio, where I have spent a lot of the past 20-plus years helping to turn our fine engineers into even greater engineers. It is our observation that, despite the accessibility and simplicity of the Core Guidelines, many developers are not especially familiar with them. We want to promote their use, and we decided to write this book because there is not enough literature about them.

The Core Guidelines can be found at https://isocpp.github.io/CppCoreGuidelines/CppCoreGuidelines. They are absolutely jam-packed with excellent advice: indeed, it is hard to know where to start. Reading from the top to the bottom is feasible, but it is a tall order to grasp the entire set of advisories without repeated reading. They are organized into 22 major sections with titles like "Interfaces," "Functions," "Concurrency," and so on. Each section is composed of individual guidelines, sometimes a few, sometimes dozens. The guidelines are identified by their major section letter, then their number within the section, separated by a period. For example, "F.3: Keep functions short and simple" is the third guideline in section F, "Functions."

Each guideline is ordered in a similar way. It starts with the title of the guideline, which is presented as an action (do this, don't do this, avoid this, prefer this) followed by a reason and some examples, and possibly an exception to the guideline. Finally, there is a note on how to enforce the guideline. Enforcement notes range from advice to authors of static analysis tools to hints on how to conduct a code review. There is a skill to reading them, it turns out; deciding which ones to prioritize in your own code is a matter of personal discovery. Let us show you how to start taking advantage of their wisdom.

There are some sharp edges in C++ as well as some dusty corners that are not visited so often in modern C++. We want to steer you away from these. We want to show you that C++ does not have to be difficult, complex, or something that most developers cannot be trusted with.

8. #include <C++>. 2021. #include <C++>. Available at: https://www.includecpp.org/ Accessed 16 July 2021.

9. Youtube.com. 2021. CppCon 2017: Kate Gregory "10 Core Guidelines You Need to Start Using Now." Available at: https://www.youtube.com/watch?v=XkDEzfpdcSg Accessed 16 July 2021.

About This Book

In this book we offer what we consider to be 30 of the best C++ Core Guidelines. By thoroughly explaining these guidelines we hope that you will at least abide by them, even if you decide against investigating the remainder. The set that we have chosen are not necessarily the most important. However, they are certainly the set that will change your code for the better immediately. Of course, we hope that you will also see that there are many other good guidelines you could also follow. We hope that you will read the remainder and try them out in your code. Just as the Core Guidelines are aimed at all C++ developers with all levels of experience, so is this book aimed at the same set of people. The material does not increase in complexity as the book progresses, nor is there a required order in which to read the chapters. They are independent of one another, although they may explicitly refer to other chapters. We kept each chapter to about three thousand words, so you may decide that this is a bedside volume rather than a textbook. The purpose is not to teach you C++, but to advise you how to improve your style.

We divided the guidelines into five sections of six chapters, following Kate's original presentation to CppCon in 2017. In Section 1, "Bikeshedding is bad," we present guidelines that allow you to simply make a decision about when to do A or B, for some particular set of As and Bs, and move on with the minimum of fuss and argument. "Bikeshedding"[10] derives from C. Northcote Parkinson's "law of triviality," an argument that organization members typically give disproportionate weight to trivial issues, such as the color to paint a bikeshed compared to the testing criteria for the nuclear power station to which it is attached, because it is the one thing everyone knows something about.

In Section 2, "Don't hurt yourself," we present guidelines for preventing personal injury while writing code. One of the problems with the residual complexity of C++ is that there are several places where you can shoot yourself in the foot with ease. For example, while it is legal to populate a constructor initialization list in any order, it is never wise to do so.

Section 3 is named "Stop using that" and deals with parts of the language that are retained for backward compatibility reasons, along with pieces of advice that used to be valuable, but which have been superseded by developments in the language. As C++ evolves, things that seemed like a good idea at the time occasionally reveal themselves as rather less valuable than was originally expected. The standardization process fixes these things, but everyone needs to stay informed about them because you may come across examples if you find yourself working with a legacy codebase. C++ offers a guarantee of backward compatibility: code written 50 years ago in C should still compile today.

10. 2021. Available at: https://exceptionnotfound.net/bikeshedding-the-daily-software-anti-pattern/ Accessed 16 July 2021.

Section 4 follows on from this with the title "Use this new thing properly." Things like concepts, `constexpr`, structured binding, and so on need care when being deployed. Again, C++ is an evolving standard and new things appear with each release, all of which require some teaching to back them up. Although this text does not aim to teach you the new features of C++20, these guidelines do give you a flavor of how to apprehend novel features.

Section 5, the final section, is titled "Write code well by default." These are simple guidelines that, if followed, will result in you generating good code without having to think too hard about what is going on. They lead to the production of good idiomatic C++ which will be understood and appreciated by your colleagues.

Throughout the book, as with any good text, themes emerge and are developed. Part of the fun of writing this book, which I hope will translate to the reading of it too, has been seeing what motivates the guidelines and introspecting about the wider application of these motivations. Many of the guidelines, when squinted at carefully with the sun in the right place, restate some of the fundamental truths of software engineering in different ways. Extracting those truths will greatly improve your programming practice.

We truly hope you enjoy and profit from this book.

Access the Code

All of the code is available at the Compiler Explorer website. Matt Godbolt has kindly reserved stable links for each chapter which are formed by joining https://godbolt.org/z/cg30-ch and the chapter number. For example, https://godbolt.org/z/cg30-ch1.3 will take you to the complete code for Chapter 1.3. We recommend you start with https://godbolt.org/z/cg30-ch0.0 for instructions on how to use the website and interact with the code.

—Guy Davidson, @hatcat01 hatcat.com
—Kate Gregory, @gregcons gregcons.com
October 2021

Register your copy of *Beautiful C++* on the InformIT site for convenient access to updates and/or corrections as they become available. To start the registration process, go to informit.com/register and log in or create an account. Enter the product ISBN (9780137647842) and click Submit. Look on the Registered Products tab for an Access Bonus Content link next to this product, and follow that link to access any available bonus materials. If you would like to be notified of exclusive offers on new editions and updates, please check the box to receive email from us.

Acknowledgments

The years 2020 and 2021 proved to be quite turbulent, and we have many people to thank for their support, both elective and incidental, during the development of this book.

Of course, we would like to thank Bjarne Stroustrup and Herb Sutter for the existence of the Core Guidelines and for their encouragement to write about them. We would also like to thank the attendees of CppCon for providing an audience to explore some of this.

Our families have provided vital support during what is a somewhat solitary process, and without them this effort would have been considerably harder.

The legion of friends on the #include discord, headquartered at includecpp.org, have continued to buoy us up in our daily C++ life since July 2017.[11] We will be donating one-tenth of our earnings from this book to you. All of you, please take a bow.

Several members of the ISO WG21 C++ committee, the body that maintains the standard, offered their help. We would like to thank Michael Wong and Tony van Eerd for their insight.

All the code examples are available at Compiler Explorer[12] with stable and intelligible links thanks to the generous efforts of Matt Godbolt, creator of this fine service. We extend our gratitude and remind him that the C++ community has profited greatly from his exertions.

Cppreference.com[13] was an excellent research tool during the initial preparation of each chapter, so we acknowledge the continuing efforts of the creator and host Nate Kohl, admins Povilas Kanapickas and Sergey Zubkov, along with Tim Song and all the other contributors, and thank them for maintaining this fine resource. They are heroes of the community.

After writing Chapter 3.6 it became clear that considerable inspiration came from an article by Arthur O'Dwyer. Many thanks to him for his continued service to the community. His blog also includes tales of his efforts to uncover some of the earliest computer-based text adventures from the 1970s and 1980s.[14]

A book like this requires an army of proofreaders, so we offer our thanks to Bjarne Stroustrup, Roger Orr, Clare Macrae, Arthur O'Dwyer, Ivan Čukić, Rainer Grimm, and Matt Godbolt.

The team at Addison-Wesley were invaluable, so we offer many thanks to Gregory Doench, Audrey Doyle, Aswini Kumar, Menka Mehta, Julie Nahil, and Mark Taber.

11. https://twitter.com/hatcat01/status/885973064600760320
12. https://godbolt.org/z/cg30-ch0.0
13. https://en.cppreference.com/w
14. https://quuxplusone.github.io/blog

About the Authors

J. Guy Davidson was first introduced to computing by way of the Acorn Atom in 1980. He spent most of his teenage years writing games on a variety of home computers: the Sinclair Research ZX81 and ZX Spectrum, as well as the Atari ST. After taking a mathematics degree from Sussex University, dabbling with theater, and playing keyboards in a soul band, he settled on writing presentation applications in the early 1990s and moved to the games industry in 1997 when he started working for Codemasters in their London office.

In 1999 he joined Creative Assembly where he is now the head of engineering practice. He works on the *Total War* franchise, curating the back catalogue, as well as improving the standard of programming among the engineering team. He serves on the IGGI advisory board, the BSI C++ panel, and the ISO C++ committee. He is the standards officer of the ACCU committee and serves on the program committee of the ACCU conference. He is a moderator on the #include<C++> discord server. He serves as code of conduct lead for several organizations. He can be found speaking at C++ conferences and meetups, particularly about adding linear algebra to the standard library.

In his bountiful spare time he offers C++ mentoring support through Prospela and BAME in Games; addresses schools, colleges, and universities through UKIE, STEMNet, and as a Video Game Ambassador; practices and teaches wu-style tai chi; studies the piano; sings first bass for the Brighton Festival Chorus; runs a local film club; is a voting member of BAFTA; has stood twice (unsuccessfully) for election to local council on behalf of The Green Party of England and Wales; and is trying to learn Spanish. You may occasionally find him at the card table playing bridge for a penny a point. There are probably other things: he is not one for letting the grass grow under his feet.

Kate Gregory met programming, some of her dearest friends, and the man she married all at the University of Waterloo in 1977 and has never looked back. Her degrees are in chemical engineering, which goes to show that you can't tell much about someone from what their degrees are in. Her rural Ontario basement has a small room with ancient computers: PET, C64, home-soldered 6502 system, and so on, as souvenirs of a simpler time. Since 1986 she has been running Gregory Consulting with her husband, helping clients across the world to be better at what they do.

Kate has done keynotes on five continents, loves finding brain-changing truths and then sharing them, and spends a great deal of time volunteering in various C++ activities. Dearest of these is #include <C++>, which is changing this industry to be more welcoming and inclusive. Their Discord server is a warm and gentle place to learn C++ as a beginner, to collaborate on a paper for WG21 to change the language we all use, or anything in between.

She is pulled from her keyboard by her grandchildren, Ontario lakes and campsites, canoe paddles and woodsmoke, and the lure of airports worldwide. A foodie, a board game player, and someone who cannot resist signing up to help with things, she is as active offline as online, but less visible. Since surviving stage IV melanoma in 2016, she worries less about what others think and what is expected, and more about what she wants for her own future. It's working well.

Section 1

Bikeshedding is bad

Chapter 1.1

P.2: Write in ISO Standard C++

What is ISO Standard C++?

This book is all about writing good code. The first piece of advice is therefore to write in ISO Standard C++. But what exactly is that?

A history of C++

C++ didn't start out as a standardized language. It started out as an extension to the C programming language, called "C with classes," invented by Bjarne Stroustrup.[1] C wasn't a standardized language at that time either: Bjarne delivered his extension as a preprocessor called Cpre. These features included classes and derived classes, with public/private access levels, friends, assignment operator overloading, constructors, and destructors. Also, inline functions and default function arguments were included, along with type-checking of function arguments.

In 1982 he started work on a fresh effort called C++, which added further features, including virtual functions, function and operator overloading, references, constants, and dynamic allocation. In addition, he created a C++ front end for C compilers called Cfront. This worked by passing in C++ code that Cfront would then compile to C. He also wrote a book called *The C++ Programming Language* (often known as *TCPL*), which was published in 1985. This served as the definitive reference on what C++ was, and commercial compilers started to appear.

1. Stroustrup, B, 1995. *A History of C++: 1979–1991*, www.stroustrup.com/hopl2.pdf.

While these compilers were becoming widely used, Bjarne continued work on C++, adding further features to what became C++2.0. These included multiple inheritance, abstract base classes, static and const member functions, the protected access level, as well as improvements to existing features. There was a big leap in the popularity of C++. By Bjarne's estimates, the number of users doubled every 7.5 months.

Conferences, journals, and books emerged, and the competing implementations of the compiler demonstrated that there needed to be something more precise than *TCPL*. In 1989 Dmitry Lenkov of HP wrote a proposal for American National Standards Institute (ANSI) standardization of C++, identifying the need for a careful and detailed definition of each language feature to prevent the growth of dialects, and also identifying necessary additional features such as exception handling and a standard library. The ANSI C++ committee, X3J16, first met in December 1989. The *Annotated Reference Manual*, or *ARM*, written by Margaret Ellis and Bjarne and published in 1990, became the single description of the whole of C++. It was written specifically to get the ANSI C++ standardization effort off to the best possible start.

It wasn't just an American concern, of course, and many international representatives attended. In 1991 the ISO C++ committee WG21 was convened and the two committees held joint meetings from then on. The goal was to write a draft standard for public review in four years with the hope of an official standard two years later. However, the first standard, ISO/IEC 14882:1998, was finally published in September 1998, not quite nine years after the first meeting.

This was not the end of the story, though. Work on bug fixes to the standard continued, and in 2003 C++03 was released. Further work was undertaken to add additional features to develop the language further. This included `auto`, `constexpr`, `decltype`, move semantics, range `for`, uniform initialization, lambdas, rvalue references, static assertions, variadic templates... the list went on, as did the development schedule. Eventually, the next version was shipped in 2011 before everyone forgot that C++ was a growing language.

Given that C++03 was a correction to C++98, this meant there was a 13-year gap between the first standard and C++11. It was clear that such a long period between standards was not in anybody's interests and so the "train model" was developed: a new standard would be shipped every three years, and if a feature wasn't ready, it would hop on the next "train" three years later. Since then, C++14, C++17, and C++20 have been shipped on schedule.

Encapsulating variations

Variations in run-time environment

The standard has very little to say about what is required of the environment in which a C++ program executes. An operating system is not a requirement. File storage is not a requirement. A screen is not a requirement. A program written for a typical desktop environment may need mouse input and windowed output, which requires specialized code for each particular system.

Writing fully portable code for such a program is not feasible. ISO Standard C++ has a very small library compared to languages like C# and Java. It is a specification for implementers of ISO Standard C++. The C# and Java standard libraries are supplied by the owners of the language, but C++ does not have a funded library development organization. You need to use the individual features of each target environment to support those parts not available in the standard library. These will be offered in the form of a header file and a library file; typically, there will be many of these per system. As far as possible, hide those away behind your own interfaces. Minimize the amount of variation between codebase versions targeting different systems.

For example, you might want to know if a particular key on the user's keyboard is being pressed. One approach might be to use the preprocessor to detect which platform you are using and execute the appropriate piece of code, like this:

```
#if defined WIN32
auto a_pressed = bool{GetKeyState('A') & 0x8000 != 0};
#elif defined LINUX
auto a_pressed = /*really quite a lot of code*/
#endif
```

This is very ugly: it is operating at the wrong level of abstraction. The code that is specific to Windows and Linux[2] should live in separate files elsewhere, exposed in a header file, so the code should look like this:

```
auto a_pressed = key_state('A');
```

The function `key_state` is an interface that encapsulates this extension. The implementation does the right thing for the appropriate platform, away from your flow of control and without the additional baggage of preprocessor macros. Separating each implementation into a separate file further supports that abstraction.

Variations in C++ language level and compiler

C++ compiler implementers must entirely and precisely support the standard if they want to announce that their compiler is standard-compliant. However, this does not tie their hands entirely, and leaves the door open for them to add additional features or extensions. For example, GCC included additional type traits such as `__has_trivial_constructor` and `__is_abstract` before they were added to the

2. https://stackoverflow.com/questions/41600981/how-do-i-check-if-a-key-is-pressed-on-c

standard. These have both been present in the type traits library since C++11 under different names: `std::is_trivially_constructible` and `std::is_abstract`.

Note that `__is_abstract` is preceded by a double underscore: the double underscore is reserved by the standard to implementers. Implementers are NOT allowed to add new identifiers to the `std` namespace. This would be a very bad idea, as they might subsequently be added to the standard with a completely different meaning. What this means in practice for C++ developers is that it is possible to accidentally write code that appears to be using standard features, but in fact is accidentally using a compiler-specific feature. A good way to guard against this is to build and test your code on more than one compiler and operating system, to discover accidentally nonstandard code.

These two features were provided for good reason: they were useful metaprogramming tools. Indeed, they were so useful that they were added to the standard. Many parts of the standard, both language and library features, start life as features in popular tools and libraries. Sometimes the use of nonstandard features is inescapable.

Extensions to C++

Some library writers also add their own extensions. For example, the Qt[3] library uses a feature called signals and slots to communicate between objects. Three symbols are added to make use of this feature: `Q_SIGNALS`, `Q_SLOTS`, and `Q_EMIT`. If you were to read a source file making use of these keywords, it would seem like any other language keyword. Qt supplies a tool called `moc` that parses these keywords to produce output that a C++ compiler can parse fully and correctly, in just the same way that Cfront would parse early C++ code so that its output could be consumed by C compilers.

The point to bear in mind is that the standard offers something that these extensions don't: rigorously defined semantics. The ISO C++ Standard is absolutely unambiguous, which is one of the reasons why it is so hard to read. You are, of course, free to use language extensions if you are mindful of the cost to portability. Qt in particular makes heroic efforts to achieve portability across different platforms. However, those extensions are not necessarily guaranteed to be present in other implementations, nor are they necessarily guaranteed to mean the same thing.

3. https://doc.qt.io/

Safety in header files

For example, consider `#pragma once`. This is a simple directive that tells the compiler not to `#include` a file a second time. It reduces the amount of time the compiler spends compiling a translation unit. Every compiler I've used over the past 20 years implements this pragma directive, but what does it actually mean? Does it mean "stop parsing until you get to the end of the file"? Does it mean "don't open this file a second time"? Although the visible effect is the same, the meaning is not precisely defined for all platforms.

You cannot assume the meaning of something will be preserved across platforms. Even if you are safe now, you cannot guarantee that you will be in the future. Relying on a feature like this is like relying on a bug. It's dangerous and may be changed or corrected at any time (although see Hyrum's Law[4]). In this case, rather than using `#pragma once`, the Core Guidelines recommend using header guards as described in SF.8: "Use #include guards for all .h files." With header guards, we know exactly what will happen.

Variation in fundamental types

Operating system implementation is not the only kind of system variation. As you may know, the width of arithmetic types like `int` and `char` is not standardized. You might think an `int` is 32 bits wide, but I remember a time when an `int` was 16 bits wide. At times I needed a type that was exactly 32 bits wide, and, fearful of making the mistake of assuming `int` would always be 32 bits wide (it had changed once, why not again?), I used the implementation headers to discover which type was that wide, and created an alias to that type:

```
typedef __int i32; // older way of doing this: do not use now
```

I introduced an identifier called `i32` that was an alias of the platform's definition of a type named `__int`. I was entirely safe if the project was ported to another platform: I could find out how the target platform defined a 32-bit signed integral type and simply update the `typedef` definition for that platform as required.

Of course, when the next standard was released, in this case C++11, new types were introduced to the library in header `<cstdint>` that defined fixed-width integral types. I was able to update the definition in two attractive ways:

```
using i32 = std::int32_t;
```

4. 2021. Available at: https://www.hyrumslaw.com/ [Accessed 16 July 2021].

First, I was able to use the new type to future-proof my definition: the type being aliased is part of the standard and is extremely unlikely to change, because backward compatibility is so important to the language. This declaration will remain valid through subsequent versions of the standard (indeed, nine years and three standards have passed, and this code is still valid).

Second, I was able to move to the new `using` keyword, which allows you to use left-to-right style for identifier and definition separated by an equals sign. You can also see this style with the `auto` keyword:

```
auto index = i32{0};
```

The identifier is introduced on the left of the equals sign and the definition is on the right of the equals sign.

As superior refactoring tools emerged, I took the plunge and swapped all instances of `i32` for `std::int32_t`, for minimum ambiguity.

Regulatory constraints

It should be mentioned that sometimes you simply can't use ISO Standard C++. Not because of some lack in the library or missing language feature, but because the host environment forbids the use of certain features. This can be for regulatory reasons, or because the implementation is incomplete for the platform you are developing for.

For example, some industry sectors forbid dynamic allocation during performance-critical functions. Allocation is a nondeterministic activity that can also throw an out-of-memory exception; that is to say, there is no guarantee how long such a call will take. Throwing exceptions is also forbidden in several sectors for similar reasons, which immediately precludes dynamic allocation since `std::operator new` throws `std::bad_alloc` on failure. In situations like this, the Core Guidelines need to be extended and customized to the specific environment.

Conversely, some sectors forbid the use of libraries that have not undergone a certification performed by the sector's regulatory body. For example, the use of Boost[5] may be problematic in some environments. This enforces widespread use of ISO Standard C++.

5. https://www.boost.org

Learning the old ways

Backward compatibility of C++

It's important to remember where this language came from, and also what motivates its development. There is code in my current project that I wrote in 2005. It looks a little peculiar to today's programmers as it uses long-discarded paradigms, no `auto`, no lambdas: it's a history lesson in source.

However, it still works. It still compiles and runs well. During your career, you will come across code of various ages. It's important to make use of the latest standard and build with the latest compiler you can find, but it's also important to know where the language came from and to plan for the future.

> *Stability over decades is a feature.*

Sometimes it isn't possible to use the latest version of the standard. In embedded development, regulation, certification of systems, or elderly infrastructure may force you to use C++11, or even C++98. C++ relies on backward compatibility. It is backward-compatible with C. It is backward-compatible with prior standards. Stability over decades is a feature. This is one of its great strengths: billions of lines of code around the world still build with a modern compiler, occasionally with a little tweaking. At some point you may be asked to maintain this code.

Forward compatibility and "Y2K"

Conversely, write code that is built to last. At the end of the last century, a problem was unearthed in much of the world's elderly computer software: only two digits were used to represent the year.[6] Memory was at a premium, and the efficient thing to do was simply store 74 rather than 1974. The developer thought nothing of it: "This piece of software will not be running in 25 years; surely it will have been replaced."

Ah, such pessimism, or perhaps optimism, depending on your point of view. Of course, once the date rolled around to the year 2000, then the year was represented as 00, spoiling time interval calculations, interest payment calculations, indeed, ANYTHING to do with the passage of time.

This was known as the Y2K bug or the millennium bug. It proved to be a bonanza for older contractors, who toured the computers of the world effecting repairs on 25-year-old systems at considerable expense. Disaster was largely averted because

6. https://www.britannica.com/technology/Y2K-bug

the problem was identified in sufficient time and there were enough engineers available to put things right.

However, if the engineers had planned for the future instead, had assumed that their code would run "forever," and were writing the code at a point in time when four-digit integers occupied the same space as two-digit integers, this would have been avoided. It would have been clear that two digits was NOT enough to represent all dates that may be required, and at least a third digit would be needed, and really a fourth digit would just be simpler all around to accommodate the turn of the millennium.

Incidentally, this is not the only date problem. Linux has a similar problem with measuring time in seconds since January 1, 1970. This was stored as a 32-bit signed integer, which means it will roll over on January 19, 2038. I say "was": from Linux 5.6 the problem was solved.

An important pair of career skills is therefore writing code for the future and learning to read code from the past.

Staying on top of developments to the standard

C++ is developing all the time. With every publication of a new standard there comes a cornucopia of new language features and library additions. There is no especial virtue in simply using the most novel features; they should be used where they give definite and concrete benefit. However, the C++ community is very fortunate to have many excellent teachers ready to unfold and reveal all these new things to us. Finding these resources is made easier in four ways.

IsoCpp

First of all, there is isocpp.org.[7] This is the home of C++ on the Web and is run by the Standard C++ Foundation. This is a Washington 501(c)(6) not-for-profit organization whose purpose is to support the C++ software developer community and promote the understanding and use of modern Standard C++ on all compilers and platforms. On this site you can find a tour of C++ written by Bjarne, a huge C++ FAQ, details about how to participate in the standardization process, and a regularly updated list of recent blog posts from the C++ community. From here, you can investigate other posts on these blogs.

7. https://isocpp.org/about

Conferences

Second, there are several conferences that take place around the world every year. It has become the habit for these conferences to record all the talks and publish them on YouTube for free public consumption. This is a truly amazing resource, and it is quite a challenge to simply keep up with them year on year.

CppCon is run by the Standard C++ Foundation. It takes place in early autumn in the US in Aurora, Colorado, and generates nearly two hundred hours of content. The Association of C and C++ Users (ACCU) holds an annual conference every spring in Bristol, UK, and occasionally also in the autumn. It focuses on C++ but also features broader programming topics and generates nearly a hundred hours of content. Meeting C++ is held in Berlin, Germany, in November, generating nearly fifty hours of content. You can afford to be quite choosy: watching one talk per day will keep you busy for most of the year, and that's before mentioning the many other smaller conferences that happen in places like Australia, Belarus, Israel, Italy, Poland, Russia, Spain...

Other resources

On top of blogs and conferences, there are many books besides this one. Some of these will appear in references throughout this text, as will quotations from conference talks.

Finally, there is day-to-day discussion available on chat servers such as Discord and Slack.[8] The Discord server is moderated by the #include[9] diversity and inclusion group for C++ programmers, which has a very welcoming community.

With so many resources available you should be able to keep pace with developments in Standard C++. Continuing to write ISO Standard C++ code is within everyone's grasp. Doing so is important not just for future maintainers, whoever they may be, including yourself, but also for future clients of your code. There is broad use of C++, serving many areas of commerce, industry, and society. A stable, reliable approach to writing code is of global importance. Step up, do the right thing, and write in ISO Standard C++.

---

8. https://cpplang.slack.com
9. https://www.includecpp.org

Chapter 1.2

F.51: Where there is a choice, prefer default arguments over overloading

Introduction

API design is a valuable skill. As you decompose a problem into its constituent abstractions, you need to identify the abstractions and design an interface for them, giving the client clear and unambiguous usage instructions in the form of a completely obvious set of carefully named functions. There is a saying that code should be self-documenting. While this is a lofty ambition, it is in API design that you should try hardest to meet this goal.

Codebases grow. They just do. There is no getting away from it. Time passes, more abstractions are discovered and encoded, more problems are solved, and the problem domain itself expands to accommodate more use cases. This is fine and perfectly normal. It is part of the usual operation of development and engineering.

As these extra abstractions are added to the codebase, the problem of unambiguously naming things rears its ugly head. Naming is hard. That phrase will come up a lot in your programming career. Sometimes you want to let the client, which is often yourself, do the same thing but in a slightly different way.

This is where overloading may seem like a good idea. The difference between two abstractions may simply be the arguments that are passed to them; in all other respects they are semantically identical. Function overloading allows you to reuse a function name with a different set of parameters. But if they are indeed semantically identical, can you express that difference in terms of a default argument? If so, your API will be simpler to understand.

Before we start, we want to remind you of the difference between a parameter and an argument: an argument is passed to a function. A function declaration includes a parameter list, of which one or more may be supplied with a default argument. There is no such thing as a default parameter.

Refining your abstraction: Additional arguments or overloading?

For example, consider the following function:

```
office make_office(float floor_space, int staff);
```

This function will return an instance of an office, with a particular area in square meters specified by `floor_space`, and facilities for a particular number of staff. The physical construction of the office takes place on a single floor and everyone is distributed nicely, with appropriate kitchen space and bathroom facilities, along with the correct number of coffee machines, table tennis tables, and massage therapy rooms. One day, during one of those problem domain expansion moments, it is announced that some offices will occupy their own two-floor building. This complicates matters rather, since you must ensure you have stairways in the right places, appropriate fire escape routes, much more complicated air conditioning, and of course, you now need a slide between floors, or maybe a fire station pole. You need to tell the constructor that you are trying to make a two-floor office. You can do this with a third parameter:

```
office make_office(float floor_space, int staff, bool two_floors);
```

Unfortunately, you must go through all your code and add `false` to all your call sites. Or you can default the final argument to `false`, which means that the calling code does not need to supply it. That looks like this:

```
office make_office(float floor_space, int staff, bool two_floors = false);
```

One speedy recompilation later and all remains right with the world. Unfortunately, the demons of domain expansion are not finished with you yet: it turns out that the single-floor offices sometimes need the name of the building they will be situated in. You, the ever-accommodating engineer, expand your function's parameter list once again:

```
office make_office(float floor_space, int staff,bool two_floors = false,
    std::string const& building_name = {});
```

You reimplement your function, but it irritates you. There are four arguments, the final argument will only be needed if the third argument is false, and it all looks messy and complicated. You decide to overload your function:

```
office make_office(float floor_space, int staff, bool two_floors = false);
office make_office(float floor_space, int staff,
    std::string const& building_name);
```

You now have what is known as a function overload set, and it is up to the compiler to choose which member of the set to invoke according to the arguments passed in. The client is forced to call the correct function when a building must be identified. Identification implies a single-floor office.

For example, some client code may wish to create an office with 24,000 square meters of space for 200 people. The office is situated on one floor in a building called "Eagle Heights." The correct invocation is therefore

```
auto eh_office = make_office(24000.f, 200, "Eagle Heights");
```

Of course, you must ensure that the appropriate semantics are observed in each function, and that they do not diverge in operation. This is a maintenance burden. Perhaps providing a single function and demanding the choice be made explicitly by the caller is more appropriate.

"Hang on," we can hear you say. "What about writing a private implementation function? I can ensure consistency of creation. I can just use one of those and all is right with the world."

You would be right. However, two functions may be viewed with suspicion by clients. They may worry that your implementation is divergent, that not everything is quite right. An abundance of caution may instill fear within them. A single function with two default arguments to switch between algorithms is a reassuring sight.

"No, you're being ridiculous now," we hear you cry. "I write great code and my clients trust me. I have unit tests everywhere and everything is fine, thank you very much."

Unfortunately, although you may indeed write great code, your client does not. Take another look at the initialization of `eh_office` and see whether you can spot the bug. Meanwhile, we shall consider overload resolution.

The subtleties of overload resolution

Overload resolution is a tricky beast to master. Nearly two percent of the C++20 standard is devoted to defining how overload resolution works. Here is an overview.

When the compiler encounters the invocation of a function, it must decide which function it is referring to. Prior to the encounter, the compiler will have made a list of all the identifiers that have been introduced. There may have been several functions with the same name but with different parameters, an overload set. How does the compiler choose which of these are viable functions and which should be invoked?

First, it will choose the functions from the set with the same number of parameters, or fewer parameters and an ellipsis parameter, or more parameters where the excess consists of default parameters. If any of the candidates has a `requires` clause (new to C++20), then it must be satisfied. Any rvalue argument must not correspond to a non-`const` lvalue parameter, and any lvalue argument must not correspond to an rvalue reference parameter. Each argument must be convertible to the corresponding parameter via an implicit conversion sequence.

In our example, the compiler has been introduced to two versions of `make_office` that differ in their third parameter. One takes a `bool` that is defaulted to `false`, and one takes a `std::string const&`. The initialization of `eh_office` matches both as far as parameter count is concerned.

Neither of these functions has a `requires` clause. We can skip over this step. Similarly, there is nothing exotic about the reference bindings.

Finally, each argument must be convertible to the corresponding parameter. The first two arguments do not even require converting. The third argument is a `char const*` and obviously converts to a `std::string` via the nonexplicit constructor that is part of the `std::string` interface. Unfortunately, we have not finished yet.

Once there is a set of functions, they are ranked by parameter to find the best viable function. A function F1 is preferred over another F2 if implicit conversions for all arguments of F1 are not worse than those of F2. In addition, there must be at least one argument of F1 whose implicit conversion is better than the corresponding implicit conversion of F2.

That word "better" is troubling. How do we rank implicit conversion sequences?

There are three types of implicit conversion sequence: standard conversion sequence, user-defined conversion sequence, and ellipsis conversion sequence.

There are three ranks for a standard conversion sequence: exact match, promotion, and conversion. Exact match means no conversion is required and is the preferred rank. It can also mean lvalue-to-rvalue conversion.

Promotion means widening the representation of the type. For example, an object of type short can be promoted to an object of type int, known as integral promotion, while an object of type float can be promoted to an object of type double, known as floating-point promotion.

Conversions differ from promotions in that they may change the value, which may cost precision. For example, a floating-point value can be converted to an integer, rounding to the nearest integer value. Also, integral and floating-point values, unscoped enumerations, pointers, and pointer-to-member types can be converted to `bool`. These three ranks are C concepts and are unavoidable if compatibility with C is to be maintained.

That partially covers standard conversion sequences. User-defined conversions take place in two ways: either through a nonexplicit constructor, or through a nonexplicit conversion operator. This is what we are expecting to happen in our example: we are expecting our `char const*` to convert to a `std::string` via the nonexplicit constructor which takes a `char const*`. This is as plain as the nose on your face. Why have we dragged you through this exposition on overloading?

Back to the example

In the above example, the client is expecting the `char const*` to participate in a user-defined conversion to a `std::string`, and for that temporary rvalue argument to be passed as a reference to `const` to the second function's third parameter.

However, user-defined conversion sequences take second priority to standard conversion sequences. In the earlier paragraph on conversions, we identified a standard conversion from pointer to `bool`. If you have ever seen older code that passes raw pointers around the codebase, you will have seen something like

```
if (ptr) {
  ptr->do_thing();
}
```

The condition of the `if` statement is a pointer, not a `bool`, but a pointer can be converted to false if it is zero. This is a brief and idiomatic way of writing

```
if (ptr != 0) {
  ptr->do_thing();
}
```

In these days of modern C++, we see raw pointers less frequently, but it is useful to remember that this is a perfectly normal, reasonable conversion. It is this standard conversion that has taken first place and been selected in preference to the seemingly more obvious user-defined conversion from `char const*` to `std::string const&`. The function overload that takes a `bool` as its third argument is invoked, to the surprise of the client.

Whose bug is this anyway: yours, or the client's? If the client had written

```
auto eh_office = make_office(24000.f, 200, "Eagle Heights"s);
```

then there would be no error. The literal suffix signals that this object is in fact a `std::string`, not a `char const*`. So, it is obviously the client's fault. They should know about the conversion rules.

However, that is not a very helpful approach. You should make an interface easy to use correctly and hard to use incorrectly. Missing out a literal suffix is a very easy mistake to make. Additionally, consider what would happen if you added the function overload taking a `bool` AFTER you had defined the constructor taking a `std::string const&`. The client code would have behaved as expected with or without the literal suffix. Unfortunately, adding the overload introduces a better conversion, and suddenly the client code has broken.

You should make an interface easy to use correctly and hard to use incorrectly.

Perhaps you remain unconvinced. You might now try replacing the `bool` with a better type. Perhaps you would like to define an enumeration to use in place of the `bool`:

```
enum class floors {one, two};
office make_office(float floor_space, int staff,
    floors floor_count = floors::one);
office make_office(float floor_space, int staff,
    std::string const& building_name);
```

We really are going to have to stop you there. You have introduced a new type simply to facilitate the correct use of an overload set. Ask yourself whether that really is clearer than this:

```
office make_office(float floor_space,int staff,bool two_floors = false,
    std::string const& building_name = {});
```

If you remain unconvinced, ask yourself what you will do when the next round of problem domain expansion heaves into view with the remark, "Actually, we would like to be able to name the buildings where the two-floor offices are commissioned."

The unambiguous nature of default arguments

The advantage of a default argument is that any conversion is immediately apparent on inspection. You can see that a `char const*` is being converted to a `std::string const&`. There is no ambiguity about which conversion might be chosen since there is only one place for a conversion to happen.

In addition, as alluded to earlier, a single function is more reassuring than an overload set. If your function is well named and well designed, your client should not need to know or worry about which version to call, but as the example shows, this is easier said than done. A default argument signals to a client that the function has flexibility about how it can be invoked by providing an alternative interface to the implementation and guarantees that it implements a single semantic.

A single function also avoids code replication. When you overload a function, you start with the very best of intentions. Of course you do. The overloaded function does a few things differently, and you plan to encapsulate the remaining similarities in a single function that both functions call. As time passes, though, it is very easy for the overloads to overlap as it becomes hard to tease out the actual differences. You end up with a maintenance problem as the functionality grows.

There is one limitation. Default arguments must be applied in reverse order through the parameter list of a function. For example:

```
office make_office(float floor_space, int staff,bool two_floors,
   std::string const& building_name = {});
```

is a legal declaration, while

```
office make_office(float floor_space, int staff,bool two_floors = false,
   std::string const& building_name);
```

is not. If the latter function is invoked with only three arguments, there is no way to unambiguously bind the final argument to a parameter: should it bind to `two_floors` or `building_name`?

We hope you are convinced that function overloading, although cute, is not to be taken lightly. We touched only lightly on overload resolution. There is plenty more detail to be pored over if you want to truly understand which overload will be selected. You will notice we did not cover ellipsis conversion sequences, nor did we discuss what happens if there is a function template in the mix. If you are supremely confident about the use of overloads, though, we have one request: please do not mix default parameters with overloaded functions. This becomes very hard to parse and sets traps for the unwary. It is not an interface style that is either easy to use correctly or hard to use incorrectly.

Alternatives to overloading

Overloading functions signals to the client that a piece of functionality, an abstraction, is available in a variety of ways. One function identifier can be invoked with a variety of parameter sets. Indeed, the function overload set has been described as the fundamental building block of the API, rather than the function, as one might expect.

However, in the admittedly somewhat contrived example for this chapter, you might find that

```
office make_office(float floor_space, int staff, floors floor_count);
office make_office(float floor_space, int staff,
    std::string const& building_name);
```

is not as clear as

```
office make_office_by_floor_count(float floor_space, int staff,
    floors floor_count);
office make_office_by_building_name(float floor_space, int staff,
    std::string const& building_name);
```

Function overloading is a great tool, but you should use it sparingly. It is a very shiny hammer and sometimes you actually need to peel an orange. The symbols are yours to define, and you should specify them as tightly as you can.

There is more to cover regarding overloading—for example, the rather long list of tie-breaks to ranking the best viable function; were this a textbook we would go into complete detail. However, it suffices to say that overloading should not be undertaken lightly.

Sometimes you must overload

The guideline starts with the phrase "Where there is a choice." There are some places where you cannot provide an alternatively named function.

For example, there is only one constructor identifier, so if you want to construct a class in a variety of ways, you must provide constructor overloads.

Similarly, operators have a singular meaning that is very valuable to your clients. If you have, for some reason, written your own string class and you want to concatenate two strings together, your clients will much prefer writing

```
new_string = string1 + string2;
```

to

```
new_string = concatenate(string1, string2);
```

The same is true for comparison operators. It is unlikely, however, that you would want a default argument when overloading operators.

The standard provides the customization point `std::swap`, where you are expected to overload the function optimally for your class. Indeed, Core Guideline C.83: "For value-like types, consider providing a `noexcept` swap function" suggests this explicitly. Again, it is highly unlikely that you would want a default argument when overloading this function.

Of course, sometimes there simply is no default argument available. So, when you MUST overload, do so consciously, and, to reiterate, do NOT mix default arguments with overloading. This falls into the chainsaw-juggling category of API design style.

Summary

We considered the growth of code and considered the impact on API design, looked at a simple example of overloading and saw where it could go subtly wrong. We looked at the subtleties of overloading and skimmed the surface of the rules on how the compiler prefers one function over another and used those rules to highlight where the example function call had not been the call we expected. Particularly, the bug was caused by offering a `bool` with a default argument in a function overload, which is very generous in allowing what can be converted to it. We used that to demonstrate that a default argument should be preferred to an overloaded function where possible, and that mixing the use of function overloads with default arguments is a very risky venture.

The example was of course a straw man, but the fact remains that dangers lurk around overload sets for the unwary engineer. You can mitigate this danger through judicious use of a default argument and delay the introduction of a function overload. You can research the full consequences of overload resolution at your favorite online resource, and we advise you to do so if ever you feel like ignoring this particular guideline.

Chapter 1.3

C.45: Don't define a default constructor that only initializes data members; use in-class member initializers instead

Why have default constructors anyway?

We will start this chapter with a scenic detour. Consider Core Guideline NR.5: "Don't use two-phase initialization." This is referring to the habit of constructing an object and then calling an initialization function. This practice dates from the last century, when C was the very thing, and one would declare an object on the stack or allocate some memory from the free store and then initialize it. If you were really on top of things, you would define a function that took a pointer to your struct and call it `my_struct_init` or something like that.

The two phases were allocate, then initialize. All sorts of things could go wrong: you could insert more and more code between the allocation and the initialization and suddenly find you were using your object prior to initialization. Then along came C++ and constructors and this problem vanished forever.

For objects with static duration, the linker would create a list of their constructors for execution prior to `main()` and a function to iterate through them. The linker would have full knowledge about how much space they would take up, so that function might allocate some address space for those objects, initialize them all by constructing them in that address space, and then invoke `main()`.

For objects with automatic duration, the compiler would allocate some stack space and initialize the object within that memory. For objects with dynamic duration, the `new` operator would invoke `operator new` to allocate some memory, followed by the constructor to initialize the object within that memory. The thread-local duration class arrived in C++11 and behaves in much the same way as static duration, except there is a per-thread instance of the object rather than a per-program instance.

We hope you can see a clear and consistent pattern here that eliminates an entire class of bugs: that of using an object before it is ready for use. By combining allocation and initialization into a single operation, the problem of two-phase initialization vanished entirely.

Except, of course, that the problem did not vanish at all. Engineers were still in the habit of instantiating an object and then modifying it after construction. Classes would be designed with a default value and clients would specialize that value according to context.

This just moves the problem around. A default constructor is not always appropriate for a class. Sadly, for a long time, the containers provided by some C++ vendor implementations would not work unless the contained class was default-constructible. A default constructor would be provided not as part of the problem domain but as part of the solution domain. Of course, that meant that it would be used in the problem domain as well, muddying the waters about what the correct use of the class should be.

Some classes should have a default constructor. For example, how would you declare an empty string? There is no meaningful API for that, unless you decide you are going to have a constructor overload especially for empty strings with a special tag parameter. The `std::string` API recognizes this and provides a default constructor that creates a string of zero length. A default constructor is the obvious solution. Indeed, all the standard containers provide default constructors that signify that the container starts life empty.

However, do not assume that your class needs to be default-constructible. Make sure you know what it means to allow your users to create an instance of your class without any kind of specification.

How do you initialize a data member?

Let's rejoin the main road and look at the process of initialization. When an object is constructed, the memory is reserved as appropriate for the storage class. The constructor is then invoked, although the rules are a little different for objects of built-in type. If no constructor is defined, then the members of the class are default-initialized. If there are any members of built-in type, then they are not initialized by default.

This is a bad thing: if you don't ensure every member of a class is initialized, then you run the risk of introducing nondeterministic behavior into your program. Good luck debugging that. I worked on a game many years ago using a C++ implementation that was very helpful when it came to dynamic storage duration. It came with two run-time libraries, one for development and one for retail. The development version of the run-time library was built with NDEBUG undefined, so asserts would fire, and all sorts of debug information was available for the standard library. When `operator new` was invoked, it would initialize the memory with the value `0xcd`. When `operator delete` was invoked, it would overwrite the memory with the value `0xdd`. This was very useful for identifying dereferencing of dangling pointers. For reasons of speed, the retail library did not do this, and simply left the memory untouched after allocation and after deallocation.

The game was a multiplayer game. Each player's machine would send their moves over the internet in the blink of an eye and each machine would have to resolve them identically. This required each machine to be in an identical state as far as the model of the game was concerned; otherwise, the models on each machine would diverge, giving confusing results and broken games. Such inconsistencies would appear less frequently in versions of the game that were built with the development version of the run-time library, because they all had the same underlying memory values for uninitialized data, `0xcd`. This led to retail-version-only crashes, which were incredibly hard to debug since any divergences would not be noticed by players until long after they occurred.

Until this point, persuading the team of the importance of initializing every data member in every constructor had been an uphill battle. When this particular penny dropped, no more persuasion was required. Determinism is your ally when it comes to debugging, so ensure determinism with deterministic construction of all objects and initialize every item of member data.

There are three places where you can initialize member data. The first place we'll take a look at is the constructor function body. Consider this class:

```
class piano
{
public:
  piano();

private:
  int number_of_keys;
  bool mechanical;
  std::string manufacturer;
};
```

We can define the constructor like this:

```
piano::piano()
{
  number_of_keys = 88;
  mechanical = true;
  manufacturer = "Yamaha";
}
```

This is perfectly adequate. Every member is initialized, and the order of initialization matches the order of declaration. This is function-body-initialization. However, it is suboptimal. Prior to the function body being executed, the members of the class were default-initialized. This meant that the `std::string` default constructor was invoked, and then the assignment operator was invoked with a `char const*`. In fact, this is overwriting, not initializing.

Now, any smart compiler will optimize away the construct-assign pattern. `std::string` is a class template, and there is a good chance that the entire execution is available to the compiler. It will see that there is a redundancy and eliminate it. However, you cannot rely on this being the case for every class. You should prefer initializing in the initializer list to initializing in the function body.

Let us change the constructor appropriately:

```
piano::piano()
  : number_of_keys(88)
  , mechanical(true)
  , manufacturer("Yamaha")
{}
```

Aside from the problem of remembering to maintain the default constructor when you add member data, this looks a lot like boilerplate code that is just bloating your source file.

There is a third place you can provide default definitions that is even closer to the action: in the definition of the class itself. Default member initializers provide a default value for an object when no other is provided in a constructor. Let's return to our class definition to take a look at this in action:

```
class piano
{
public:
  // piano(); // no longer needed

private:
  int number_of_keys = 88;
  bool mechanical = true;
  std::string manufacturer = "Yamaha";
};
```

This is much better. You have managed to get rid of a surplus member function and you have also specified what you expect a default piano to look like: an 88-note mechanical Yamaha piano. There is a cost that cannot be ignored, though, which is that these default values are exposed in a class declaration that is likely to be a dependency of other source files. Making a change to any of these values may require recompilation of an unknown number of files. There are, however, good reasons for paying this price.

What happens when two people maintain a class?

It is to be hoped that in the normal run of things, one person will maintain a class. They will have identified the abstraction, encoded it in a class, designed the API, and will have full knowledge of what is going on.

Of course, Things Happen. A maintainer might be moved to another project temporarily, or worse, suddenly leave without the opportunity for a proper handover. Several things can complicate matters without the strict discipline of thorough communication via documentation, meetings, and all the other time-sinks that plague the typical engineer.

Hotch-potch of constructors

When several people work on a class, inconsistencies start to creep in. A lot of the Core Guidelines material is about reducing the opportunity to be inconsistent. Consistent code is easier to read and contains fewer surprises. Consider what might happen to the piano class were three maintainers let loose upon it:

```
class piano
{
public:
  piano()
    : number_of_keys(88)
    , mechanical(true)
    , manufacturer("Yamaha")
  {}
  piano(int number_of_keys_, bool mechanical_,
        std::string manufacturer_ = "Yamaha")
    : number_of_keys(number_of_keys_)
    , mechanical(mechanical_)
    , manufacturer(std::move(manufacturer_))
  {}
  piano(int number_of_keys_) {
    number_of_keys = number_of_keys_;
    mechanical = false;
    manufacturer = "";
  }


private:
  int number_of_keys;
  bool mechanical;
  std::string manufacturer;
};
```

Default constructors should be an active choice.

This is a sample class, but I have seen things like this in the wild. Usually, the constructors are separated by many lines. Perhaps they are all defined in the class definition, so it is not immediately obvious that there are three very similar constructors because they are obscured by many lines of implementation. Indeed, you can tell a couple of things about the different maintainers. The implementer of the third constructor does not appear to know about initialization lists. Also, assigning the empty string to the manufacturer member is redundant, so they are possibly unaware of how constructors and default initialization works.

More importantly, though, the first and third constructors have different defaults. While you may have spotted that in this simple example, we are sure you can imagine circumstances where it would not be so obvious. Calling code can pass in one, two, or three arguments with unexpectedly different behavior, which is not what any user wants. The presence of default arguments in the constructor overloads should also worry you.

What happens if we adopt the in-class member initializers? The code becomes this:

```
class piano
{
public:
  piano() = default;
  piano(int number_of_keys_, bool mechanical_, std::string manufacturer_)
    : number_of_keys(number_of_keys_)
    , mechanical(mechanical_)
    , manufacturer(manufacturer_)
  {}
  piano(int number_of_keys_) {
    number_of_keys = number_of_keys_;
  }


private:
  int number_of_keys = 88;
  bool mechanical = true;
  std::string manufacturer = "Yamaha";
};
```

We now have consistent defaults. The constructor authors have been told by the presence of in-class member initializers that defaults have been chosen and they do not need to, nor should they, choose their own.

Default parameters can confuse matters in overloaded functions

Default parameters in constructors are confusing beasts. They imply a default value for something, but there is a cognitive distance between that default and the member declaration. There exist plausible reasons for adding a default parameter to a constructor; perhaps a member has been added, and rather than change all the client code you decide to take on the technical debt of maintaining a default value. However, you need to recognize it as technical debt that needs to be repaid, ideally by adding an additional constructor that takes all the required parameters and deprecating the existing constructor.

Summary

Default constructors should be an active choice. Not all classes have meaningful default values. Member data initialization can happen in three places: the constructor function body, the constructor initialization list, and at the point of declaration of the member data, known as default member initializers.

Default member initializers define a default value at the point of declaration. If there is a member that cannot be defined in such a way, it suggests that there may be no legal mechanism by which a default constructor can be defined. This is fine. As remarked earlier, there is no necessity for default constructors.

Constructors provide a variation from the default. Providing default member initializers gives each variation increased specificity. This is a bonus for the client as they have fewer things to worry about regarding the state of the object: it can be more closely tailored to their requirements.

Chapter 1.4

C.131: Avoid trivial getters and setters

An archaic idiom

Trivial getters and setters are a hangover from the early days of C++. Typically, they look like this:

```
class x_wrapper
{
public:
  explicit x_wrapper(int x_) : x(x_) {}
  int get_x() const { return x; } // this is a getter
  void set_x(int x_) { x =  x_; } // this is a setter

private:
  int x;
};
```

The get and set functions simply reach into the implementation of the class and return or modify the value. On the surface there are some things to commend in this approach. You can search your codebase for `get_x` and `set_x` to see where the code changes `x`. Alternatively, it is easy to set a breakpoint in the function so that you can trap every instance of where the value is retrieved or modified. It honors the idea of keeping data private: the data is encapsulated behind an API.

These are trivial functions. They simply put a roadblock in the way of direct access to `x`. The guideline advises against this approach. Understanding why this is poor design is impossible with a meaningless class like `x_wrapper`, though, so we will demonstrate some more realistic examples later. First of all, though, we need to talk about abstraction, what it is for, and why it is so important to programming in C++. Along the way we will look at some history, encounter class invariants, and consider the importance of preferring nouns and verbs to get and set for member function identifiers.

Abstraction

The purpose of language is abstraction. So, what is it that we are actually doing when we abstract with the C++ programming language?

We are turning chunks of memory, containing numbers, into representations of things that inhabit our problem domain. This is one of the core strengths of C++, as well as one of its primary motivations.

A house can be represented as a collection of numbers. They might include the dimensions of the plot of land on which it is situated; the height; the size of the floor space; the quantity of floors, rooms, and windows; and the quantity of attics. This last item is likely to be zero or one, unless your house is particularly grand.

This abstraction is implemented as a series of numbers, or fields, arranged into a record. The record dictates the order in which the fields are arranged, which means that if you have a set of records stored consecutively in memory, then you can trivially navigate to any record from the first record, and any field within that record, with some simple arithmetic.

In the early days of computing, a lot of time was spent wrangling these collections of records, or tables. Simple data processing would involve either collecting some data and making some records or reading some records and producing more data. These were happy, simple days.

If you are at all familiar with C++, you will recognize the struct as a record, member data as fields, and tables as arrays of structs. For simple data processing, it seems sensible to read and write directly to the records.

However, what happens when you want to do more than wrangle records? Before the arrival of classes, you would hold data in structs, and invoke functions on that data. Before the arrival of copy constructors and assignment operators, you could not pass instances of structs to functions, only pointers to those instances. Before the arrival of access levels, you could directly modify any field in the struct. It was really, really important to know what you were doing with the data and what everyone else expected of the data. This could be a considerable cognitive load.

Significantly, it was usual for data that was not in the scope of the currently executing function to be directly available for modification. Data would be shared between functions by placing it at file scope, allowing one function to write to the data and other functions to read from the data. It would look like this:

```
int modifying_factor;

void prepare_new_environment_data(int input)
{
  int result = 0;
  /* … prepare the new environment data using input */
  modifying_factor = result;
}

int f2(int num)
{
  int calculation = 0;
  /* … perform f2-relevant calculations */
  return calculation * modifying_factor;
}
```

If the engineer was lucky enough to be the only person expected to modify such data, they would be able to reason about it with a valuable degree of certainty. They knew where the data was modified, and they knew where the data was read, and they would therefore be able to identify bugs related to the data.

Sadly, as teams grew bigger, and individual pieces of data became more important, keeping hold of responsibility for them became harder. The data would be declared in a header file, making it accessible to many engineers. Reasoning about the data would become a lost cause, coding guidelines would be written about the data, arguments would break out in the kitchen about who was mucking about with it, meetings would be called to set policy once and for all about who was allowed to write to the data and under what conditions. Documentation would be added to the declaration, and everyone would hope that it was being kept up to date by someone who wasn't them. Everyone would hope that all the other engineers were reasoning about the data in the same way. Everyone would hope, six months later, that all the other engineers were continuing to reason about the data in the same way.

The important thing to remember is that once data is declared in a header file as an `extern` declaration, not only is all control lost, but all hope of control is also lost, and whatever you think you might mean by this piece of data, Hyrum's Law applies:

> "With a sufficient number of users of an API, it does not matter what you promise in the contract: all observable behaviors of your system will be depended on by somebody."[1]

1. https://www.hyrumslaw.com

You no longer own the data, and yet you remain responsible for it. Searching the codebase for an identifier with a useful and therefore common name becomes a nightmare of context assessment.

Eventually, a bright engineer would hide away the piece of data behind a pair of functions, one to write to the data and one to read from the data. It would not make reasoning about the data any easier, but a search through the codebase for the call sites of those functions, along with a breakpoint at those functions, would combine to reveal under what circumstances the data was being changed.

If they were REALLY clever, they would find a way of naming the functions to reflect what their purpose was in the problem domain, in an attempt at producing self-documenting code. For example, if the piece of data was an elevation above sea level, they might name the functions like this:

```
/* elevation.h */
void change_height(int new_height);
int height();

/* elevation.c */
int height_ = 0;

void change_height(int new_height)
{
  height_ = new_height;
}

int height()
{
  return height_;
}
```

This would not prevent people from arbitrarily changing heights at inopportune moments throughout the codebase, but at least it would signal what they were doing and perhaps improve client readability by using nouns for functions that queried values and verbs for functions that modified values. Gatekeeping the data in this way allows you to search for its uses, and you get the added bonus of being able to set breakpoints in your debugger so that you can keep a careful watch over it.

However, these were dark times.

Mere Encapsulation

Along came C with classes, with access levels and member functions. Access levels! Finally, the data belongs to me. I can make it mine by declaring it private. Then nobody can touch it except through one of the public member functions. Member functions! In C it was possible to store pointers to arbitrary functions in structs, but member functions with an implicit instance pointer as the first function parameter were a leap in usability. The world was a brighter, shinier place.

The programming style of hiding your data behind a pair of functions was no longer simply a bright idea: it became normal practice, enforceable by the language itself. New advice was offered, loud and clear: "Make all your data members private." A new keyword was added, `class`, to distinguish from `struct`. For backward compatibility, members of structs remained public by default, while members of classes were private by default, reinforcing the idea that data should be private.

With the ability to keep data in a private interface came the opportunity to prevent, trivially, people from interfering with that data. You could create an object and provide get/set functions to get at the data. This, in a nutshell, is encapsulation.

Encapsulation is one of the core principles of object-oriented programming: restricting access to the object's parts and combining data with the functions that operate on that data. It's a safety feature that easily improves the ability of the engineer, and the users of the encapsulation, to reason about what is going on. Suddenly, encapsulation was available to C engineers, and this sort of thing happened:

Before:

```
struct house
{
  int plot_size[2];
  int floor_area;
  int floor_count;
  int room_count;
  int window_count;
};
```

After:

```
class house
{
public:
  int get_plot_x() const;
  int get_plot_y() const;
  int get_floor_area() const;
  int get_floor_count() const;
  int get_room_count() const;
  int get_window_count() const;

  void set_plot_size(int x, int y);
  void set_floor_area(int area);
  void set_floor_count(int floor_count);
  void set_room_count(int room_count);
```

```
  void set_window_count(int window_count);

private:
  int plot_size[2];
  int floor_area;
  int floor_count;
  int room_count;
  int window_count;
};
```

> *There is no point in making data private if you're simply going to expose it through other means.*

Coding standards emerged with edicts like "all data should be private and should have a get and set method." There may even be an insistence that get functions should be `const`-qualified. The sunlit uplands of bug-free code were just over the next hill. The drinks were on the house.

But hang on, what have we actually gained here? This sounds no different from the problems we used to have. We are still stuck with having to worry about the data being modified by other people. What is the point of the functions to get at the data?

This is the core of this guideline. Don't do this. Don't write getters and setters that do nothing more than forward data between the call site and the object. There is no point in making data private if you're simply going to expose it through other means. You may as well simply make the data public. Nothing is added to the user's comprehension of your class by putting the data behind get and set functions. If we simply get and set everything, then we aren't using the full power of C++. Worse, we have exchanged a compact if potentially dangerous API, the public member data of the struct house, for a bloated API. It's harder to take in at a glance. Also, what does it even mean to change the number of floors? That sounds like a very odd thing to do.

Adding get and set functions doesn't make this interface safer or less error prone. It's just another way in for bugs.

The question you need to ask is WHY you care about people modifying the data. Does arbitrary tweaking of member data invalidate instances of your class? Is there some restriction on your data? If so, then your setter function needs to do a little work. For example, the floor area should not exceed the area of the plot:

```
void house::set_floor_area(int area)
{
  floor_area = area;
  assert(floor_area < plot_size[0] * plot_size[1]);
}
```

Now this setter function is no longer trivial, and it has a reason to exist.

Consider another example: the bank account. The wrong way to do this would look like:

```
class account
{
public:
  void set_balance(int);²
  int get_balance() const;

private:
  int balance;
};
```

A better way of doing this is to introduce business logic:

```
class account
{
public:
  void deposit(int);
  void withdraw(int);
  int balance() const;

private:
  int balance_;
};
```

Now, you change the balance by doing what the business logic dictates. The deposit function will increase the balance, and the withdraw function will decrease the balance.

Class Invariants

The condition that the floor area cannot exceed the size of the plot is known as a class invariant. More generally, a class invariant is a condition that must hold for all valid instances of a class. It is established at construction and maintained between calls to public member functions. A class invariant for the account class may be that the balance may not fall below 0, or that the sum of all the deposits and withdrawals equals the balance. The class invariant for the house class is that the plot size must exceed the floor size, as expressed in the function `void house::set_floor_area(int area)`. It is the expression of that class invariant that makes the setter nontrivial.

2. Please, never use floats for money. Rounding errors and representation errors will propagate and degrade your output.

See whether you can find any class invariants in the following example.

```
class point
{
public:
  void set_x(float new_x) {
    x_ = new_x; }
  void set_y(float new_y) {
    y_ = new_y; }
  float get_x() const {
    return x_; }
  float get_y() const {
    return y_; }

private:
  float x_;
  float y_;
};
```

There are none. Changing the x-coordinate has no bearing on the y-coordinate. They can vary independently, and the point remains a point. The member functions add nothing to the class. This is precisely what the guideline is telling you not to do.

Try this example:

```
class team
{
public:
  void add_player(std::string name) {
    if (players_.size() < 11) players_.push_back(name); }
  std::vector<string> get_players() const {
    return players_; }

private:
  std::vector<string> players_;
}
```

The class invariant is that a team can have no more than 11 players.

Access levels allow a class designer to easily preserve class invariants by checking the effect of operations on the member data and ensuring that all the data retains valid values.

This guideline gives as its reason "A trivial getter or setter adds no semantic value; the data item could just as well be public." As we can see from the house example and the point example, that is exactly the case. There is no semantic difference between struct house and class house. The member functions in class point are redundant. There is an operational difference in that there is an opportunity to set breakpoints where the member data is read and written, but that has no impact on the semantic nature of the house abstraction or the point abstraction.

When creating a class and designing its interface it is quite usual to think of aspects of the abstraction being modeled with numbers: this is a computer you're writing for, after all. The temptation becomes simply to make those aspects numerical data members. If a client wants to change something, they call the function to set the new value and, after some checking to maintain class invariants, the corresponding data member is modified appropriately.

Nouns and Verbs

But this is rather missing the point of good class design. A class is an abstraction of an idea, not a bundle of data. The reason why `change_height` and `height` are good function identifiers is because they convey, in English, what is going on. The client engineer doesn't care that they are changing an `int` by some amount: they care that they are changing the height of the object. They don't want to know the value of the `height_` member, they want to know the height of the object. These two things operate at different levels of abstraction, and leaking abstraction details is bad practice, unnecessarily increasing the cognitive load of the client engineer.

The private data, the implementation, models the abstraction. The public member functions are expected to have meaning related to the abstraction, not to the implementation of the abstraction. Get and set functions precisely don't do this. The public/private divide identifies the different levels of abstraction.

Particularly, this approach helps to model the Model-View-Controller concept. As a real-world example, consider an elderly nuclear reactor consisting of a reactor core, and a control room that might have many panels of buttons, switches, and sliders and rows and rows of lamps and gauges. The lamps and gauges give you information about the reactor core; they are views. The buttons, switches, and sliders change the reactor core in some way; they are controllers.

This is observed in API design. Member functions that are `const`-qualified give you a view of the object. Other member functions control the object. Member data models the object. When choosing identifiers for the view and controller functions, it makes sense to choose nouns for the former and verbs for the latter rather than get and set functions.

Since private member data is used for the model, that implementation can be updated as the design evolves. This is very hard to do with get/set pairs: updating the implementation means updating all the call sites that call the get/set functions. One of the significant benefits of a correctly specified public interface is that it is much more stable than the private interface, which means that client code is less likely to need modifying if the implementation of the abstraction changes.

Of course, having said all this, sometimes you simply want to fling bundled data around without going to all the trouble of building a class: it might not be necessary, since the data could simply be bytes read from a file or a network socket. This is when you would use a struct. The data is public, and getters and setters are neither necessary nor relevant.

Summary

In summary:

- Trivial getters and setters add nothing to an interface.
- Nontrivial setters should preserve class invariants.
- Nouns and verbs provide superior function identifiers that better reflect the abstraction.
- Unrelated data without class invariants can be bundled into a struct.

Chapter 1.5

ES.10: Declare one name (only) per declaration

Let me introduce you

A declaration introduces a name into the program. It can also reintroduce a name: multiple declarations are entirely permissible, for without them we would be unable to have forward declarations. A definition is a special kind of declaration, since it provides enough detail to be able to use the thing that has been named.

There are a surprising number of types of declaration. You can declare functions, like this:

```
int fn(int a);
```

This is a very common use of declarations. A name is being introduced, `fn`, which is of type "function taking an integer and returning an integer." You can use this function in your code without having to define it first. You can declare a function or class template, like this:

```
template <class T, class U>
int fn(T a, U b);

template <class T>
class cl {
  public:
    cl(T);

  private:
    T t;
};
```

This is a function taking any types `T` and `U` and returning an `int`, and a class constructed with any type `T`. You can also declare partial and explicit template specializations, as well as explicit template instantiations:

```
template <class T> int fn(T a, int b); // Partial specialization
template <> int fn(float a, int b); // Explicit specialization
template class cl<int>; // Explicit instantiation
```

You can declare a namespace:

```
namespace cg30 {
… // more declarations
}
```

You can declare a linkage, to enable interoperation with other languages:

```
extern "C" int x;
```

You can declare an attribute:

```
// Warn if the return value is discarded rather than assigned
[[nodiscard]] int fn(int a);
```

There is also a set of declarations that can only be made inside a block; for example, within a function body. These include `asm` declarations, where you can specify explicit assembly language instructions for the compiler to insert into the output stream:

```
asm {
        push    rsi
        push    rdi
        sub     rsp, 184
}
```

Type alias declarations can introduce brief names for verbose types:

```
using cl_i = cl<int>;
```

Namespace aliases can shorten verbose nested namespaces:

```
namespace rv = std::ranges::views;
```

`using` declarations can introduce names from other namespaces into the current block:

```
using std::string // Now you no longer need to type the
                  // std:: prefix in this block for string
```

using directives, different from using declarations, inject entire namespaces into the current block:

```
using namespace std; // Never do this at global namespace scope. Ever.
                     // Ever, ever. Not with ANY namespace.
```

using enum declarations introduce the contents of an enumeration into the current block:

```
using enum country; // country may be defined earlier elsewhere
```

static_assert is a declaration. This can be made in a block:

```
static_assert(sizeof(int) == 4); // Assert that an int is four bytes big
```

Opaque enum declarations allow you to declare an enumeration without defining it, simply by specifying the underlying type and thus its size:

```
enum struct country : short;
```

You can even declare nothing at all:

```
;
```

Finally, there is the simple declaration. We are going to focus on declaring objects. You should be able to make sense of this declaration:

```
int a;
```

Here we have an instance of an integer named a. So far, so good. Of course, it is uninitialized (unless it is declared at global namespace scope), and the identifier is not very meaningful, but we'll let that pass.

Uniquely to this type of declaration, the standard allows the declaration of a comma-separated list of identifiers. Each identifier is treated as a stand-alone declaration with the same specifiers. For example:

```
int a, b, c, d;
```

Here we have four instances of an integer, named a, b, c, and d.

Backward compatibility

Look at this:

```
int* a, b, c, d;
```

Of what type are these objects?

We are hoping you spotted the trap and said that `a` is a pointer to an `int`, while `b`, `c`, and `d` are `int`s (this is one reason why you will often see pointers declared with the asterisk next to the identifier rather than the type). Of course, you spotted it because you were looking for trouble; historically I have uncovered compilation errors where the programmer has assumed that they are all pointers to `int`.

This is legal, but not wise. It is an accident waiting to happen and it should be excised from the language. At least, that is what one of my colleagues said when I told him about this. Unfortunately, this is legal for reasons of backward compatibility. The C programming language permits this because it used to require you to declare all your objects at the top of the function. This told the compiler how much the stack should grow by and provided addresses for all the data at the point of entry to the function. It was a handy optimization. However, the wiser thing to do instead is to write declarations on separate lines, like this:

```
int* a;
int b;
int c;
int d;
```

Backward compatibility cannot be overvalued. One of the fundamental reasons for the success of C++ is that it was already able to build millions of lines of code. When you introduce a new language like Rust or Go the outstanding body of code is tiny, consisting only of samples that the inventor has designed. With C++, you could select parts of existing programs and incrementally replace them with clearer abstractions. For example, the technique of late function binding has been available to C from the outset: it has always been possible to store function pointers in structs and invoke a particular member of a struct. The advance that C++ made was to formalize this approach and introduce the `virtual` keyword to signal that this was the intent of the programmer. You can still do things the old way, without using the `virtual` keyword:

```
using flump_fn_ptr = void(*)(int);

struct flumper {
  flump_fn_ptr flump;
  …
};

void flump_fn(int);

void fn()
{
```

```
  flumper fl { flump_fn; }
  fl.flump(7);
}
```

There are an extremely limited number of occasions where you might consider taking this approach rather than using virtual functions, but they are still legal. This doesn't make it a good idea, but it can still be done.

Similarly, as the C++ language develops, old code can still be compiled and run, with a few notable deprecation exceptions such as `std::auto_ptr`, for which `std::unique_ptr` is a drop-in replacement.

Writing clearer declarations

Back to the theme of this guideline, requiring early declaration can lead to some quite busy function preludes. The guideline presents the following example:

```
char *p, c, a[7], *pp[7], **aa[10];
```

If multiple names per declaration were not permitted, this would expand to

```
char *p; char c; char a[7]; char *pp[7]; char **aa[10];
```

or, more likely:

```
char *p;
char c;
char a[7];
char *pp[7];
char **aa[10];
```

Five lines of cognitive real estate would be consumed instead of one.

"But," you may be thinking, "what if my function has lots of state? What am I supposed to do then? List it, one line at a time, over half a screen? I need to group relevant parts together, and rather than having them on different lines, they will need a whole blank line between them. There will be so much stuff before we get to the actual function. This doesn't aid readability. This is a stupid idea."

The key there is "group relevant parts together," which sounds to me a lot like "form an abstraction." If you have state that is already related in some way, then formalize that relationship by defining a struct, and name, it in such a way as to capture and identify that relationship. Push the relevant functionality into the struct. Then you can replace those few lines of declarations with a single declaration: an instance of that struct. You should, at all times, remain vigilant for the opportunity to create a useful abstraction.

Structured binding

There is an exception to this guideline, which applies when it comes to the use of structured bindings. This innovation was introduced in C++17, and allows you to bind an array or a nonunion class type to a list of names. For example, in the simplest case:

```
int a[2] = {1, 2};
auto [x, y] = a;  // x = a[0], y = a[1]
```

Binding to a tuple like type is also simple:

```
std::unordered_map<std::string, int> dictionary;
auto [it, flag] = dictionary.insert({"one", 1});
        // it points to the element
        // flag signals whether the insertion was successful
```

Binding to a struct to unpack it works in the same way:

```
struct s {
  int a;
  float b;
};

s make_s();

auto [sa, sb] = make_s();  // sa is an int
                           // sb is a float
```

In each case, you will have observed multiple names in each declaration. However, we can mitigate any confusion by declaring the names on separate lines, thus:

```
std::unordered_map<std::string, int> dictionary;
auto  [it,     // it points to the element
       flag]   // flag signals whether the insertion was successful
      = dictionary.insert({"one", 1});
```

One person's simplification can be another person's complication, so this is a matter of taste and style, of course.

Summary

This is a fairly simple guideline which attends to old habits. Many of the Core Guidelines lead you toward writing more readable code that can be apprehended quickly. This guideline boils down to three considerations.

- There are many kinds of declaration.
- Names can be introduced anywhere.
- Do not confuse declarations by introducing more than one name per line unless the language requires it.

Chapter 1.6

NR.2: Don't insist to have only a single `return`-statement in a function

Rules evolve

It astonishes me that, 20 percent of the way through the 21st century, people still argue about this. This section of the Core Guidelines is called "Non-rules and myths." The remarkably prevalent advice that there should be only one return statement in a function falls right into this category.

Mandating a single return statement is an old, old rule. It is easy to forget the advances that have been made in programming. I bought my first computer, or rather, my parents did, back in 1981. It was a Sinclair ZX81, powered by an NEC Z80 CPU running at 3.25MHz. The operating system, supplied on 8KB of read-only memory (ROM), included a BASIC interpreter which enabled me to write simple programs in the meager 1KB of RAM.

Of course, I was 14 years old and I wanted to write games, and I discovered that the best way to do that was to bypass the BASIC interpreter entirely and write in native Z80 assembly language. With the help of *Mastering Machine Code on Your ZX81* by Toni Baker,[1] the astounding *Programming the Z80* by Rodnay Zaks,[2] and an assembler, I was able to write and sell my first games to my friends at school.

I found it much harder to write things in Z80 assembly language than I did in BASIC. Particularly, BASIC had line numbers and the concept of subroutines. I could branch by executing GOTO, or I could branch by executing GOSUB, which would take me back to where I came from when the interpreter parsed the RETURN

1. Baker, T, 1982. *Mastering Machine Code on Your ZX81*. Reston, VA: Reston Publishing Company, Inc.
2. Zaks, R, 1979. *Programming the Z80*. Berkeley, CA: Sybex.

keyword. As I grew more proficient with Z80, I could see common concepts between it and BASIC and started to grasp the nature of programming languages, and I could map the idea of line numbers to the program counter, and GOTO and GOSUB to "jp" and "call."

Z80 also allowed me to do some quite ghastly things. For example, I developed the habit of writing my code such that if there were two steps, A and B, and B was a useful piece of functionality by itself, I would put A before B so that I wouldn't have to call B; I could simply run on into B after A had finished. This had the side effect of making it unclear how I had got to B, whether it was from A or from some other place, but that did not matter to me because I knew everything that was going on.

No, really.

Another thing I could do was alter the stack so that I could return up the call stack by an arbitrary number of callers for the price of one instruction. It was faster. Since I knew everything that was going on, I could speed up my games. These things mattered.

No, really, they did.

I moved on to a ZX Spectrum: it came with more RAM (16KB) as well as color and sound! However, as my platform increased in scope, my ambition grew along with my code, and it became increasingly hard to debug. I was unable to work out where I had come from, and what code had already been executed. I quickly realized that I was making my life very, very difficult by indulging in these shenanigans. I considered the trade-off between execution speed and code comprehension. I decided that the extra cycles gained were not worth the loss of comprehension if I could never eliminate all bugs. I learned that it is fun and quite easy to write super-fast Z80 code, but it is next to impossible to debug it: there is a middle ground between performance and legibility. This was a valuable lesson.

As a result, I changed the way I wrote code. I organized it into reusable parts and was rigorous about documenting in the source where the parts started and finished. No more decrementing the stack pointer. No more jumping about to useful parts of larger functions. Life became considerably easier.

I graduated to an Atari ST, with a Motorola 68000 CPU running at 8MHz, and a truly extraordinary 512MB of RAM. My programming style of well-organized parts kept me sane. There was one and only one place to start a piece of code, and you would always go back to where you came from. I told everyone it was the one true way: I was religious in my zeal.

It turned out I was not the only person to write code like this. FORTRAN and COBOL programmers could tie themselves in similar knots if they decided not to take the same kind of care. This led to a simple piece of wisdom: "Single Entry, Single Exit." There should be one and only one entry point for a function. There should be only one place it returns to: where it was called from.

Single Entry, Single Exit was part of the structured programming philosophy, which emerged from Edsger Dijkstra's letter to the editor titled "GOTO statement considered harmful."[3] The book *Structured Programming*[4] is still an excellent read and you should consider reading both of these. They informed how programming was done for over a decade.

Unfortunately, old habits die hard. Not only that, but the motivation behind those habits starts to recede from memory with the passage of time. New innovations diminish the importance of old wisdom. Functions in C++ obviate the need to pay attention to the idea of "Single Entry." The syntax of C++ makes it impossible to jump halfway into a function. Similarly, there is no way to return to anywhere other than the call site (exception handling and coroutines aside).

You might be asking yourself what this has to do with multiple return statements. Well, unfortunately, there was a mix-up with the prepositions in the minds of the programmer community, and single exit came to mean "return FROM one place only" rather than "return TO one place only."

Disaster.

Ensuring cleanup

Let's look at an example demonstrating the wisdom of a single return statement. Assume this function is calling an old C library exporting functions for acquiring, manipulating, and displaying resources based on an integer identifier:

```
int display(int ID)
{
  auto h = get_handle_to_resource(ID);
  if (h == 0) {
    return 0;
  }
  auto j = manipulate_resource(h);
  if (j < 0) {
    release_handle(h);
    return 0;
  }
  auto k = supply_resource_to_system(h, j);
  if (k < 0) {
    return 0; /* forgot to release handle */
  }
  display_resource(h);
```

3. www.cs.utexas.edu/users/EWD/ewd02xx/EWD215.PDF

4. *Structured Programming* by Ole Johan-Dahl, Edsger W. Dijkstra, and Charles Anthony Richard Hoare.

```
  release_handle(h);
  return 1;
}
```

In this snippet of code, we see a very common situation: a handle to a resource is acquired and must subsequently be released before the handle falls out of scope. The engineer has forgotten to release the handle at the third return statement. One solution is to have a single return statement, preceded by the release of the handle, thus:

```
int display(int ID)
{
  auto result = 0;
  auto h = get_handle_to_resource(ID);
  if (h != 0) {
    auto j = manipulate_resource(h);
    if (j >= 0) {
      auto k = supply_resource_to_system(h, j);
      if (k >= 0) {
        display_resource(h);
        result = 1;
      }
    }
  }
  release_handle(h);
  return result;
}
```

Ah, no, hang on, that's wrong. The call to `release_handle` should only be made if the handle was successfully gotten. Let's try again:

```
int display(int ID)
{
  auto result = 0;
  auto h = get_handle_to_resource(ID);
  if (h != 0) {
    auto j = manipulate_resource(h);
    if (j >= 0) {
      auto k = supply_resource_to_system(h, j);
      if (k >= 0) {
        display_resource(h);
        result = 1;
      }
    }
    release_handle(h);
  }
  return result;
}
```

This approach does not scale well for longer functions with many conditional branches, since each condition will introduce a further indentation, reducing legibility; but functions should be small anyway, which weakens this argument. It also introduces additional state in the form of the return value, which increases the reader's cognitive load a little when reasoning about the function which, although this is not too great a burden, runs the risk of it being modified after the correct value has been calculated, a risk that will increase as the function grows. This has the advantage of `release_handle` being called whatever happens, although it needs to be called within the correct `if` branch. This argument of reliable cleanup remains a strong case for a single return statement. It is sensible advice.

For C programmers.

The bug in the first implementation of display was that the resource handle was not released in every pathway before leaving the function. The fix was to ensure all appropriate paths through the function ended with a single call to `release_handle`, after which return could safely be called.

The preeminent feature of C++ is deterministic, programmer-definable cleanup, provided by destructors. You will not convince me otherwise. At a stroke, an entire class of errors was eliminated with the introduction of this feature. It is deterministic in that you know precisely when it will be called. In the case of automatic objects, which are created on the stack, it is when the name falls out of scope.

Using RAII

Rather than use flow control to ensure code is executed, it is safer to make use of the idiom known as Resource Acquisition Is Initialization, or RAII. In this case, we bundle the acquire and release functions with the handle into a single struct:

```
int display(int ID)
{
  struct resource {
    resource(int h_) : h(h_) {}
    ~resource() { release_handle(h); }
    operator int() { return h; }

  private:
    int h;
  };

  resource r(get_handle_to_resource(ID));
  if (r == 0) {
    return 0;
```

```
  }
  auto j = manipulate_resource(r);
  if (j < 0) {
    return 0;
  }
  auto k = supply_resource_to_system(r, j);
  if (k < 0) {
    return 0;
  }
  display_resource(r);
  return 1;
}
```

Note that this code is not signaling errors by throwing exceptions but by using multiple return statements with different values to signal success. If this were a C++ library rather than a C library, we might expect the functions to throw an error rather than return. What would our example look like then?

```
void display(int ID)
{
  struct resource {
    resource(int h_) : h(h_) {}
    ~resource() { release_handle(h); }
    operator int() { return h; }

  private:
    int h;
  };

  resource r(get_handle_to_resource(ID));
  auto j = manipulate_resource(r);
  supply_resource_to_system(r, j);
  display_resource(r);
}
```

Of course, we might also expect the functions to take user-defined types rather than `int`s, but please let that pass for the sake of this example.

Now we have no explicit return at all. This is to be expected; after all, this function simply does something, not even signaling success or failure. With exceptions used to signal failure there is no need for a return statement: the code assumes success and invisibly throws if it fails. It doesn't calculate a value and return it.

This struct is so useful it should be pulled out of that function and made available to other users. Indeed, I've seen many codebases that interface with C libraries that contain something like this:

```
template <class T, class release_fn>
struct RAII
{
  RAII(T t_) : t(t_) {}
  ~RAII() { release_fn r; (t); }
  operator T() { return t; }

private:
  T t;
};
```

where `T` is usually a built-in or other trivial type.

It behooves me to acknowledge that exceptions are not universally deployed in C++ codebases. Throwing an exception requires the program to unwind the stack; that is, to destroy every automatic object created between the try site and the catch site. This introduces extra bookkeeping to the program to achieve this, which occupies memory. C++ is used in the broadest variety of environments, some of which are extremely sensitive to memory constraints or execution times. I have witnessed a stand-up fight in a parking lot over a 1KB buffer suddenly becoming available after some cunning optimization.

I have witnessed a stand-up fight in a parking lot over a 1KB buffer suddenly becoming available after some cunning optimization.

Compilers, as a matter of course, offer options to disable exception handling, which produces smaller, faster binaries. This is a dangerous thing to do. First, this will cost you in incomplete error handling. `dynamic_cast` throws an exception if a cast to a reference fails. The standard library throws an exception if allocation fails. Accessing a `std::variant` object incorrectly will generate an exception.

Second, you are not guaranteed smaller and faster binaries. The introduction of complex, explicit error-handling code may soak up all your advantage and yield additional cost. However, if it is important enough, if it is worth the trade-off, engineers will write code to accommodate the absence of exception handling. It's not a pretty sight, but needs must when the devil drives.

However, if your codebase does permit exception handling, then single return statements carrying the successfully computed value back to the call site become the normal way of things. Multiple return statements might signal a function that is trying to do too much.

Writing good functions

There are nearly fifty Core Guidelines about functions. We give two of them their own chapter, but it's worth considering some others here in the context of multiple return statements. For example, Core Guideline F.2: "A function should perform a single logical operation." Although this guideline talks about splitting larger functions into smaller component functions, and viewing large numbers of parameters with suspicion, one of the side effects of following this advice is that your functions are likely to have a single return instruction, which is the result of the function.

In the same vein, Core Guideline F.3: "Keep functions short and simple." The function that acts as a counterexample stretches over 27 lines of text and includes three return statements. However, the final example, which puts some of the logic into two helper functions, is nearly a third of the size but still contains three different return instructions, decided upon by the input parameters.

Core Guideline F.8: "Prefer pure functions." This is a tall order but excellent advice. A pure function is one that does not refer to state outside of its scope. This makes them parallelizable, easy to reason about, more amenable to optimization, and, again, likely to be short and simple.

The important point is that there are very, very few rules that are cast-iron. Rules like that tend to end up being encoded in the language itself. For example, "don't leak resources" is encoded in the destructor feature and in the library smart pointers. A single return statement might be a sign of other good practices being observed, but it isn't a universal rule. It's a matter of taste and style. Consider the following function:

```
int categorize1(float f)
{
  int category = 0;
  if (f >= 0.0f && f < 0.1f) {
    category = 1;
  }
  else if (f >= 0.1f && f < 0.2f) {
    category = 2;
  }
  else if (f >= 0.2f && f < 0.3f) {
    category = 3;
  }
  else if (f >= 0.3f && f < 0.4f) {
    category = 4;
  }
  else {
    category = 5;
  }
```

```
  return category;
}
```

Now compare it with this function:

```
int categorize2(float f)
{
  if (f >= 0.0f && f < 0.1f) {
    return 1;
  }
  if (f >= 0.1f && f < 0.2f) {
    return 2;
  }
  if (f >= 0.2f && f < 0.3f) {
    return 3;
  }
  if (f >= 0.3f && f < 0.4f) {
    return 4;
  }
  return 5;
}
```

Which of these is "better"? They both do the same thing. Any compiler is likely to yield identical output for each. The second contains multiple return statements but fewer characters. The first contains extra state but clearly identifies a series of mutually exclusive conditions, rather than hiding that information away after an indentation. Depending on your programming experience, what programming languages you've been exposed to, what coding advice you've already absorbed in your professional life, and a whole host of other conditions, you will have a slight preference for one over the other. Neither is objectively better; nor is "each function should have only one return statement" a reasonable rule.

Summary

We all want hard and fast rules that we don't have to think about, but these golden edicts are few and far between and usually end up becoming encoded within the programming language anyway. The single-return rule is old and due for retirement in the context of C++.

- Understand the source of received wisdom.
- Differentiate between returning results and throwing exceptions.
- Identify rules that are matters of taste.

Section 2

Don't hurt yourself

Chapter 2.1

P.11: Encapsulate messy constructs, rather than spreading through the code

In the course of this chapter we'll learn about encapsulation, and also about the closely related concepts of information hiding and abstraction. These three are often used interchangeably, usually at the cost of clarity. Before we start, we want to set the scene by building a parser. We will return to these three concepts in a moment.

All in one gulp

One of the qualities that marks out a great engineer is the ability to notice when things start to get out of hand. We are all excellent at spotting when things have got completely out of hand: who has not started a code review with the phrase, "There's quite a lot going on here and I found it hard to follow." Sadly, that skill rarely stretches to anticipating the bloom of messy code.

Let's walk through an example. Early in the execution of my program, I want to read in some options from an external file identified on the command line. They are declared as key-value pairs. There are only a dozen possible options, but being a smart engineer, I decide to create a separate function for doing this. I am going to call it `parse_options_file`. It will take a filename which I will pull out of the command line. If none is declared, I will not call the function. This leads me to the function signature:

```
void parse_options_file(const char*);
```

The function body is simple: open the file, read each option line by line, and update the state appropriately, until we reach the end of the file. It will probably look something like this:

```
void parse_options_file(const char* filename)
{
  auto options = std::ifstream(filename);
  if (!options.good()) return;
  while (!options.eof())
  {
    auto key = std::string{};
    auto value = std::string{};
    options >> key >> value;
    if (key == "debug")
    {
      debug = (value == "true");
    }
    else if (key == "language")
    {
      language = value;
    }
    // and so on...
  }
}
```

This is great! I can easily add new options in one place and withdraw old options without any hassle. If the file contains invalid options, I can just notify the user in the final `else` declaration.

A couple of days later, a new option is defined whose value could be several words. That's fine, I can just read until the end of the line in that option. I'll create a 500-character buffer and make a string from it. That will look like this:

```
else if (key == "tokens")
{
  char buf[500];
  options.getline(&buf[0], 500);
  tokens = std::string{buf};
}
```

I totally rock. I've come up with a simple, flexible way of parsing options. I can just add code for each option! Great!

The following week, a colleague tells me that some of the tokens are only valid if the user has set the debug flag. That's also fine: I set the debug flag at the top of the function, so I can query it later in the function and be sure that I only apply tokens when they're applicable. Mind you, I'm keeping track of state now, and that is something to be mindful of.

Mmm...

The next month, incorrect preferences files are causing a stir. I am asked to apply the preferences only if they are all valid. I sigh. That is fine. I can create a preferences object containing all the new state and return that if it is valid. `std::optional` will come in useful here. I go to modify the function and discover that my lovely, neat, tidy, elegant, beautiful, special function has been the target of considerable interest as other engineers have thrown their preferences tokens into the mix. There are now 115 preferences being interrogated. That is going to be quite the maintenance issue, but that is fine, it is just a set of values that I am going to set in the function and then transfer piecewise at the call site...

Stop. Just stop. Look at yourself. You have a 600-line function full of lots of state and a bajillion conditional statements. Are you really the new Donald Knuth?[1] What happened here?

You have created, or allowed the creation of, a messy construct. A single function, many screens long, several tabs deep, and still steadily growing is the very definition of such a thing. This function has suffered from appalling scope creep and you need to find some way of effecting scope retreat before it all comes crashing down around you: you know full well that it's only a matter of time before the bugs start pouring in and you are enslaved to the constant maintenance of this beast. You must plead for time to refactor before disaster engulfs the codebase and your career.

What it means to encapsulate a messy construct

We mentioned encapsulation, information hiding, and abstraction at the start of this item. As promised, we will take a look at these concepts now.

Encapsulation is the process of enclosing one or more things into a single entity. Confusingly, that entity is called an encapsulation. C++ offers a number of encapsulation mechanisms. The class is the most obvious: take some data and some functions, wrap them up in a pair of braces, and put `class` (or `struct`) and an identifier at the front. Of course, there is also the enumeration: take a bunch of constants, wrap them up in a pair of braces, and put `enum` and an identifier at the front. Function definitions are a form of encapsulation: take a bunch of instructions, wrap them up in a pair of braces, and put an identifier and a pair of parentheses, optionally containing parameters, at the front.

How about namespaces? Take a bunch of definitions and declarations, wrap them up in a pair of braces, and put `namespace` and an optional identifier on the outside. Source files work in a similar way: take a bunch of definitions and declarations, put

1. https://en.wikipedia.org/wiki/Donald_Knuth

them in a file, and save it to your file system with a name. Modules are the first new encapsulation mechanism in a long time. These work in a similar way to source files: take a bunch of definitions and declarations, put them in a file, add the `export` keyword at the top, and save it to your file system with a name.

Information hiding implies that some encapsulation is taking place, but encapsulation does not imply that information hiding is taking place.

Encapsulation is only part of the story, as anyone with any experience of modules will tell you. All we have done in each of these examples is gathered things together and named them as a single entity. If we are smart, we will have gathered related things together. Information hiding is a more subtle activity, requiring you to make more careful decisions. In addition to gathering, you must decide which items you are going to reveal to the outside world, and which you are going to hide. Information hiding implies that some encapsulation is taking place, but encapsulation does not imply that information hiding is taking place.

Some of the encapsulation mechanisms of C++ support information hiding. The class offers us access levels. Members within the private implementation are hidden from clients of the struct. This is how we relieve clients of the burden of enforcing class invariants: by hiding the implementation and thus preventing clients from breaking them. The enumeration offers no information hiding: there is no way of exposing only a few members of an enumeration. Functions hide information perfectly, by merely exposing an identifier and a return type, while hiding away the implementation. Namespaces can expose declarations and hide definitions by distributing over more than one file. Header and source files do the same thing, as do modules.

Consider the problem at hand. How will encapsulation help us? We have lots and lots of options being handled in a single function. Perhaps we can have a different function for each option. We then call the correct function within the `if` statement that checks the key. The function could return a `bool` depending on whether or not the parameter data was valid.

This looks good: we have encapsulated all the different options in their own function and we can easily add further functions for new options; we just need to grow the parsing function for each one. We can even capture the return value to validate the options file. We still have to create an object which can apply the options if they are all valid, so we'll need to update that when we add a new option, but that's an easy thing to document, and anyway, other engineers will get the pattern when they look at other examples of these option functions.

Mmm...

Your Spidey-Sense should be kicking off about the places where this can go wrong. You are still relying on the other engineers to do the right thing when they add new options. They might misunderstand the nature of the validation process, or forget to check for the function in the `if` statement, or misspell the option text. You have improved matters considerably, but sometimes encapsulation and information hiding are not enough. To solve these remaining problems, we are going to have to bring out the big guns: abstraction.

The purpose of language and the nature of abstraction

Abstraction is a tricky word. Matters aren't helped by the fact that the result of abstraction is an abstraction, just as an encapsulation is the result of encapsulation. Let us consider the process of abstraction, in the same way that we just considered the processes of encapsulation and information hiding.

Literally, abstraction means to draw off from. In a programming context, it means identifying and isolating the important parts of a problem, drawing them off, and discarding the remainder. We separate them from the details of implementation. We label abstractions with identifiers. Again, consider the nature of functions: we bundle a set of instructions into a single entity and label it. The function is an abstraction with a name meaningful to the problem domain. Similarly with classes: the class is an abstraction with a name meaningful to the problem domain, containing relevant functionality to model behavior implied by the name.

However, the art of abstraction is deciding what should lie within the scope of the abstraction and what should stay outside. This is where it differs from mere encapsulation. Also, we use the word "art" advisedly: there is no mechanical method for deciding where to draw the line between what is relevant to the abstraction and what is not. That ability comes with practice and experience.

Returning to our problem, we are trying to parse a file of key-value pairs and apply the results to the environment if they are valid. The function is well named: `parse_options_file`. The problem we have is safely adding arbitrary key-value pairs. Is the identity of the full set of pairs actually relevant to `parse_options_file`? Is it within scope? Can we separate the options from the function?

At the moment we are simply pulling keys from the file and checking each in an ever-growing if-else statement since we cannot switch-case on strings. This sounds like an associative container. In fact, a map of keys against function pointers sounds perfect here. Suddenly our function has lost a huge amount of repetition and been replaced with a single interrogation of a map and a corresponding function call.

```
auto options_table = std::map<std::string, bool(*)(std::string const&)>
{{"debug"s, set_debug},
 {"language"s, set_language}}; // Extend as appropriate

void parse_options_file(const char* filename) {
  auto options = std::ifstream(filename);
  if (!options.good()) return;
  while (!options.eof()) {
    auto key = std::string{};
    auto value = std::string{};
    options >> key >> value;
    auto fn = options_table.find(key);
    if (fn != options_table.end()) {
      (*(fn->second))(value);
    }
  }
}
```

The important part of this function is that it parses an options file and does something with each key. Unfortunately, along the way, we have lost the capability for values to contain spaces. The chevron operator will stop extracting when it reaches white space. We'll return to this shortly.

However, this is certainly feeling better. All we must do is initialize the map of keys and function pointers. Unfortunately, we have just moved the problem around. The initializer is another point where users can trip up: it is easy to forget to update the initializer. Perhaps we can automate that?

We absolutely can. Rather than mapping keys against function pointers, we can map them against function objects with constructors, and create static objects rather than functions. The constructor can insert the address of the object into the map. In fact, we can derive all the function objects from a base class that will do that for us. Also, now that we have a base class, we can add a validation function and perform a validation pass followed by a commit pass. It all seems to be coming together.

```
auto options_table = std::map<std::string, command*>{};

class command {
public:
  command(std::string const& id) {
      options_table.emplace(id, this);}
  virtual bool validate(std::string const&) = 0;
  virtual void commit(std::string const&) = 0;
};

class debug_cmd : public command {
public:
```

```
  debug_cmd() : command("debug"s) {}
  bool validate(std::string const& s) override;
  void commit(std::string const& s) override;
};
debug_cmd debug_cmd_instance;

class language_cmd : public command {
public:
  language_cmd() : command("language"s) {}
  bool validate(std::string const& s) override;
  void commit(std::string const& s) override;
};
language_cmd language_cmd_instance;
```

What next? Although we are parsing an options file, we are only reading a series of characters. They do not have to come from a file: they could come from the command line itself. We should rename the function `parse_options` and change the input parameter to a `std::istream`. If a key is not found, it could be treated as a filename and an attempt could be made to open the file. Then we could simply recurse.

```
void parse_options(std::istream& options) {
  while (options.good()) {
    auto key = std::string{};
    auto value = std::string{};
    options >> key >> value;
    auto fn = options_table.find(key);
    if (fn != options_table.end()) {
      if ((*(fn->second))->validate(value)) {
        (*(fn->second))->commit(value);
      }
    } else {
      auto file = std::ifstream(key);
      parse_options(file);
    }
  }
}
```

Now that we have separate function objects for each key, we are not limited to initializing data. We can treat each key as a command, and suddenly, we have a basic scripting facility. Whereas at the start of this chapter the engineer had to extend a function in an unbounded fashion, all they must do now is derive a new class from `command` and override `validate` and `commit`.

We have now moved from a single, potentially enormous parsing function to a small bounded function and a dictionary of parsing objects. We have also gained command-line parsing at very little cost as an added extra. This was all achieved by considering what was relevant to which part of the problem. What started life as a messy construct has become a clean and easily maintainable scripting facility with bonus content. Everybody wins.

Levels of abstraction

Another way of moving from the single parsing function to smaller bundles of functionality might have been to group related activities in separate functions, something like this:

```
void parse_options_file(const char* filename)
{
  auto options = std::ifstream(filename);
  if (!options.good()) return;
  while (!options.eof())
  {
    auto key = std::string{};
    auto value = std::string{};
    options >> key >> value;
    parse_debug_options(key, value);
    parse_UI_options(key, value);
    parse_logging_options(key, value);
    // and so on...
  }
}
```

This does indeed address the issue of encapsulating a messy construct: you now have several functions, each labeled by category. However, this has only moved the problem around rather than improved matters. Future maintainers must decide which is the correct function to add their parser to. Decisions need to be made when those functions get too big about how to divide them further. Such an approach does not respect levels of abstraction.

To explain levels of abstraction, consider the seven-layer OSI model.[2] This model partitions a communication system into abstraction layers. Each layer exposes an interface to the next layer, but not to the previous layer. Engineers work in the layer that fits their specialty. For example, I am a software engineer rather than an electronics engineer. I would feel very uncomfortable working in layer 1, the physical layer, and much happier working in layer 7, the application layer. You may have heard the term "full-stack engineer." This engineer is comfortable in all the layers. They are mythical creatures.

2. https://en.wikipedia.org/wiki/OSI_model

The levels of abstraction in the parsing problem can be described thus:

1. The streaming layer, which delivers a stream of data to...
2. The parsing layer, which delivers individual symbols to...
3. The dictionary layer, which matches symbols to tokens and delivers them to...
4. The token layer, which validates input and updates values

These abstractions are all distinct, nonoverlapping parts of the problem.

Abstraction by refactoring and drawing the line

The key to abstraction is knowing where to draw the line that separates the different layers. As we remarked earlier, it is an art, not a science, but there are three things you can look for.

First, excessive detail. Does the code spend time carrying out tasks that seem singularly unrelated to the task at hand? The Core Guideline for this chapter uses a busy `for` loop involving reading a file, validating, and performing reallocation as an example: there is too much going on in there. One can also consider designing baroque data structures especially for local use. Is this data structure of any use outside of this context? Will it ever be? If the answer is yes, take this data structure and move it from the code under examination to a more generic library. Separating detail into different libraries is a form of abstraction that is applicable to both the guideline example and the notion of pulling out data structures.

Second, verbose repetition. What sort of patterns can you see? Has there been some devious copying and pasting? Are you able to express them as an individual function or function template? Pull that code out into a function, give it a name, and rejoice in having identified an abstraction.

Third, and we would love a better word for this, wheel reinvention. This is slightly different from repetition and is a combination of the first two items. A lot of time has been spent identifying and naming the fundamental algorithms of computing. Make sure you are familiar with what they are and how they are offered through the standard library.

Repetition is a hint that there is an algorithm waiting to be uncovered, and a good algorithm is merely a concise description of what a piece of code does. In 2013 Sean Parent gave a talk called C++ Seasoning,[3] which spent much of the first half

3. https://www.youtube.com/watch?v=W2tWOdzgXHA

addressing the mantra "no raw loops." His advice was to use an existing algorithm such as `std::find_if`, or implement a known algorithm as a function template and contribute it to an open source library, or devise a brand-new algorithm, write a paper about it, and become famous giving talks. This is excellent advice that will guide you on your way to eliminating messy code.

Summary

Messy code stops the reader from understanding at a glance what is going on. Avoid this by:

- Identifying patterns of existing code or existing algorithms, preferably as they happen, and lifting them out of the mess and abstracting them into their own function
- Identifying the different levels of abstraction
- Identifying how to encapsulate all these parts

Chapter 2.2

I.23: Keep the number of function arguments low

How much should they earn?

Here's a function declaration:

```
double salary(PayGrade grade, int location_id);
```

It's nice to see "double salary" at the start of a line of code; sadly, the purpose of this function is not to double your salary, but to report a salary for a particular pay grade at a particular location. Also, as remarked earlier, you should use integral types for money, so we shall redeclare this function, thus:

```
int salary(PayGrade grade, int location_id);
```

You might see this sort of thing in a government contract: civil servant salaries are often pegged to a pay grade but will vary by location. In the UK, for example, some civil servants in London are paid more because of the increased cost of living in the capital.

This is a perfectly normal, ordinary function. It doesn't appear to rely on external information and in all likelihood simply queries a database table to retrieve the data. It has the look and feel of a first attempt at a function: simple, unambiguous, quiet, unassuming.

Then one day, by act of parliament or some other great immovable object of irresistible progress, the requirements change, and salaries are now calculated based not only on pay grade and location, but also on length of service. Perhaps as an aid to retention, it has been decided that a small multiplying factor should be included for long-serving members of staff.

This is not a problem: we can simply add a parameter to the function to represent length of service. This is measured in years, so an `int` will do. We now have

```
int salary(PayGrade grade, int location_id, int years_of_service);
```

You might be looking at the pair of `int`s and answering the question "what could possibly go wrong" with "parameter inversion." You make a mental note to see how many different locations there are, with a view to creating an enumeration so that the second parameter can be converted into a more narrowly focused type.

Time passes and, with a crashing inevitability, pay mechanisms change again, and another consideration emerges. This one is based on team size. There has been grumbling that management pay grades don't reflect the additional burden of managing a team of more than 10 people. Rather than add a new pay grade, which would represent an enormous amount of bureaucratic negotiation, a new rule has been added for employees in the management pay grades that, as with long service, adds a small multiplying factor. This is a simple matter of passing in the number of reports, so we add a fourth parameter.

```
int salary(PayGrade grade, int location_id, int years_of_service,
           int reports_count, bool* large_team_modifier);
```

The `reports_count` boundary depends on the pay grade. Above a certain pay grade, the multiplier comes into effect for managers of larger teams. However, the information about whether the multiplier is applied is important to other functions. After extensive discussion on a lengthy email thread about the merits of returning `std::pair<int,bool>` versus adding a pointer to `bool` to the parameter list, team `std::pair` loses the day and the function signature is now amended to

```
int salary(PayGrade grade, int location_id, int years_of_service,
           int reports_count, bool* large_team_modifier);
```

It turns out there are several dozen locations whose boundaries are rather flexible, so an enumeration isn't appropriate for the second parameter type.

This function is now rather overworked. The presence of three consecutive `int`s in the function signature is a trap for the unwary. If we have five reports after seven years of service, swapping those two values around would likely yield a credible but incorrect value. This kind of bug is desperately hard to spot as word-blindness starts affecting your reading of the code.

In addition, not only is it querying a database for information, but it is also performing a couple of additional calculations, one of which is conditional on other state. The function is called `salary`, which seems innocuous, but in fact a fair amount of activity is going on under the hood. If this is performance-sensitive code, that may be relevant.

Simplifying matters through abstraction

The guideline suggests that the two most common reasons for functions having too many parameters are

1. Missing an abstraction
2. Violating "one function, one responsibility"

Let's look at those in detail.

The purpose of the `salary` function is to calculate a value given some state. The function started off taking two pieces of state and grew as requirements changed. However, one thing that remained constant was that the function calculated a salary according to an employee's details. On reflection, once that third parameter made an appearance in the function signature, the smart thing to do would have been to encapsulate the parameters into a single abstraction and call it `SalaryDetails`.

Once you have a collection of state serving a purpose, possibly with some relationships between them, there is a chance that you have discovered an abstraction. Collect that state together into a single class, give it a name, and form those relationships into class invariants.

This is what is meant by missing an abstraction. Once you have a collection of state serving a purpose, possibly with some relationships between them, there is a chance that you have discovered an abstraction. Collect that state together into a single class, give it a name, and form those relationships into class invariants.

Applying this process to the `salary` function, we now have a struct called `SalaryDetails` that looks like this:

```
struct SalaryDetails
{
  SalaryDetails(PayGrade grade_, int location_id_, int years_of_service_,
                int reports_count_);

  PayGrade pay_grade;
  int location_id;
  int years_of_service;
```

```
  int reports_count;
};
```

and a function signature that looks like this:

```
int salary(SalaryDetails const&);
```

This is only a partial improvement. There are still three ints in the constructor ready to trap the unwary. Indeed, there is a Core Guideline warning against this practice, I.24: "Avoid adjacent parameters that can be invoked by the same arguments in either order with different meaning." However, techniques exist, such as strong typing, to mitigate this problem, so all is not lost.

As changes were made to the original salary requirements function, those changes could be reflected in the SalaryDetails struct instead. Indeed, you might decide to make salary a member function of the SalaryDetails abstraction. You could also make large_team_modifier a predicate, that is, a function that returns true or false, and create a class:

```
class SalaryDetails
{
public:
  SalaryDetails(PayGrade grade_, int location_id_, int years_of_service_,
                int reports_count_);
  int salary() const;
  bool large_team_manager() const;

private:
  PayGrade pay_grade;
  int location_id;
  int years_of_service;
  int reports_count;
};
```

Client code would now look like this:

```
auto salary_details = SalaryDetails(PayGrade::SeniorManager, 55, 12, 17);
auto salary = salary_details.salary();
auto large_team_manager = salary_details.large_team_manager();
```

If you decide against the member function approach, then the member data would be public and the client code would look like this:

```
auto salary_details = SalaryDetails(PayGrade::SeniorManager, 55, 12, 17);
auto salary = calculate_salary(salary_details, &large_team_manager);
```

Let's reiterate what went on there. Functionality was required to produce a value from some state. The quantity of state grew. That state was abstracted into a class, and member functions were added to reflect what was originally wanted from the function.

It's worth taking a moment here to consider where the data being used to call the function came from. We explicitly provided 55, 12, and 17 in the example, but that would be an unlikely use case. It is more likely that there is an `Employee` class containing this information and it was simply being passed to the `salary` function, perhaps like this:

```
for (auto const& emp : employees)
auto final_salary = calculate_salary(
   PayGrade::SeniorManager, emp.location, emp.service, emp.reports);
```

When I see a function call like that, I immediately wonder why it isn't a member function of the data source's class. In this case I would be asking "why isn't `salary` a member function of the `Employee` class?"

Perhaps the author is unable to modify the `Employee` class; it may be in third-party code. In that case, it is better to pass the entire `Employee` class to the `salary` function via a `const` reference and let the function query the class rather than the engineer calling the function, like this:

```
for (auto const& emp : employees)
auto final_salary = calculate_salary(PayGrade::SeniorManager, emp);
```

Both solutions reduce the quantity of parameters that the `salary` function takes, and that's the aim of this guideline.

Do as little as possible, but no less

Does this mean that you should always convert a bundle of parameters to a class?

It does not. The guideline says keep the number of function arguments low. If you are working within the x64 ABI, there is a four-register fast-call calling convention by default. A four-parameter function will execute slightly faster than a function taking a class by reference. It is up to you to decide if the trade-off is worth it. Of course, if you have a dozen parameters, then creating a class to encapsulate the state is an obvious choice. There is no hard-and-fast rule, just a guideline that should be interpreted in the context in which you are working.

The second part of the guideline discussion focuses on violating the "one function, one responsibility" rule. This is a simple rule that says that a function should do one thing only, which enables it to do it well. The poster child for violation of this principle is the `realloc` function. There is a good chance that if you are a well-behaved C++ programmer you will never have encountered this beast. It exists in the C Standard Library, where it is declared in the header `<stdlib.h>` with this signature:

```
void* realloc(void* p, size_t new_size);
```

It does a number of things. Principally, it resizes the memory pointed to by `p`. More precisely, it will grow or contract the raw memory block pointed to by `p` to `new_size` bytes, allocating a new block if it can't grow the existing block, and then copying the contents of the old memory block to the new memory block. This copy ignores the semantics of copy construction and simply copies the bytes, which is why a well-behaved C++ programmer is unlikely to encounter it.

If you pass zero to the `new_size` parameter, the behavior is implementation defined. You might think that it would simply free the block entirely, but that is not necessarily the case.

The function returns the address of the new block of memory, or the address of the expanded block of memory. If a bigger block is requested and there is not enough memory to allocate this new block, the return value is the null pointer.

There are two things going on here. The memory is resized, and the contents may be moved. Different levels of abstraction are being mixed up, and the second action is conditional on the first failing. If I were to offer this functionality from scratch, I would offer a single function, called `resize`, like this:

```
bool resize(void* p, size_t new_size);
```

This would simply attempt to grow or shrink the block. If it failed, I could then allocate a new block myself and move everything over. There would be no need for implementation-defined behavior. I would be respecting levels of abstraction by separating reallocation from moving stuff around.

The principle of "one function, one responsibility" is related to cohesion. In software engineering, cohesion refers to the degree to which things belong together. We hope that the example above demonstrates high cohesion in a function. High cohesion is a good thing. It leads to improved readability and reusability while diminishing complexity. When you cannot give your function a good name, there is a good chance that it is doing too many things. Naming is hard, particularly when you are naming something complicated.

In the case of a class, high cohesion implies that the member functions and data are intimately related. Cohesion is increased when the member functions carry out a small number of related activities with a small set of data rather than with unrelated sets of data. High cohesion and loose coupling often go together. You can read more about them in the book *Structured Design,*[1] a text over forty years old but still worth reading today.

---

1. Yourdon, E, and Constantine, L, 1978. *Structured Design: Fundamentals of a Discipline of Computer Program and Systems Design* (2 ed.). New York: Yourdon Press.

Real-life examples

If you squint in the right way, you will see that the second guideline discussion is really another way of expressing the first. When a function accumulates responsibilities, it costs abstraction, becoming a very specific entry in the glossary of the problem domain. Let us look at the examples shown in the guideline itself.

The first of these is the `merge` function. This behemoth has the following signature:

```
template <class InIt1, class InIt2, class OutIt, class Compare>
constexpr OutIt merge(InIt1 first1, InIt1 last1,
                      InIt2 first2, InIt2 last2,
                      OutIt dest, Compare comp);
```

While the signature is arguably readable, I had to abbreviate it slightly to fit on the page, type it several times, correct several errors, and proofread it with care and attention before getting it right, even while copying it from cppreference.com.

There is scope for identifying abstractions. The function takes a selection of iterators which mark a pair of ranges. Since C++20, we are now able to identify ranges explicitly as a pair of iterators marking the beginning and the end of the range. This allows us to simplify the function by bundling together the first four iterator parameters:

```
template <class InRng1, class InRng2, class OutIt, class Compare>
constexpr OutIt merge(InRng r1, InRng r2, OutIt dest, Compare comp);
```

The detail of the range is at a lower level of abstraction. We are merely interested in merging two ranges. Another way of defining a range is as a pointer to the beginning of some items, along with the number of items. The second example in the guideline offers this function signature:

```
void f(int* some_ints, int some_ints_length);
```

Another object introduced in C++20 is `std::span`. The Core Guidelines are accompanied by a support library, called the Guidelines Support Library. This is a collection of classes defined in the namespace `gsl` that can be used to support enforcement of some of the Core Guidelines. `std::span` was developed from `gsl::span`, and it is precisely as described above: a pointer to some data, and a length, bundled together into a single object, yielding the following signature:

```
void f(std::span<int> some_ints);
```

In both examples, we have induced abstractions from the parameters.

There is another way of identifying a range, which is with a pointer and a sentinel value. This method is built into the language in the form of the string literal. This is expressed as a pointer to an array of characters with a null terminator. That terminator is the sentinel character. The more specialized version of `std::span`, `std::string_view`, can be constructed from a pair of iterators, a pointer and a count, and a pointer and a sentinel.

Summary

There are many ways of building abstractions, but often there comes a time when the client wants more from their function. We cannot simply say, "Nope, I'm not going to add another parameter, that violates Core Guideline I.23," and fold our arms, glaring at them. This is not very kind to your colleagues. What, then, do we do when there are no further meaningful abstractions to be induced?

The presence of a surplus of parameters is a signal that complexity is getting out of control and that something needs attention. If there are no more abstractions to be induced from them, then perhaps the problem lies with the function identifier itself. If a lot is being demanded of it, then it is clearly a very important identifier in the problem domain. Rather than try and encapsulate that importance in a single abstraction, perhaps it is time to consider broadening the function. Perhaps the function should be overloaded according to how its use is intended, or varying function names can be used to accommodate the different types of operation. Maybe a function template is required. There are always other options besides adding additional parameters.

The important thing to remember, whatever the reason for adding additional parameters to a function, is that it is not to be undertaken lightly and should be considered a last resort, and a place to start reconsidering the nature of the function itself. Keep the parameter count low, separate similar parameters, minimize complexity, and rejoice in the discovery of abstractions.

- Multiple parameters increase the burden of understanding on the user.
- Gather parameters together in structs, perhaps with a view to discovering a latent abstraction.
- View multiple parameters as a sign that the function may be trying to do too much.

Chapter 2.3

I.26: If you want a cross-compiler ABI, use a C-style subset

Creating libraries

Writing libraries in C++ is a simple matter. Compile your source files, glue them together into a library, expose your exports in a header, or module if your compiler supports it, and supply the library file and header or module definition to your client.

Unfortunately, that is not the end of the story. There is a substantial amount of detail to get right. The purpose of this guideline is to show you a way to minimize this overhead, to prevent a truly overwhelming amount of work from landing on your desk at some random point in the future, and to enable you to create libraries that will serve the community for many years to come.

Recall the operation of the linker. It matches missing symbols from object files or libraries with exported symbols other object files or libraries. The declarations in the header point to definitions in the library file.

For example, imagine you have written a library that contains, among other items, the function

```
id retrieve_customer_id_from_name(std::string const& name);
```

and a header that declares it. This is a handy way of doing things: it allows you to create a package of functionality with a header, and your user does not need to spend time recompiling. Maybe your source is proprietary, and you are not allowed to share it.

The likely operation of this function is that it will retrieve the character buffer from the string reference, query a database Somewhere In The Cloud with it, and return an `id` formed from the result of the query. A string implementation may contain a length followed by a pointer to a buffer, so retrieving the character buffer and passing it to the database is a trivial matter.

Now, imagine that your library becomes insanely popular: perhaps the database is full of particularly useful information and everyone wants a piece. You have hundreds, then thousands, then tens of thousands of clients, all cheerfully parting with their cash in exchange for this functionality. Suddenly, a trickle of complaints come in telling you that the library is crashing during the execution of this function. The trickle becomes a torrent and then a veritable flood of ire. You investigate and notice that there has been a toolset upgrade: the compiler, linker, and standard library have changed.

The next thing you do is rebuild the library and the unit tests with the new toolset and run everything. It all passes. There is no crash. You attempt to reproduce the bug report, but to no avail. What has happened?

The answer is that the definition of `std::string` has changed. When you first shipped the library, `std::string` was implemented as a length followed by a pointer. Unfortunately, your clients have upgraded to a new toolset which now implements `string` as a pointer followed by a length. They are now supplying a `std::string const&` to your function whose memory layout is different from what it is expecting. On attempting to dereference the pointer, it is in fact dereferencing the length, reaching into forbidden memory, and engendering a hasty exit.

Of course, when you recompiled the library and the unit tests, they were all built with the new toolset, so the definition of `std::string` agreed throughout, as a pointer followed by a length. Everything passed. It is only when new code called your old code that things went wrong.

What is an ABI?

What happened was that there was a change to the ABI. The API for your library did not change, but the ABI did. The term "ABI" may be new to you. It stands for application binary interface. Just as an API, an application programming interface, is a guide to humans about what you can do with a library, so is an ABI a guide to machines about how libraries interact. Think of it as the compiled version of an API.

An ABI defines several things: not just how objects are laid out in the standard library, but also how things are passed to functions. For example, the System V AMD64 ABI[1] specifies that the first six integer or pointer arguments are passed in registers RDI, RSI, RDX, RCX, R8, and R9. This ABI is followed by Unix and Unix-like operating systems. Other considerations include how exceptions are handled

1. https://wiki.osdev.org/System_V_ABI

and propagated, function prolog and epilog code, the `virtual` table layout, `virtual` function calling conventions, and so on.

The need for an ABI is one of the reasons why code compiled for one operating system will not work with another operating system: although they might have the same processor architecture, for example x86, they may have different ABIs. Of course, if there were one unifying ABI this would not matter, but ABIs are intimately bound up with the performance characteristics of the hardware. Pinning everything to one ABI would come at a performance cost. A library that does not use types from another library in the signatures of its functions cannot suffer an ABI break if that library changes. Eventually, all libraries change, and this is a rather problematic fact of development.

A library that does not use types from another library in the signatures of its functions cannot suffer an ABI break if that library changes. Eventually, all libraries change, and this is a rather problematic fact of development.

It is therefore important to keep your ABI stable. Changing a function in any way, the return type or the types, the quantity and order of arguments, or the `noexcept` specification, is an ABI break. It is also an API change. Changing definitions of data types or data structures in the private interface is not an API change but it IS an ABI break.

Even name mangling isn't immune from ABI breaks. An ABI can define a standard way of uniquely identifying the name of a function so that libraries built with different languages, for example C and Pascal, can be linked together. If you have ever seen the declaration `extern "C"` in a header file, that is a signal to the compiler that the function names within the declaration should have their names inserted into the exports table using the same naming scheme as a C compiler on that platform would use.

The earlier hypothetical problem with a library that takes a `std::string` is unlikely to trouble you. Today's linkers will simply prevent clients of different standard libraries from linking. There are a number of ways to do this: the ABI version can be embedded in the mangled name of the symbol, or the compiler can insert the ABI version into the object file and emit an error should anyone try to link conflicting versions together. The labor of dealing with conflicting ABIs is not eliminated, but it is exposed and added to the engineer's plate.

Recall the guideline: "If you want a cross-compiler ABI, use a C-style subset." We have now explained the nature of a cross-compiler ABI, and why observing it is important for both today and the future. Let us now move on to the C-style subset.

Paring back to the absolute minimum

So, what does a C-style subset consist of? The C types are often referred to as the built-in types. They are the types that are not made up of any other types. I would say they are the atomic types, but sadly that has another meaning in C++. You can, however, think of them as the fundamental building blocks of all your types. The list consists of[2]

```
void
bool
char
int
float
double
```

Some of these types can be modified by sign or by size. The keywords `signed` and `unsigned` can be applied to `char` and `int`. The keyword `short` can be applied to `int`. The keyword `long` can be applied to `int` and `double`. This keyword can also be applied twice to `int`. In fact, the keyword `int` can be omitted entirely and replaced with the sign or size modifiers. The modifiers can also be applied in any order: the type `long unsigned long` is entirely valid.

This might seem at first glance to be somewhat cumbersome, although if I saw `long unsigned long` in any code submitted for review, I would return it with a request for justification. The presence of the size modifier gives rise to a favorite interview question of mine: "How big is an `int`?" the answer to which is, "It depends." The standard offers some guarantees.

- A `short int` and an `int` are at least 16 bits wide.
- A `long int` is at least 32 bits wide.
- A `long long int` is at least 64 bits wide.
- 1 == `sizeof(char) <= sizeof(short) <= sizeof(int) <= sizeof(long) <= sizeof(long long)`.

The implementation decides on these widths. This set of choices is known as the data model. There are four models that have found wide acceptance:

- LP32 or 2/4/4 (`int` is 16-bit, `long` and pointer are 32-bit) as used in the Win16 API

2. https://en.cppreference.com/w/cpp/language/types

- ILP32 or 4/4/4 (`int`, `long`, and pointer are 32-bit) as used in the Win32 API and some Unix systems
- LLP64 or 4/4/8 (`int` and `long` are 32-bit, pointer is 64-bit) as used in the Win64 API
- LP64 or 4/8/8 (`int` is 32-bit, `long` and pointer are 64-bit) as also used in some Unix systems

This highlights the significance of the word "cross-compiler" in the guideline. Your library needs to work on your compiler today, but it also needs to work a year from now, and on the compiler used by your clients. If the compilers have different opinions on the size of an `int` or a pointer, then their behavior will differ in ways that you did not intend.

The floating-point types are simpler than the integral types, since they are defined by reference to another standard, particularly ISO/IEC/IEEE 60559:2011, which is the same as IEEE 754-2008. This makes them utterly reliable between platforms. `char` can be signed, unsigned, or neither; all three are distinct types. `unsigned char` is used for dealing with raw memory.

It is clear from this that changing data models is an ABI break: I first encountered ABI breaks (although I didn't understand the problem in this way) when I first installed Win32s on my Windows 3.11 machine in the early 1990s. Suddenly, all my `int`s took up twice as much memory and some of my programs fell over. More recently, the slight difference between LLP64 and LP64 (width of `long`) caused me pain writing for Windows and MacOS, the former using LLP64 and the latter using LP64.

You may now relax, breathe out, and raise an eyebrow. The advice is "If you want a cross-compiler ABI, use a C-style subset" and yet we have just demonstrated how fragile the built-in types are. However, this fragility is only present when you are trying to move between data models. Also, there is a way to overcome the data model hazard and that is with the use of fixed-width integer types. These embed the width of the type in the identifier, and have names like `int32_t` and `uint8_t`. These are defined in C in the header <stdint.h> and in C++ in the header <cstdint>.

To be clear, the original function declaration at the start of this chapter should not have taken a `std::string` across an ABI boundary, because the definition of string can change. It changed in GCC for C++11, and the pain was considerable. The function should have taken a `char*` and an `int`, or better still a `uint8_t`, because those will never change.

Exception propagation

This sounds like the job is done: pass and return fixed-width built-in types and there should be no problems. However, there is another way that data passes between functions, which is via the exception-handling machinery. When an exception is thrown, the compiler will allocate space for the exception and then start unwinding the stack via a call to a special function in the standard library implementation. On some platforms, this function will iterate through each catch statement via data inserted by the compiler corresponding to each function body. It's looking for a catch statement that will handle the type of exception that has been thrown.

There are two possible outcomes: either a matching catch statement is found, or no matching catch statement is found. In the latter case, the standard library implementation will call `std::terminate` which, by default, will call `std::abort`. This returns control to the host environment without cleaning up. If the stack unwinder is fortunate enough to find a matching catch statement, it will then go back through the stack and clean up each function, calling destructors and restoring the stack, before resuming execution at this matching catch statement. After the catch statement is executed, the memory allocated for the exception is released.

Setting aside the matter of what might happen when the exception is thrown because of a lack of memory, this behavior is deeply implementation specific. The mechanism used to allocate space for the exception, and the format of the data inserted by the compiler after each function body, will depend on the implementation, as will the means by which each catch statement is described to the stack-unwinding function. This information is all written by the toolset at compile time, and if two libraries built with two compilers differing by even the version number coexist in the same program, there is a risk of ABI incompatibility. The risk is quite small, however: the exception-handling info format is defined by the platform ABI, and the exception types are defined by the library, and the vendors go to great lengths not to change those things. However, if you are feeling particularly cautious, the only option here is to ensure that exceptions do not leave your library, and to decorate each function in the API with `noexcept` or `noexcept(true)` depending on your local style.

As you can see, some work is required to ensure a cross-compiler ABI for a library. This is a manifestation of the perils of binary dependency. You may decide to distribute (or consume) a library as source or as a prebuilt binary. In the example above the notion of proprietary code was observed, along with compilation time for your client. This can be a serious matter: a GUI library I use at my studio takes most of the day to configure and build. Binary versions of the library are available. I simply have to identify which version of the toolset I am using and press the download button on their website. This delivers a variety of libraries contained in a directory structure which reflects whether or not NDEBUG is defined, and whether the binaries are statically or dynamically linked. This set of four permutations may be in danger of becoming a set of 12 permutations, since at the time of writing there is a contracts proposal that offers three different configurations. Supplying for NDEBUG definition choice, static versus dynamic linking, and contract configuration will be a nontrivial task.

This does not apply to libraries distributed as source. If your library consists solely of class templates and function templates, then you cannot distribute your library as a prebuilt binary: class and function templates require full definitions to be instantiated. If the responsibility of building is delegated to your consumer, then all ABI considerations are delegated to them as well unless your library is itself dependent on a prebuilt binary library.

Summary

You might decide, perhaps somewhat pessimistically, that your library will not have the life span necessary to require considerations of ABI stability. Perhaps it is merely a short-term patch until a more comprehensive solution is available.

Please, please, never, ever think that.

In 1958 the United States Department of Defense launched a computerized contract management system that it dubbed Mechanization of Contract Administration Services, or MOCAS. It was written in COBOL, and was still in use in 2015, having enjoyed a green screen upgrade to replace the punched card input and latterly the introduction of a web interface. Good things are built to last and see a lot of use. Trillions of dollars have passed through MOCAS.[3]

C has been with us for 50 years, and C++ has been with us for 40. The ubiquity of C has led to C interfaces being emitted and consumed by other languages, such as Perl, Python, Lua, PHP, Ruby, Tcl, and many others. The C interface has become the de facto lingua franca of language interoperability. Libraries and programs exist with "ancient" pedigrees. For example, a library I use very often, libcurl, was first released in 1997. I first used it in the early 2000s. It is still a critical part of the infrastructure of the game franchise I have been involved with since 2000. Windows developers may be familiar with MFC, the Microsoft Foundation Classes. It is a set of classes for developing with the Windows SDK. Version 1 of this library dropped in 1992, and it is still in wide use. Anyone writing image manipulation software is very

3. https://www.technologyreview.com/2015/08/06/166822/what-is-the-oldest-computer-program-still-in-use

likely to be using libjpeg. The initial release was in October 1991. The iostreams library was written in 1985. Despite it being superseded in part by the fmt library in the C++20 standard, it is still in wide use. It seems unlikely that, at release time, any of the authors thought their creations would be in use 20, 30, or 60 years later. We ask you to develop with the future in mind and to remove every possible barrier to the use of your library in future. Follow this guideline and your libraries may join the elders of the C++ ecosystem. Your fame will be assured as legend status is conferred upon you. Avoid ABI problems and build your ABI from a C-style subset.

Chapter 2.4

C.47: Define and initialize member variables in the order of member declaration

There is only one order of initialization of member data, which is the order of declaration. You cannot change this. There are very good reasons for this being an immutable rule, which we will describe in this chapter.

But first, an example. Bryn, a new engineer at a large firm, is asked to write a population service for finding out how many people are in the building. A server locked away in the bowels of the building handles admissions and exits. It is old and slow. Etched on the front in red lettering is the name of a forgotten hardware company long ago sold to a rapacious and overfunded startup. Queries are rather cumbersome and time consuming. New safety regulations require the number to be available instantaneously, but since it takes about a minute for someone to sign in at the front desk it is considered safe to query the server, cache the value, and retain it for 30 seconds. This will stop queries from building up faster than they can be handled.

I know you're laughing. This is a true story, although I have changed the names. Bryn produces this simple solution:

```
class population_service {
public:
  population_service(std::string query);
  float population() const;

private:
  mutable float current_population;
  mutable std::time_t expiry;
  std::string query;
};
```

The class is constructed with the server query. A call to population will check the expiry time of the population value and update it using the query if necessary. This lazy evaluation is a typical use case of mutable.

Bryn writes the constructor:

```
population_service::population_service(std::string query_)
{
  query = std::move(query_);
  expiry = std::chrono::system_clock::to_time_t(
                      std::chrono::system_clock::now());
  current_population = population();
}
```

The population function is a simple matter. All the tests pass, and Bryn submits it for code review. He is asked to migrate initialization out of the constructor body and into the initialization list. Keen to make a good impression, Bryn turns this around in short order and produces this:

```
population_service::population_service(std::string query_)
  : query(std::move(query_))
  , expiry(std::chrono::system_clock::to_time_t(
                      std::chrono::system_clock::now()))
  , current_population(population())
{}
```

He submits it and gets a knock on the door from his lead, Beth.

"Bryn," she asks, "did you test this?"

"Yup, all green," he answers, innocently.

"Did you test this AFTER you migrated everything to the initialization list?" she persists.

"Well, there was no need, was there?" he responds. "I've just moved everything before the braces."

Beth dies a little on the inside. In her mind she is preparing the "automate your tests and always test prior to submission" lecture in the face of this answer. She did not need to run the code to see that there was a problem.

Unfortunately, moving everything up changes the behavior of the code. The first thing that happens now is that current_population is initialized by a call to population. Setting aside the questionable wisdom of calling a member function from an initializer list, this was not the original intent of the engineer. He wanted to initialize the query and the expiry time first. Without those values correctly initialized, the call to population is vanishingly unlikely to succeed.

To be absolutely clear, member data is initialized in order of declaration. That is the only order. There is no magical choosing going on, nor is there any variation available to you. In this case, `current_population` was declared first, so that was initialized by the call to the member function `population`. The expiry member was initialized next, but `std::time_t` has no constructor and usually consists of a built-in integral type, so it was not initialized to a deterministic value. Finally, `query` was initialized by move construction.

There are two ways to fix the problem. The correct way to initialize this object is to initialize `current_population` to zero and expiry to `now()`, and then move-construct the query, thus:

```
population_service::population_service(std::string query_)
  : current_population(0)
  , expiry(std::chrono::system_clock::to_time_t(
                    std::chrono::system_clock::now()))
  , query(std::move(query_))
{}
```

You could optionally call `population` in the constructor body. Given that it is an expensive function that requires caching, though, we would not call it until the value was needed.

The other way to fix the problem is to reorder the member data in the class definition, thus:

```
class population_service {
public:
  population_service(std::string query_);
  float population() const;

private:
  std::string query;
  mutable std::time_t expiry;
  mutable float current_population;
};
```

With this ordering, `population` can be safely invoked in the initialization list, although for the same reason I would not do this.

This leads us to an interesting aside about class layout and alignment. Consider this program:

```
#include <iostream>
struct int_two_bools {
  bool m_b1;
  int m_i;
```

```
  bool m_b2;
};
int main() {
  std::cout << sizeof(int_two_bools);
}
```

What answer would you expect to see?

We built and ran this program using x64 MSVC 19.28 on Compiler Explorer and got the answer 12. Each member takes up four bytes.

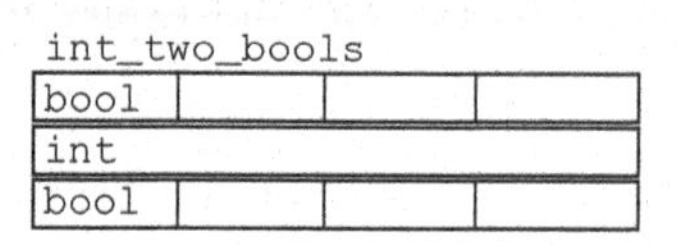

Figure 2.4.1. *Layout for storing an integer and two bools*

Then we exchanged the second and third members, thus:

```
struct int_two_bools {
  bool m_b1;
  bool m_b2;
  int m_i;
};
```

Now what answer would you expect to see? You can check the output on Compiler Explorer and observe that the answer is 8.

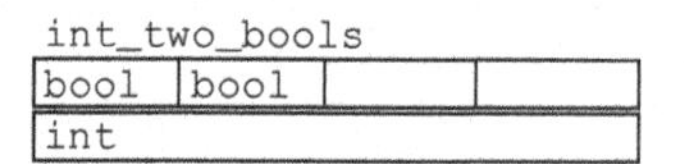

Figure 2.4.2. *Optimized layout for storing an integer and two bools*

Indeed, if you add a third bool after `m_b2` thus:

```
struct int_two_bools {
  bool m_b1;
  bool m_b2;
  bool m_b3;
  int m_i;
};
```

you STILL get the answer 8.

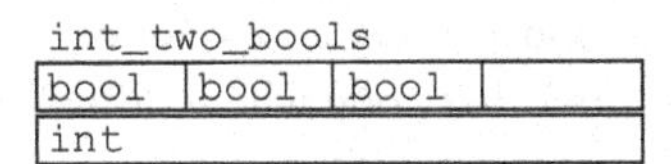

Figure 2.4.3. *Optimized layout for storing an integer and three bools*

This may come as a surprise. The standard has a few things to say about alignment, which you can find at [basic.align].[1] In summary, individual objects must be aligned on boundaries matching their size. In this example, and for this implementation, `sizeof(bool)` is 1 and `sizeof(int)` is 4. In the first definition of `int_two_bools`, the first `bool` member occupies one byte. Three bytes of padding are then added so that the `int` member will lie on a four-byte boundary. In the second definition, the two `bool` members are consecutive and only need to be aligned on a one-byte boundary. This means that only two bytes of padding are required before the `int` member. In the third definition, only a single byte of padding is required since all three `bool` members can fit in four bytes.

This demonstrates that layout order is significant with regard to the size of an instance of a class. This is particularly relevant if you are in a size-constrained situation and have a million objects: those extra four bytes may be very valuable. Solving initialization order problems may not be as simple as reordering the members, since that may increase the size of the object.

You may ask yourself, "Why does the order matter? Why must it match the order of declaration? Why can't I dictate the order of initialization?" Indeed, some compilers will in fact warn you if the order is wrong. The answer is that C++ guarantees that members are destroyed in the reverse order of construction.

If you were to specify that order in the constructor, this would make matters rather difficult for the compiler. If no destructor were declared in the class definition, the compiler would have to define one in the same translation unit as the constructor, using the constructor to infer what the destruction order should be. If a destructor were declared in the class definition, you would need to add something like a deinitialization list to the language, executed at the end of the destructor body. It would be up to you to ensure that you kept your constructor and destructor synchronized. The scope for catastrophe is considerable.

"No, that's fine, I'm up to the job," you reply, with a cheerful smile. You may very well be, but this is not the only problem. The language allows for the constructor to be overloaded. You have already decided that initialization order is sensitive to performance in some way, as is member order. Are you able to guarantee that each constructor is going to remain synchronized?

1. https://eel.is/c++draft/basic.align

"Yes, yes I am," you reply. You are very confident of your abilities, it seems. However, there may be situations in other code where different constructors carry different dependencies. In those cases, you will be unable to remain synchronized.

"Ah-ha! We could have multiple destructors! Each constructor would have a matching destructor so that each pair could correctly create and destroy the members in the right order. It's brilliant! I'm going to write a proposal to the committee!"

Your tenacity is admirable, but this won't fly. What if an object is to be destroyed in a different translation unit from that in which it was created? The compiler will not know which destructor to call. There is simply an object falling out of scope without any information about the constructor.

"Easy, we just add a tag to the class that describes how the object was built and examine that at the time of destruction, and then we call the correct destructor."

You're just making this up as you go along now. The trouble with this solution is that you have now added another field to the class to support a feature that is rarely used. You have introduced a run-time overhead for every class. You have created an abstraction that you must pay for regardless of whether or not it is used. This goes against one of the fundamental principles of the design of the language: do not pay for what you do not use. There are billions and billions of lines of C++ out there. If you were to introduce this feature to the language, then you would impact negatively on millions of projects. It is not going to happen. There will not be multiple destructors and there will not be specifiable initialization order. Members are initialized in the order in which they are declared, and in no other order. We do hope that is clear.

The preeminent feature of C++ is, in my opinion, deterministic destruction. There are many languages out there, many of which manage lifetimes for you. With C++ YOU decide when the lifetime of an object comes to an end, and when all its resources are released. When the name of an object of automatic storage duration falls out of scope, its destructor is invoked, and the destructors of the members are invoked. When you explicitly delete an object of dynamic storage duration, its destructor is invoked, and the destructors of the members are invoked. When a program ends, all objects of static storage duration are destroyed in the reverse order of their construction: their destructors are invoked, and the destructors of their members are invoked. When a thread is destroyed, all thread-local instances of objects are destroyed in the reverse order of their construction: their destructors are invoked, and the destructors of their members are invoked.

You may feel that we are belaboring the point here, but this is an extremely valuable property of the language, and if you have been exposed to managed lifetimes before you will appreciate why. For example, imagine that you have a connection to a database stored as a member of an object, and that connections are a limited resource. You rely on that connection being closed when the destructor is invoked. It should not be closed before the object is destroyed; it should be closed only when it is certain that it is no longer needed. This is precisely what a destructor is for. It is the function invoked at the end of the life of an object. It is guaranteed to be invoked at scope exit, something that garbage collection simply cannot offer. Using scope, you can minimize the lifetime of an object and maximize your resource usage efficiency. If you are working in some other language, and that lifetime is managed by some other system, such as the language runtime, then you are in danger of holding open a connection to the database while you wait for the runtime to do the garbage collection. This can be outstandingly frustrating, and the only solution is to manually close the connection when you are pretty sure that the object is ready to be destroyed. This kind of manual lifetime management was endemic in C and is precisely what C++ aims to get away from.

Deterministic destruction cannot be achieved without the one constraint that informs this guideline: all objects must be constructed deterministically, in an order that can be determined statically, at compile time. To achieve this, construction order is inferred from the class definition, which may only exist once, and from the order of declaration of member data. There are other ways that the order could have been chosen: reverse order of declaration, alphabetical order of member identifier, a special member that specifies the order with numeric tags… we are sure you can think of plenty of others. However, these all seem somewhat perverse when a clear order already exists: the order of definition.

There is a related Core Guideline, C.41: "A constructor should create a fully initialized object." One way of avoiding this error is to write a constructor that constructs every member in its initialization list. If you recall Bryn's feedback from his lead, she asked him to move everything into the initialization list, possibly in recognition of this handy approach. By matching the initialization list with each one of the members, you guarantee that every item is initialized before you reach the constructor body, where any additional work involving objects outside of the class may be involved, such as logging construction or subscribing to callback handlers.

If you adopt this approach, be mindful of the role of in-class member initializers. These provide default initial values for objects so that a default constructor is unnecessary. If any member data has such a value, make sure you choose your value appropriately.

We should mention what is known as "leading punctuation style" here. If you review the code earlier, you will see that the initialization list of each constructor was written in such a way that each member was on its own line, preceded by a comma, or a colon in the case of the first member. Other ways of writing a constructor might include putting everything all on one line within the class definition or using a more natural-looking approach to punctuation and putting the commas and colon at the end of each line. The advantage of leading punctuation style is that reordering members can be easily achieved by moving the entire line up or down, without leaving a trailing comma at the end of the list. This is a small thing, but it is an annoying compilation bug to be caught by.

You may be wondering about the compilation overhead this may incur: if you initialize a member in the initializer list and then modify it in the constructor body, surely this will generate redundant code? Fortunately, we have the as-if rule. This is described in the standard at [intro.abstract],[2] which says that "...conforming implementations are required to emulate (only) the observable behavior of the abstract machine..." This allows the compiler to make code transformations for the purpose of optimization. In the example above, the `current_population` member could be initialized to zero in the initialization list, then the population function could be called in the constructor body, and the compiler, if it could see the definition of the population function, would know that the first initialization is redundant.

Do not fear putting apparently redundant code in the initialization list. If it is redundant the compiler will eliminate it if it can. The purpose of writing code is to tell the compiler what to do, and to give it as much information and context as possible. By maximizing this, you give the compiler the best chance of generating optimal code. A constructor should create a fully initialized object, ready to go and safe to use, with no members flapping in the wind. If a constructor cannot do that, you have a failure in your abstraction that should be remedied as soon as possible. This is a warning that needs attending to immediately, either by redesigning the class, or narrowing the abstraction so that the class *can* be fully initialized.

There are some, and we use this word hesitantly, tricks you can use if you *really* need to carry out any somewhat exotic initialization in the initialization list. Recall that the initialization list is formed of a series of initialization expressions. In the example, `current_population` was simply initialized to `0`, `expiry_time` was initialized with a call to `std::chrono::system_clock::to_time_t(std::chrono::system_clock::now())`, and `query` was move-initialized from the constructor parameter. You are not allowed to execute arbitrary code in the initialization list, only call existing functions. Use of the ternary operator is also permitted since it is an expression.

This historically led to private static functions being declared in classes that were used as helpers for construction. This was a disappointing sight to behold: the interface was populated with functions that only had one use, increasing cognitive load and maintenance burden.

C++11 changed the landscape with the introduction of lambda expressions. There is a technique called IILE or Immediately Invoked Lambda Expression that looks like this:

```
example::example(int a, int b, int c)
  : x([&](){
```

2. https://eel.is/c++draft/intro.abstract

```
    …function body…
  }())
{}
```

The `example` class constructor takes three arguments and initializes `x` by first declaring a lambda expression and then immediately invoking it by adding a pair of parentheses after it. This technique is useful for initializing `const` objects: sometimes you need extensive calculations for initialization which cannot be successively applied to a `const` value.

However, in the case of initialization, all this has done is moved the problem around. What were once private static helper functions are now initialization lambdas. You have used a shiny new hammer to solve an old problem, but the correct solution is still to reconsider your abstraction. If there is a need for extensive state manipulation at initialization time, then perhaps a companion abstraction is lurking somewhere in the data. In the review of Core Guideline I.23: "Keep the number of function arguments low," we discussed minimizing the number of function parameters, perhaps by forming a struct to pass to the constructor. Do not ignore these kinds of clues when writing your code. Finding abstractions is the best thing you can do when developing software.

Summary

In summary:

- The constructor body is less constrained than the initialization list.
- Member initialization is sensitive to order of declaration, supporting deterministic destruction.
- Resolve dependencies by reordering your member declarations unless alignment is a consideration.
- Avoid solving the problem by throwing code at it: treat dependency issues as signposts to an undiscovered abstraction.

Chapter 2.5

CP.3: Minimize explicit sharing of writable data

Traditional execution model

The concurrency and parallelism section of the Core Guidelines addresses a well-known fact of programming life for C++ developers: multithreaded programming is harder than single-threaded programming. It introduces a unique class of errors to bemuse the unwary. It is ferociously hard to debug multiple threads of execution since the primary tool of debugging, stepping through code line by line, is a strictly serial process.

Let us consider how we got here. You will almost certainly have encountered a diagram like that shown in Figure 2.5.1.

The CPU steps through the instructions of the program, one at a time. Some instructions will load data from primary storage, others will manipulate data, and others will store data to primary storage. Some instructions will control the order in which the processor executes subsequent instructions.

This is a great way of teaching the fundamentals of programming. Data retrieval, manipulation, storage, and control flow is everything you need to write programs.

Of course, once you start to deal with actual hardware, things change a little. For example, different types of storage have different performance characteristics. You cannot assume that it will take the same amount of time to retrieve data from arbitrary locations. The introduction of caches to mainstream desktop processors in the 1990s highlighted the large amount of waiting incurred by the processor for loading and storing. Even worse is reading from and writing to external storage such as disk drives or SSDs. Worse still is reading from and writing to arbitrary storage over network cables or Wi-Fi.

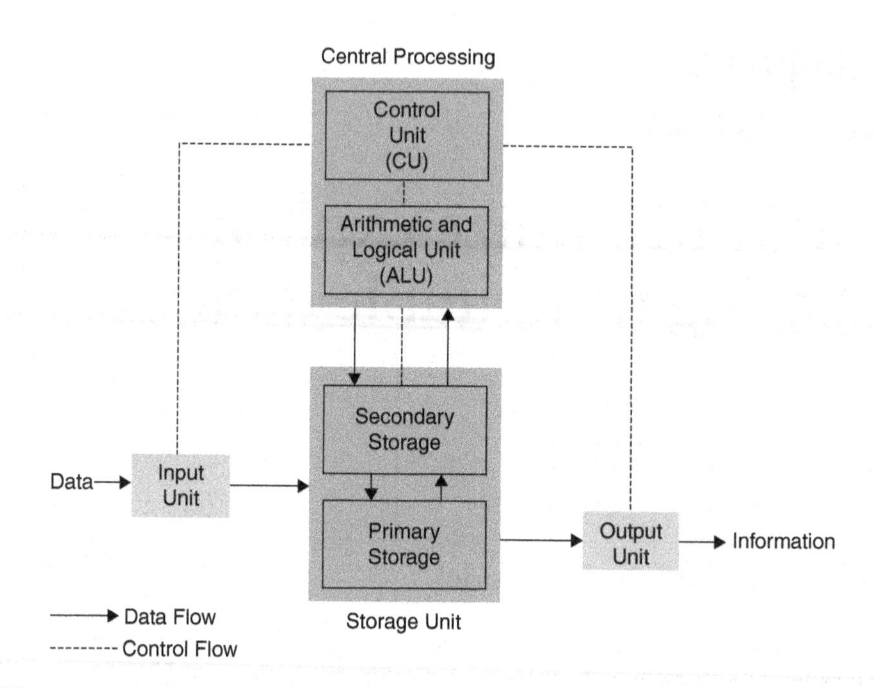

Figure 2.5.1. Block diagram of a computer

Typically, during the operation of your program there exists some data stored outside main memory, on a remote device. There also exist operating system calls which open connections to these devices. We will consider a file on a local disk drive.

The program will create a buffer of memory to receive the data, and then direct the operating system to open a file on the local disk drive, read the data into the buffer, and close the file. It would be ideal if the program could leave the operating system to its own devices, and then receive a notification when the data from the disk drive has filled the buffer. Such a facility is in fact available on all modern operating systems. Two threads of execution exist, one which creates the buffer and one which fills the buffer.

This kind of concurrency is relatively simple. If you handle I/O errors correctly, if you do not read the buffer prematurely, and if you periodically check for completion, all is well. Reading the buffer early is a class of error known as a data race. Precisely, a data race occurs when these conditions are met:

- Two or more threads access the same memory location concurrently.
- One of the threads is writing to the memory.
- The threads are not using anything to control or schedule their accesses to that memory.

Sadly, as programs increase in complexity, it is too easy to create a data race. A branch of your code may not be checking if the buffer has been filled. Perhaps a newcomer to the codebase doesn't realize that I/O is handled in this way, believing that once they have asked for a file, the program waits, or blocks, until it has been read into the buffer.

The error here is exposing the unfilled buffer to two threads, allowing the thread that created the buffer access to the data before it is ready. One solution to this problem is to hide the buffer until it is full: instruct the I/O thread to create and fill the buffer, and then hand it back to the calling thread when it has been filled.

Wait, there's more

In the early 1990s, fresh from university, I became a Windows developer, working on Windows machines. I wrote a lot of multimedia software: I really wanted to write games, but I took what I could get. It was fun.

One of the features of developer life back then was the sudden, unexpected freeze of your system. A badly written program would bring your session down, and if you couldn't bring up the Task Manager and kill the offending process, the only option was to hit the reset button. Sadly, the environment I worked in meant that I was, in fact, rarely able to bring up the Task Manager in the case of a freeze. Although I quickly learned to save often, it was a quite maddening aspect of software development.

I wrote presentations for workstation manufacturers (among other businesses) to assist their sales teams, and one day a Windows NT 3.51 workstation with two Intel Pentium processors turned up on my desk. I was used to servers with multiple processors, but not desktop machines. The transition was amazing. After a day or so of installing my development environment, I was up and running and the first thing I noticed was how often I was able to bring up the Task Manager and kill stalled processes. I could just do my work. It was an utter joy to develop on.

Of course, being an inquisitive developer, the first thing I did was see if I could make use of both processors in a single program. I decided to write a decoder that would decompress backups from the network and write them to the local disk. One processor would read and write, the other would decompress.

It took me less than an hour to stall my program entirely. I had no idea why. I was being super careful waiting for my buffers to fill before decompressing them: each one had its own lock, which was released when the buffer was filled. I spent ages trying to work out what was causing the problem. Maddeningly, if I single-stepped through the code, everything worked fine. Worse still, when I ran the code on other machines it also worked fine.

I'm not going to detail the descent into madness that I endured over the following 12 days (and nights) as I tried to work out what on earth was going on. It turned out that the problem was an artifact of timing, and both threads were waiting for a buffer owned by the other thread. This timing artifact was unique to multiprocessor machines, it turned out. I could reproduce it nowhere else in the building.

I had encountered my first deadlock.

A deadlock occurs when two threads of execution are waiting for a resource held by the other. Each thread was waiting on the other buffer before completing its work and releasing its lock. On the single-processor machines, things proceeded as expected: one buffer would fill and release its lock, allowing the other thread to carry on. With two processors it was possible, and in fact usual, to block both threads at the same time, each waiting for the other to finish.

Once I realized what was happening, I reconsidered my logic and fixed everything. That wasn't the end of it, though. Other code I had written earlier would also fail on this machine. Situations that were very rare on single-processor machines were suddenly frequently exposed on this multiprocessor machine.

It became clear to me that the purpose of multiprocessor machines was for running multiple processes and making Windows a nicer place to be. Running multiple threads in a single program was clearly not worth the trouble. It was an interesting academic exercise, but I had been bitten badly and I wasn't planning on returning to that particular idiom.

One of the features of developing in the 1990s was the steady growth in speed of the processors. My first work PC featured an Intel 80286 processor running at 8MHz. This was 1992 and it was somewhat underpowered but still in wide use. By the end of the decade the Pentium III could run at up to 1.13GHz. I grew very used to processors Just Getting Faster. I even discovered that there was a name for this: Moore's Law, which stated that the number of transistors on a chip doubles every two years.[1]

It isn't a law, of course. It's an observation of engineering practice. Unfortunately, all good things come to an end and eventually physics took over. In December 2004 Herb Sutter, one of the authors of the C++ Core Guidelines, wrote an article titled "The Free Lunch Is Over."[2] He highlighted the problem with Moore's Law, predicting the necessity of a hard turn toward concurrency in software to exploit the full potential of upcoming CPUs with increasing numbers of cores. He observed the lack of understanding of concurrency among most programmers, and how efficiency and optimization would become more important than ever.

1. https://www.intel.com/content/www/us/en/silicon-innovations/moores-law-technology.html

2. www.gotw.ca/publications/concurrency-ddj.htm

Cramming more and more transistors onto a processor was no longer an option for achieving faster compute speeds. At around the end of 2006 I encountered my first dual-core processor. Processors might not be able to get faster, but they could do more things at once, which is just as good, right?

Of course it isn't. Two cores only execute your code twice as fast if they are not waiting for each other. My heart sank a little. I knew what was coming and I was not disappointed. Race conditions and deadlocks became part of the life of a developer as we tried to squeeze more and more out of the processor. I had become comfortable with I/O threads: now the world was filling up with compute threads. Multithreaded programs have become the new normal, particularly in my domain of games. Processors with dozens of cores are common. Core Guideline CP.1: "Assume that your code will run as part of a multi-threaded program" acknowledges this truth.

Avoiding deadlocks and data races

Deadlocks and data races are caused by breakdowns in turn-taking. Two threads are competing for a single resource: access to a piece of data. That is the motivation for this guideline. If writable data is not shared, then races and deadlocks will not be a problem. Unfortunately, threads need to communicate with one another. What is needed is a way of reading and writing data with a guarantee of no interference from other threads.

C++11 introduced `std::atomic`, a library type that supports this. Particularly, if one thread writes to an atomic object while another thread reads from it, the behavior is well defined, and all is well with the world. But what happens if two threads want to write to the object? Now we need a flag to warn other threads that the object is being written to and no other threads should attempt to write to it. This is problematic: how do we know if it is safe to write to the flag? Two threads may write to the flag and spoil everything.

Fortunately, we have the concept of a mutex. This is an abstraction of the single-thread-access flag. C++11 also introduced `std::mutex`, a library type that allows you to secure exclusive access to something. The API is simple: there are two lock functions, `lock()` and `try_lock()`, and one unlock function, `unlock()`. Once a thread successfully locks a mutex, no other thread may do so.

Problem solved! Why all the bother? Sadly, it is quite easy to find yourself in a position where two threads are both waiting on each other to release a mutex.

```
void thread1()
{
  // Lock writing mutex
```

```
  // Lock logging mutex
  // Do writing
  // Do logging
  // Unlock writing mutex
  // Unlock logging mutex
}

void thread2()
{
  // Lock logging mutex
  // Lock writing mutex
  // Do writing
  // Do logging
  // Unlock writing mutex
  // Unlock logging mutex
}
```

If both threads start simultaneously, thread 1 can lock the writing mutex while thread 2 can lock the logging mutex. Now both threads are waiting for the other thread to unlock their mutex before continuing.

"That's silly," you say. "They should simply lock the mutex they need, do the thing they need it for, and unlock it before locking the next mutex."

```
void thread1()
{
  // Lock writing mutex
  // Do writing
  // Unlock writing mutex
  // Lock logging mutex
  // Do logging
  // Unlock logging mutex
}

void thread2()
{
  // Lock writing mutex
  // Do writing
  // Unlock writing mutex
  // Lock logging mutex
  // Do logging
  // Unlock logging mutex
}
```

"Surely, nothing can go wrong now. The guideline should read 'Don't lock more than one mutex at a time.' Honestly, I could write this stuff."

Well, yes, that would be a useful guideline, but how would you enforce it? What if the writing function locks another mutex? Are you suggesting that we need a way of decorating functions, like the `const` keyword, that does not lock mutexes? Isn't this rather a severe constraint to enforce on multithreaded software development? There is in fact another Core Guideline, CP.22: "Never call unknown code while holding a lock (e.g., a callback)," that addresses this situation.

Unfortunately, this is not a solved problem. You could call `std::lock()`, or make use of the `std::scoped_lock` class, but as a programming style, sharing writable data is an accident waiting to happen, and so you should minimize it if not avoid it entirely. In fact, all this mutex infrastructure is solving the wrong problem: we should not be communicating by sharing memory, we should be sharing memory by communicating.

Setting aside locks and mutexes

The phrase "Don't communicate by sharing memory; share memory by communicating" is the first Go proverb: it is a piece of wisdom as old as concurrency. The application of this wisdom in C++ requires setting aside mutexes and associated data entirely and embracing a different way of communicating between threads. This is achieved by passing messages.

Messages are small objects passed by value to message queues. Each thread will maintain a message queue and periodically inspect it for new messages, acting upon them as appropriate. Messages are sent when one thread has finished something and needs to tell another thread that the results of its activity are now available. The result may be referenced in a `std::unique_ptr` object—not a `std::shared_ptr` object, as that would defeat the point of the approach.

Of course, we've just moved the problem around. Ultimately, we can't get away from sharing some data somewhere, but what we have done here is abstracted it into a queue object. The queue object is the only place where there will be any kind of write-sharing shenanigans, relieving you from the risk of shooting yourself in the foot.

However, by using `std::unique_ptr` objects as handles to data, and by moving them from thread to thread through a message queue,[3] we can treat each thread as a self-contained unit of work, minimizing shared writable data to the management of the queue.

3. As of writing, there is no standard concurrent queue, although a paper has been in development for several years; see www.open-std.org/jtc1/sc22/wg21/docs/papers/2017/p0059r4.pdf.

So, in summary:

- Shared writable data can cause data races and deadlocks
- Correct synchronization is a hard problem
- Minimize sharing by, for example, exchanging messages

Although this is the end of this guideline, this is not the end of the chapter. We have taken a journey of abstractions which we haven't quite finished.

Our first abstraction was the atomic object: an object that couldn't be written to by two different threads simultaneously. The next abstraction was the mutex: an atomic object signaling permission to access a resource. Our third abstraction was the message queue: a mechanism for safely communicating between threads. Our final abstraction turns threads into tasks and is the theme of Core Guideline CP.4: "Think in terms of tasks, rather than threads."

Consider the earlier job of filling a buffer from an I/O device. The heart of the complexity associated with multithreading is the matter of sharing memory. If a thread is completely insulated from the rest of the program, then nothing can go wrong. The thread is very easy to make safe: do not share the buffer being filled until it has been filled. The task could be described as "given a filename, return a buffer filled with the contents of that file." That can easily be encapsulated in a single class, like this:

```
class file_contents
{
public:
  file_contents(std::string const& filename);
  ~file_contents();
  std::pair<std::byte*, size_t> buffer() const;

private:
  …
};
```

The class is constructed with a filename. The constructor looks at the file, finds out how large it is, creates a buffer, and starts a thread, requesting notification when it completes. Before completion, `buffer()` will return `{nullptr, 0}`. After completion, `buffer()` will return the address of the buffer and the number of bytes it contains. Error handling can be a tricky matter: you could decide to throw an exception when `buffer()` is called to signal errors, or add a `good()` predicate.

There is private implementation to consider as well, but it is clear that there is no scope for a data race or a deadlock here: access to the buffer is carefully ordered by the I/O completion and no mutexes can cause any trouble.

A more complex example is a typical phone, console, or PC game. While a game is running, there are different pieces of hardware to be mindful of. The game collects input from a controller, and possibly from a network port. It collects data in the form of graphics data, audio data, and text from offline storage. It runs a model of the world the game takes place in, updating at a particular frequency. These tasks all run concurrently. The model ticks over, examining input, and meanwhile the video renderer draws a snapshot of it and the audio renderer plays sound effects. The input task sends data to the model task, which sends data to the renderers. It's all tasks, all the way down.

Consider the dual-processor workstation: the operating system was able to treat each process as a separate "task," with no communication between them (aside from perhaps the clipboard, Dynamic Data Exchange, OLE, and so on, all of which were scheduled by the operating system). If a task failed, the system could recover easily. It was not dependent on any one task.

Creating and destroying threads can be an expensive activity. A superior approach to sending messages between threads is to create a pool of threads that simply wait, sleeping. Periodically the pool is notified with bundles of instructions and data, whereupon it prods a thread into life. It executes the instructions using the data, returns the value to the sender, and goes back to sleep.

Besides saving on the thread creation and destruction overhead, this is an immensely scalable approach. I first started concurrent computation with two processors each with one core. Today I can buy processors whose cores number well into double figures. Exploiting all these cores can only be achieved by completely factoring your problem into tasks that can be run independently of one another.

The secret is to stop thinking in terms of threads, which are part of the solution domain, and think in terms of tasks, which are part of the problem domain. Particularly, the Core Guideline says, "A thread is an implementation concept, a way of thinking about the machine. A task is an application notion, something you'd like to do, preferably concurrently with other tasks. Application concepts are easier to reason about."

Tasks are the substance of your program, the set of things that you want your program to achieve. Make your tasks independent and describe them as bundles of instructions and data. Core Guideline CP.4: "Think in terms of tasks, rather than threads" addresses this. The standard will eventually add thread pools to the concurrency support library, at which point there will be no need for you to think about threads at all. Until then, only involve yourself with threads at the appropriate level of abstraction, and don't share writable data.

Summary

There are several things to think about here. Concurrent programming still remains the most taxing area of software development in C++. Data races and deadlocks are beastly problems to resolve and migrating to tasks will make your life much easier. Until then:

- Beware of holding multiple mutexes.
- Build loosely coupled abstractions that reflect the tasks you want to carry out.
- Minimize the need to use the lowest level abstractions of the concurrency library.

Chapter 2.6

T.120: Use template metaprogramming only when you really need to

I have served on the program committee of several annual C++ conferences. This means that I participate in choosing what talks are presented to conferences from the many that are submitted. Choosing takes the form of voting: in the usual case there are about a dozen members on the committee. One topic that is guaranteed to get a high score is template metaprogramming, which I shall henceforward refer to as TMP. This is an exciting field of development in C++ because it promises so much, and yet it often does more harm than good: this is yet another manifestation of the shiny hammer syndrome.

There are several things that make TMP rather complex, as well as attractive to conference organizers and developers alike, but also an unattractive proposition to engineering managers.

First, TMP happens at compile time, and the nature of compile-time programming means that there is no mutable state available. This means that it is rather like functional programming, which can be a tricky paradigm to master.

Second, there is no flow control except through recursion. Again, recursion takes some effort to understand; indeed, there is an expression that "to iterate is human, to recurse is divine."

Third, debugging is not available through conventional means. If your code fails, you must simply look at the problem until the answer occurs to you. There are no other options. If you are lucky, you will get some compiler error output, which rapidly explodes into messages that are hundreds of characters long.

Fourth, I would have to be feeling extremely charitable to describe a piece of TMP as self-documenting. The constructs required to deliver TMP are opaque and require a broad understanding of some dusty corners of the language and the standard library.

Fifth, the impact on compilation time can be dramatic. Template instantiation takes time, and if it happens inside a header, then that time cost will be exacted many times over. Of course, function and class templates require inline definitions to operate, so this is the usual case.

Unfortunately, the sheer exhilaration of getting a piece of TMP to work is hard to beat. Also, TMP can offer superior representations of the problem domain at hand, delivering generic and reusable solutions. It is very tempting to reach for TMP when it is not necessary to do so.

But what IS metaprogramming, and how does TMP model it?

In a nutshell, metaprogramming blurs the line between state and execution by treating code as data. The program can see and understand its own code and reason about it, making decisions based on its own structure and content. This leads to things like self-modifying code. For example, and this is going back many years, knowledge of Z80 assembly has allowed me to change code while it's running. I was able to change jump destinations while code was running to change the behavior of algorithms at runtime.

In the case of C++, the compiler knows about the language and treats all the declarations as data. It works on this data to produce the final program. This means there is scope for metaprogramming, which is realized through templates. Templates are customization points for the language, yielding new types depending on how they are instantiated. These types can be thought of as the result of calculations based on the programmer's input. For example, given the function template declaration:

```
template <class T> void fn(T);
```

the declaration

```
fn<int>(17);
```

can be thought of as the result of applying `int` to the function template. This makes C++ its own metalanguage, a facility known as reflection. As we shall see, the reflection facilities offered by C++, though Turing complete, are rather obscure and obfuscate rather than clarify code.

Here is a trivial example, for generating the sum of all integers from `1` to `N`:

```
// Recursive calculation delivers iteration
template <int N> struct sum_integers {
  static constexpr int result = N + sum_integers<N-1>::result;
};

// Explicit specialization forms the recursion base case
// Note that if constexpr may also suffice
```

```
template <> struct sum_integers<1> {
  static constexpr int result = 1;
};

int main () {
  return sum_integers<10>::result;
}
```

This will simply return 55: that value will be calculated at compile time. You can try this out and see how big `N` can get before compilation fails, and look at why it fails.

The state is contained in the result member and is a `const` value. Repeated explicit instantiation of `sum_integers` with a successively reducing parameter achieves the recursion required. If you comment out the base case, the compiler should emit an error related to the complexity of the instantiation context. Here it is using clang 12.0.0, edited slightly for presentation:

```
<source>:3:37: fatal error:
recursive template instantiation exceeded maximum depth of 1024
  static constexpr int result = N + sum_integers<N-1>::result;
                                    ^
<source>:3:37: note:
  in instantiation of template class 'sum_integers<-1014>' requested here
<source>:3:37: note:
  in instantiation of template class 'sum_integers<-1013>' requested here
<source>:3:37: note:
  in instantiation of template class 'sum_integers<-1012>' requested here
<source>:3:37: note:
  in instantiation of template class 'sum_integers<-1011>' requested here
<source>:3:37: note:
  in instantiation of template class 'sum_integers<-1010>' requested here
<source>:3:37: note:
  (skipping 1015 contexts in backtrace;
  use -ftemplate-backtrace-limit=0 to see all)
<source>:3:37: note:
  in instantiation of template class 'sum_integers<6>' requested here
<source>:3:37: note:
  in instantiation of template class 'sum_integers<7>' requested here
<source>:3:37: note:
  in instantiation of template class 'sum_integers<8>' requested here
<source>:3:37: note:
  in instantiation of template class 'sum_integers<9>' requested here
<source>:12:10: note:
  in instantiation of template class 'sum_integers<10>' requested here
  return sum_integers<10>::result;
         ^
<source>:3:37: note:
```

```
  use -ftemplate-depth=N to increase recursive template instantiation depth
  static constexpr int result = N + sum_integers<N-1>::result;
                                     ^
1 error generated.
Compiler returned: 1
```

Here with GCC 11.1:

```
<source>:
In instantiation of 'constexpr const int sum_integers<-889>::result':
<source>:3:56:
   recursively required from 'constexpr const int sum_integers<9>::result'
<source>:3:56:
   required from 'constexpr const int sum_integers<10>::result'
<source>:12:28:
   required from here
<source>:3:56: fatal error:
template instantiation depth exceeds maximum of 900
(use '-ftemplate-depth=' to increase the maximum)
    3 |    static constexpr int result = N + sum_integers<N-1>::result;
      |                                                        ^~~~~~
compilation terminated.
Compiler returned: 1
```

The MSVC compiler timed out on Compiler Explorer, although to its credit it produced the best assembly when compiling the correct source code:

```
main    PROC
        mov     eax, 55                              ; 00000037H
        ret     0
main    ENDP
```

If you are familiar with recursion and base cases, or with proof by induction, this should be clear to you, but the documentation helps here.

There are plenty of resources out there that demonstrate how you can use partial specialization for conditional compilation and use types for returning values. These two features along with iteration via recursion yield TMP as Turing complete, which is a frankly terrifying idea.

This is a trivial example, so let's look at a genuine use case: expression templates.[1] These are sometimes used in linear algebra implementations. Consider this vector class, and by vector we mean the mathematical object rather than the

---

1. I am delighted to credit my committee colleague Daveed Vandevoorde, as well as Todd Veldhuizen, as detailed at https://en.wikipedia.org/wiki/Expression_templates.

standard container. It is likely to be used in three-dimensional geometry. We shall call it `vector_f` because it is a vector of floats:

```
template <size_t N>
class vector_f {
public:
  vector_f();
  vector_f(std::initializer_list<float> init);
  float operator[](size_t i) const; // read-only accessor
  float& operator[](size_t i); // read-write accessor
  size_t const size(); // extract the size parameter

private:
  std::array<float, N> data;
};
```

We want to be able to add `vector_f` objects together. This means we will need an addition operator function template:

```
template <size_t N>
vector_f<N> operator+(vector_f<N> const& u, vector_f<N> const& v) {
  vector_f<N> sum;
  for (size_t i = 0; i < N; i++) {
    sum[i] = u[i] + v[i];
  }
  return sum;
}
```

No rocket science here. It's a raw loop, but we want to highlight something: the code creates the return value, populates it, and returns it. The compiler can do some loop unrolling for small values of `N`. We cannot initialize the return value using the initializer list constructor, but it seems entirely sufficient.

A common activity when dealing with vectors is to add several together in a single operation:

```
vector_f<3> v = a + b + c;
```

This will result in two loop iterations and a discarded temporary object, the result of a + b. As `N` gets bigger this cost will become increasingly apparent. The solution is to defer the generation of the addition operator as far as possible. This is achieved by having the addition operator return a special type that evaluates the addition on demand rather than immediately. It's a kind of lazy evaluation. Strap in...

First, we need an expression class:

```
template <struct E> class vector_expression {
```

```
  public:
    float operator[](size_t i) const {
      return static_cast<E const&>(*this)[i]; }
    size_t size() const {
      return static_cast<E const&>(*this).size; }
};
```

This uses the curiously recurring template pattern, possibly the first piece of TMP to be published. It delegates the bracket operator and the `size` call to the class which is the parameter of this class template.

We now need to derive `vector_f` from this class:

```
template <size_t N> class vector_f
  : public vector_expression<vector_f<N>> {
public:
  vector_f();
  vector_f(std::initializer_list<float> init);
  template <class E>
  vector_f (vector_expression <E> const& e);
  float operator[](size_t i) const; // read-only accessor
  float& operator[](size_t i); // read-write accessor
  size_t const size(); // extract the size parameter

private:
  std::array<N, float> data;
};
```

We have added a new constructor which takes the parent as a parameter. This is where we construct an instance from an expression type rather than a list of values. It looks like this:

```
template <size_t N>
template <class E>
vector_f<N>::vector_f(vector_expression<E> const& e)
  : data(e.size()) {
  for (size_t i = 0; i != e.size(); ++i) {
    data[i] = e[i]; //(1)
  }
}
```

This is where the evaluation takes place. The final part is the actual addition expression class. This looks like:

```
template <class E1, class E2> class vector_sum
  : public vector_expression<vector_sum<E1, E2>> {
  E1 const& u;
```

```
  E2 const& v;

public:
  vector_sum(E1 const& u, E2 const& v);
  float operator[](size_t i) const { return u[i] + v[i]; } //(2)
  size_t size()              const { return v.size(); }
};

template <typename E1, typename E2>
vector_sum<E1, E2> operator+(vector_expression<E1> const& u,
                             vector_expression<E2> const& v) {
  return vector_sum<E1, E2>(*static_cast<E1 const*>(&u),
                            *static_cast<E2 const*>(&v));
}
```

That is everything required for addition. The expression

```
a + b + c
```

is now no longer of the type `vector_f<3>`, but of the type

```
vector_sum<vector_sum<vector_f<3>, vector_f<3>>>
```

When this expression is assigned to a `vector_f<3>` object, the constructor that takes a `vector_expression` is invoked, which assigns the expression elements to the data elements (1). The bracket operator for `vector_sum` returns the sum of the two objects (2), which recurses to the sum of another two `vector_sum` objects, which finally expands to the sum of three elements.

As you can see, this requires no temporaries and only one loop, which is exactly what we were looking for. This sort of lazy evaluation is also used in the ranges library: expression types are built during compilation and evaluated at the moment of assignment.

Now, that example took a lot of exposition. It is clear that the amount of documentation required to explain what is going on is considerable, and the biggest problem I have with code reviews is the lack of documentation, which means that the chances of sufficient documentation for tricks like this are low. However, this is a popular pattern that can yield benefits, so, if you are going to deploy it (because you really need to), make sure you do so with thorough documentation. Also, make sure that you do really need to deploy this pattern. Compiler writers are clever. Check that there is indeed a shortfall in performance. Look at the generated assembly before and after. Measure performance. Measure build time. What yielded advantage three years ago may no longer have the edge, so look before you leap, or rather, check before you commit.

std::enable_if => requires

Let's look at another popular technique.

When C++98 emerged, one of the first things I did was look at the interactions of the containers with the algorithms. At the time, I was working for a game company in London and trying to persuade some of the engineers that C++ was the way to go (I was possibly a little premature). I demonstrated tiny functions that would search and sort their way through our collections of stuff. The big problem, though, was `std::vector`. Whenever its capacity was exceeded and a resize was triggered, it would copy the contents, one by one, to the new location using a `for` loop, and then it would destroy the prior versions. Of course it did: the standard required the contents be copy constructed to their new location and then their destructors invoked. In the majority of situations, though, there was an obvious optimization, and that was to use `memcpy` rather than per-item copying.

`memcpy` is a C function that you should never use directly, since it simply duplicates the contents of memory somewhere else, without any regard for the copy constructor. This means that although the data is correct, any additional initialization, for example registering objects with a notification service, or destruction, for example deregistering from the notification service, is skipped. `memcpy` is an implementation detail that should not be part of your daily use.

My colleagues turned and walked away. I was crestfallen and decided to write a vector that would use `memcpy` rather than copy constructing and destructing as it should have done. I called it `mem_vector`. This was only for use with types that had no constructor or destructor, and it was great. Everyone was excited about it and put it to good use in combination with the algorithms. I was on cloud nine for about three days until someone broke everything by adding a constructor to a type. The `mem_vector` was no longer fit for purpose in that case, and soon it became clear that it was not fit for purpose unless the code was finished, by which point The Old Ways had been followed anyway.

What I REALLY needed was a way of choosing between using `memcpy` and individual per-element copy-and-destroy. This was a bit of a head scratcher, since it meant providing a member function overload that would be chosen for families of types rather than specific types. I wanted to be able to declare:

```
template <class T>
void mem_vector<T>::resize(size_type count);
```

(this was before C++11) along with

```
template <class Trivial>
void mem_vector<Trivial>::resize(size_type count);
```

and have the compiler call the appropriate `mem_vector` depending on the nature of the template parameter rather than the specific type of the template parameter. One day I heard about SFINAE (Substitution Failure Is Not An Error) and suddenly it dawned on me: I could embed an empty struct called `trivial` in all the appropriate types. Then I could redeclare the second `resize` function:

```
template <class T>
void mem_vector<T>::resize(size_type count, T::trivial* = 0);
```

If the trivial member struct did not exist, then the function would not be considered. But all I had done was move the problem around. There was still no way of enforcing the trivial member struct would be removed if the class were no longer trivial. This was especially obvious when structs were inherited from other trivial structs and the parent struct became nontrivial. I despaired.

It wasn't all bad: we were able to fudge something together using compiler-specific intrinsics, and then C++11 arrived. Suddenly everything was fixed by the awesome power of `std::enable_if` and the `type_traits` header. Oh, frabjous day!

There was one teensy little problem, though. The code was nearly illegible. Types like this:

```
std::enable_if<std::is_trivially_constructible<T>::value>::type
```

(yes, that's a type) became scattered throughout the codebase, introducing further cognitive load.

Again, the problem with this TMP technique is that it obfuscates the code and puts the brakes on rapid apprehension of what is going on. Frankly, it looks like transmission noise to me. Yes, with practice, we became able to read it with some ease, but there was a big learning phase for new programmers.

This complexity did not prevent the widespread adoption of this technique. A quick tour through older GitHub repositories will reveal swathes of code with carefully crafted function overloads differentiated by `std::enable_if` clauses of varying verbosity. The committee was not blind to this problem, though, and in C++17 a new facility was added to the language: the `constexpr` if statement.

This beauty solved a few classes of problems that would historically have seen you reaching for `enable_if`. It enables you to evaluate an expression at compile time and choose execution based on the result. You can use it like this:

```
if constexpr(sizeof(int) == 4)
{
  // ints are 32 bits wide.
}
```

but particularly you can use it where you might have used `enable_if`, for example:

```
if constexpr(std::is_move_constructible_v<T>)
{
  // the function template is being specialized for a move-constructible type
}
```

Rather than having function template overloads for different types, you were now able to express the difference in a single function. For example, the following pair of overloads:

```
template <class T, typename =
    std::enable_if<std::is_move_constructible_v<T> >::type>
void do_stuff()
{
  …
}
template <class T, typename =
    std::enable_if<!std::is_move_constructible_v<T> >::type>
void do_stuff()
{
  …
}
```

can be replaced with:

```
template <class T>
void do_stuff()
{
  if constexpr(std::is_move_constructible_v<T>)
  {
    …
  }
  else
  {
    …
  }
}
```

The committee didn't stop there, though. After a long gestation period concepts were added to the language, which brought with them constraints and `requires` clauses. This makes it much clearer to specify the restrictions on types for specialization. A `requires` clause looks like this:

```
template <class T>
requires std::is_move_constructible_v<T>
void do_stuff()
{
  …
}
```

This function will only be available to types that are move constructible. This is conceptually identical to `std::enable_if` but it is a lot easier to apprehend This gives us a way of avoiding TMP and being explicit with our intentions.

There is still more to come. One of the committee study groups, SG7, is devoted to reflection. This is what is being attempted with much of TMP. The intention is to add to the language many of the facilities that are being handcrafted using TMP, and eventually to eliminate the need for TMP. Reflection is a big part of metaprogramming, and the study group is bringing together many ideas to deliver a coherent metaprogramming strategy and solution. Even more features are being worked on that rely on reflection, one of which is metaclasses. This enables the programmer to define the shape of a class rather than just the substitutable types, allowing clients of the metaclass to instantiate types of classes without worrying about boilerplate code.

All of these features will deliver better clarity for everyone: rather than adding burdensome additional things to learn, it will enable the simplification of a lot of existing code and the elimination of unnecessary angle brackets.

We hope that this guideline has impressed upon you the complexity of TMP and why it should be deployed as a last resort. Of course, there are places where metaprogramming can only be delivered through the careful use of templates. The Hacker's Delight of solving problems in such a way is strong but, in time, you should be able to deliver clearer code.

There is an aphorism that every engineer should hold close to their heart.

Clever code is easy. Easy code is clever.

The best code is that which is presented to the reader who, upon examining it, says, "What's so special about this? It's obvious." I get the Hacker's Delight when someone says this to me. It is very unusual for anyone to say that about template metaprogramming.

Summary

In summary:

- Metaprogramming in C++ is modeled via function and class templates.
- This self-awareness offers reflection.
- Metaprogramming techniques, while useful, have been adopted into the language more explicitly.
- This trajectory is continuing, obviating the need for metaprogramming via templates.

Section 3

Stop using that

Chapter 3.1

I.11: Never transfer ownership by a raw pointer (`T*`) or reference (`T&`)

Using the free store

Ownership is important. It implies responsibility which, in C++, means cleaning up after yourself. If you create something, you clean it up. While this is a completely trivial matter for objects of static and automatic storage duration, it is a minefield for objects of dynamic duration which are allocated from the free store.

Once memory is allocated from the free store it can be very easily lost. It can only be returned to the free store using the pointer to which it was assigned. This pointer is the only available handle to the memory. If that pointer falls out of scope without being copied, then the memory can never be recovered. This is known as a memory leak. For example:

```
size_t make_a_wish(int id, std::string owner) {
  Wish* wish = new Wish(wishes[id], owner);
  return wish->size();
}
```

At the end of the function the `Wish` pointer falls out of scope, leaving the memory unrecoverable. We can change the function a little by returning the pointer so that the caller can take ownership and delete the object later, freeing the memory.

```
Wish* make_a_wish_better(int id, std::string owner) {
  Wish* wish = new Wish(wishes[id], owner);
  return wish;
}
```

This is perfectly well-formed code, although we would not call it modern in the idiomatic sense. Unfortunately, it carries a burden: the caller must take ownership of the object and ensure that it is destroyed via the delete operator when they are finished with it, freeing the memory. There is also a danger of deleting it before everyone has finished with the object it points to. If `make_a_wish` takes a pointer from another object, how should it be signaled that the other object has finished with it and no longer needs it?

Historically, this type of function led to the free store being exhausted by zombie objects whose ownership was not clearly signposted and for which the necessary deleting never took place. This signposting might take several forms. The function author might name the function `allocate_a_wish`, hinting to the client that an allocation had taken place and it was their responsibility now.

This is a rather weak way of signaling ownership; it is unenforceable, and it relies on the client remembering that they have this responsibility and discharging it appropriately. It also requires the author to embed the implementation in the interface. This is a bad habit since it implicitly exposes implementation details to the client and prevents you from changing them without introducing confusion.

While constrained naming may seem weak, it is not as weak as remarking on it in some documentation on a server somewhere remote, dark, and uninviting. Nor is it as weak as a note in a header file that nobody ever reads. While it is a lesser evil, it is certainly not foolproof.

Worse still is returning a value via a reference rather than a pointer. How does the caller know when the object has been destroyed? All that the caller can do with such a value is hope that another thread doesn't destroy it in the meantime, and ensure the object is used before calling another function that may trigger its destruction. This is a lot of context to keep in mind while writing your code.

If you work with particularly elderly codebases you may see instances of `std::auto_ptr`. This is the first attempt at solving this problem which ended up being standardized in C++98. The `std::auto_ptr` would contain the pointer itself and provide overloaded pointer semantics, acting as a handle to the object. The `std::auto_ptr` could be passed around, releasing ownership when it was copied from. When it fell out of scope while retaining ownership it would delete the contained object. However, these unusual copy semantics meant `std::auto_ptr` objects could not be safely contained in standard containers, and the class was deprecated in the second standard (C++11) and removed in the third (C++14).

The committee doesn't deprecate things without replacements, though, and the introduction of move semantics made it possible to create pointer owning objects for which containment was not a problem. As `std::auto_ptr` was deprecated in C++11, `std::unique_ptr` and `std::shared_ptr` were introduced. These are known as "smart" pointers or "fancy" pointers, and entirely solve the ownership problem for you.

Your default choice for holding objects with dynamic storage duration should be a `std::unique_ptr`. You should only use `std::shared_ptr` where reasoning about lifetime and ownership is impossibly hard, and even then, you should treat it as a sign of impending technical debt caused by a failure to observe the appropriate abstraction.

When you receive a `std::unique_ptr` object you become the owner of what the object points to. When its name falls out of scope it deletes the contained object. However, unlike the `std::auto_ptr`, it does not contain a flag identifying ownership, so it can be safely contained in a standard container. The reason it doesn't need a flag is because it cannot be copied, it can only be moved, so there is no ambiguity about who is currently responsible for the object it contains.

When you receive a `std::shared_ptr` object you gain an interest in what the object points to. When it falls out of scope that interest is withdrawn. The instant that nothing any longer has an interest in the object, it is deleted. Ownership is shared between everything that has an interest in the contained object. The object will not be destroyed until no objects remain that hold an interest in it.

Your default choice for holding objects with dynamic storage duration should be a `std::unique_ptr`. You should only use `std::shared_ptr` where reasoning about lifetime and ownership is impossibly hard, and even then, you should treat it as a sign of impending technical debt caused by a failure to observe the appropriate abstraction. One example of this could be a Twitter viewer that organizes tweets into different columns. Tweets may contain images that make them large, and they may also be shared across columns. A tweet only needs to continue to exist while it is in view in one of the columns, but the user decides when a tweet is no longer needed by scrolling it away from all columns. You might decide to keep a container of tweets and use counts, effectively reference counting the tweets manually, but that is simply duplicating the `std::shared_ptr` abstraction at another level of indirection. Particularly, though, the user is making the decision about the lifetime of the tweet, not the program. It should be rare that such a situation arises.

The performance cost of smart pointers

Sometimes you might decide that you do not want to use smart pointers. Copying a `std::shared_ptr` is not without cost. A `std::shared_ptr` needs to be thread safe, and thread safety costs cycles; only the control block of a `std::shared_ptr` is thread safe, not the resource itself. It may be implemented as a pair of pointers, one of which points to the thing being contained and the other pointing to the bookkeeping mechanism. It remains cheap to copy in terms of moving memory around, but the bookkeeping mechanism will have to acquire a mutex and increment the reference count when it is copied. When it falls out of scope it will have to acquire the mutex again and decrement the reference count, destroying the object if that count reaches zero.

The `std::unique_ptr` is a simpler, cheaper beast. Since it can only be moved, not copied, only one instance of it can exist, so when it falls out of scope it must delete the object it is containing. No bookkeeping is required. However, there is still the overhead of containing a pointer to the function that will delete the object. The `std::shared_ptr` contains such an object too as part of the bookkeeping.

This is not something you should worry about until it turns up as a hot spot in your profiling measurements. The safety of a smart pointer is a very valuable part of your engineering effort. However, if you find that using smart pointers registers in your profile, you might look at where you are passing them and discover that sharing or transferring ownership is unnecessary. For example:

```
size_t measure_widget(std::shared_ptr<Widget> w) {
  return w->size(); // (We're assuming that w is non-null)
}
```

This function does not require any kind of ownership considerations. It is simply calling a function and returning that value. This function would work just as well:

```
size_t measure_widget(Widget* w) {
  return w->size(); // (We're still assuming that w is non-null)
}
```

Pay particular attention to what has happened to `w`, or rather what has not happened to `w`. It has not been passed on to another function, or used to initialize another object, or indeed had its lifetime extended in any way. If the function were to look like this:

```
size_t measure_widget(Widget* w) {
  return size(w); // (You guessed it…)
}
```

then that would be a different matter. You do not own `w`, so it is not yours to pass around. The size function may take a copy of `w` and cache it for later use, so unless you are certain of the implementation of that function and you are also in charge of how it might change, passing `w` is unsafe. If the object `w` points to is destroyed later, then that copy of `w` will be pointing to nothing and dereferencing it will be potentially disastrous.

This function takes an object by pointer and then passes it to another function. This implies ownership, which is not conveyed in the function signature. Do not transfer ownership by a raw pointer.

The correct way to implement this function is:

```
size_t measure_widget(std::shared_ptr<Widget> w) {
  return size(w);
}
```

You are now giving the `size()` function an interest in the `std::shared_ptr`. If the calling function subsequently destroys `w`, the `size()` function can still retain a copy.

Using unadorned reference semantics

A raw pointer is not the only way to pass an object by reference rather than by value. You can also achieve this using a reference. Using a reference is the preferred mechanism of passing by reference. Consider this version of `measure_widget`:

```
size_t measure_widget(Widget& w) {
  return w.size(); // (References cannot be null without evil intent)
}
```

This is superior because it passes the burden of checking that the object exists to the caller. They must dereference the object and pay the penalty of dereferencing a null pointer. However, the same ownership problem exists if `w` is passed on. If the reference is stored as part of another object, and the referent is destroyed, then that reference will no longer be valid.

The function signature should tell the caller everything they need to know about ownership. If the signature includes a `T*`, then the caller can pass a pointer to an object, or a null pointer, and not worry about its lifetime. The caller is simply passing an object by reference to the function and then carrying on with things. If the signature includes a `T&`, then the caller can pass a reference to an object, and not worry about its lifetime. The same benefits apply.

If the signature includes a `std::unique_ptr<T>`, then the caller must surrender ownership of the object. If the signature includes a `std::shared_ptr<T>`, then the caller must share ownership of the object with the function. This implies the caller cannot be sure when the object will be destroyed.

If you deviate from these rules, you can introduce painfully subtle bugs into your codebase which will result in tiring arguments about ownership and responsibility. Objects end up being destroyed early or not at all. Do not transfer ownership by raw pointer or reference. If your function takes a pointer or a reference, do not pass it on to a constructor or another function without understanding the responsibilities of so doing.

gsl::owner

We've covered passing and returning values by raw pointer and by reference and seen that it is not a good idea. Users might infer ownership when they shouldn't. Users might want ownership rights when they can't have them. The correct course of action is to use smart pointers to indicate ownership.

Unfortunately, you may be working in legacy code that can't be modified very much. It may be part of a dependency of other legacy code that is relying on the ABI. Exchanging pointers for smart pointers would change the layout of any objects that contain them, breaking the ABI.

It's time to introduce properly the Guidelines Support Library (GSL). This is a small library of facilities designed to support the Core Guidelines. There are a lot of items in the Core Guidelines, some of which are very hard to enforce. The use of raw pointers is a case in point: how do you signal ownership of a pointer if you can't use smart pointers? The GSL provides types to aid enforcement.

The GSL is divided into five parts.

- GSL.view: these types allow the user to distinguish between owning and non-owning pointers, and between pointers to a single object and pointers to the first element of a sequence.
- GSL.owner: these are ownership pointers, which include `std::unique_ptr` and `std::shared_ptr` as well as `stack_array` (a stack allocated array) and `dyn_array` (a heap allocated array).
- GSL.assert: these foreshadow the contracts proposal by providing two macros, Expects and Ensures.
- GSL.util: no library is complete without a homeless bag of useful things.
- GSL.concept: this is a collection of type predicates.

The GSL predates C++17, and parts of the GSL, particularly the concept section, have been superseded by Standard C++. It's available on GitHub at https://github.com/Microsoft/GSL. Simply `#include <gsl/gsl>` to get the full set of objects.

This chapter is most concerned with one of the view types, `gsl::owner<T*>`. Let's look at an example:

```
#include <gsl/gsl>

gsl::owner<int*> produce()      // You will become the proud owner
{
  gsl::owner<int*> i = new int; // You're the owner
  return i;                     // Passing ownership out of the function
}

void consume(gsl::owner<int*> i) // Taking on ownership
{
  delete i;                     // It's yours, you can destroy it
}

void p_and_c()
{
  auto i = produce();           // create…
  consume(i);                   // …and destroy
}
```

As you can see, enclosing the pointer with `owner<>` signals that ownership is being established. Let's change things a little:

```
int* produce()                  // Just a raw pointer
{
  gsl::owner<int*> i = new int;
  return i;
}
```

What happens now?

You might be forgiven for thinking that the compiler will warn you that you are passing to an unowned pointer from an object signaling ownership. Unfortunately, this is not the case. The definition of owner is:

```
template <class T,
          class = std::enable_if_t<std::is_pointer<T>::value>>
using owner = T;
```

As you can see, there is no magic here. The definition of `gsl::owner` is very simple: if `T` is a pointer type, then `gsl::owner<T>` is an alias to `T`, otherwise it is undefined.

The purpose of this type is not to enforce ownership, but rather to hint to the user that there is a change in ownership going on. Rather than embedding this information in the function name, it is embedded in the type. While it is quite possible to create a type named `owner` that does all the required enforcement to correctly track and maintain ownership, there is no need: `std::shared_ptr` and `std::unique_ptr` do this job entirely adequately. The `gsl::owner` type is merely syntactic sugar that can be dropped into an existing codebase with no impact to the code, the ABI, or the execution, but with a large impact on readability and comprehension, as well as a contribution to the efficacy of static analyzers and code reviews.

As the GSL becomes more widely used we might expect IDEs to learn about its types and warn about abuses of ownership through signals in the editor, such as red underlining or floating lightbulb hints. Until then, do not use `gsl::owner` as an enforcement type, but rather as a documentation type. Ultimately, treat `gsl::owner` as a last resort when you are truly unable to use higher-level ownership abstractions.

Summary

In summary:

- Owning something means being responsible for something.
- C++ has smart pointers for unambiguously signaling ownership.
- Use smart pointers to signal ownership, or `gsl::owner<T>`.
- Do not assume ownership from a raw pointer or a reference.

Chapter 3.2

I.3: Avoid singletons

Global objects are bad

Global objects are bad, m'kay? You will hear this all the time, from programmers young and old, recited as an article of faith. Let's look into why this is.

A global object lives in the global namespace. There is only one of these, hence the name "global." The global namespace is the outermost declarative region of a translation unit. A name with global namespace scope is said to be a global name. Any object with a global name is a global object.

A global object is not necessarily visible to every translation unit of a program; the one-definition rule means that it can only be defined in one translation unit. However, a declaration can be repeated in any number of translation units.

Global objects have no access restrictions. If you can see it, you can interact with it. Global objects have no owner other than the program itself, which means no single entity is responsible for it. Global objects have static storage duration, so they are initialized at startup (or static initialization) and destroyed at shutdown (or static deinitialization).

This is problematic. Ownership is fundamental to reasoning about objects. Since nothing owns a global object, how can you reason about its state at any time? You might be calling functions on that object and then, suddenly and without warning, another entity may call other functions on that object without your knowledge.

Worse still, since nothing owns global objects, their construction sequence is not determined by the standard. You have no idea in which order global objects will be constructed, which leads to a rather frustrating category of bug that we shall cover later.

Singleton Design Pattern

Having convinced you of the harm that global objects cause to your codebase, let us turn our attention to singletons. I first encountered this term in 1994 when the book *Design Patterns*[1] was published. This venerable tome was a tremendously exciting read at the time and is still a very useful book to have on your shelf or your e-reader. It describes patterns that recur in software engineering, in much the same way that patterns recur in conventional architecture, such as cupola, portico, or cloister. What was so welcome about this book was that it identified common patterns in programming and gave them names. Naming is hard, and having someone do the naming for us was a great boon.

The book categorizes the patterns in three ways, as creational, structural, or behavioral patterns. It is within the creational division that we find the singleton, which restricts object creation for a class to only one instance. Of course, with such a fabulous text outlining such a well-used pattern, it was taken for granted that using a singleton was A Good Thing. After all, we had all been using something like singletons for years, we just had not yet given them a name that we could all agree on.

A popular example of a singleton is the main window. The main window is where all the action happens, collecting user input and displaying results. You should only create one main window, so it might make sense to prevent the creation of another. Another example is the manager class. This is characterized by including the name "manager" in the identifier. This is a strong sign that in fact a singleton has been created, and that there are problems deciding about ownership of whatever is being managed.

Static initialization order fiasco

Singletons are prone to the static initialization order fiasco.[2] This term was coined by Marshall Cline in his C++ FAQ and characterizes the problem of dependent objects being constructed out of order. Consider two global objects, A and B, where the constructor of B uses some functionality provided by A and so A must be constructed first. At link time, the linker identifies the set of objects with static storage duration,

1. Gamma, E, Helm, R, Johnson, R, and Vlissides, J, 1994. *Design Patterns*. Reading, MA: Addison-Wesley.
2. "Fiasco" is possibly an unfair characterization. Static initialization was never supposed to offer a topological ordering of initialization. That was infeasible with separate compilation, incremental linking, and linkers from the 1980s. C++ had to live with the existing operating systems. This was a time when systems programmers were used to living with sharp tools.

sets aside an area of the memory for them to exist in, and creates a list of constructors to be called before `main` is called. At runtime, this is called static initialization.

Now, although you can identify that B depends on A and so A must be constructed first, there is no standard way to signal to the linker that this is the case. Indeed, how could you do that? You would need to find some way of exposing the dependency in the translation unit, but the compiler only knows about the translation unit it is compiling.

We can hear your brow furrowing. "Well, what if I told the linker what order to create them in? Could the linker be modified to accommodate that?" In fact, this has been tried. Long ago I used an IDE called Code Warrior, by Metrowerks. The edition I was using exposed a property that allowed me to dictate the order of construction of static objects. It worked fine, for a while, until I unwittingly created a subtle circular dependency that took me the better part of twenty hours to track down.

By keeping your object dependencies in a single translation unit, you avoid all of these problems while maintaining clarity of purpose and separation of concerns.

You aren't convinced. "Circular dependencies are part and parcel of engineering development. The fact that you managed to create one because you got your relationships wrong shouldn't preclude the option to dictate the creation order at static initialization." Indeed, I did actually resolve the problem and carried on, but then I needed to port the codebase to another toolchain which didn't support this feature. I was programming in nonstandard C++ and paid the price when I attempted portability.

"Nonetheless," you continue, "this is something the committee COULD standardize. Linkage specifications are already in the purview of the standard. Why not initialization order specification?" Well, another problem with static initialization order is that there is nothing to stop you starting multiple threads during static initialization and requiring an object before it has been created. It is far too easy to shoot yourself in the foot with dependencies between global static objects.

The committee is not in the habit of standardizing footguns. Dependency on the order of initialization is fraught with peril, as demonstrated in the prior paragraphs, and allowing programmers to command this facility is unwise at best. Additionally, it militates against modular design. Static initialization order IS specified per translation unit by order of declaration. Specification between translation units is where it all falls down. By keeping your object dependencies in a single translation unit, you avoid all of these problems while maintaining clarity of purpose and separation of concerns.

The word "linker" appears ONCE in the standard.[3] Linkers are not unique to C++; linkers will bind together anything of the appropriate format, regardless of what compiler emitted it, be it C, C++, Pascal, or other languages. It is a steep demand to require that linkers suddenly support a new feature solely for the benefit of promoting a dicey programming practice in one language. Cast the idea of standardizing initialization order from your mind. It is a fool's errand.

Having said that, there is a way around the static initialization order fiasco, and that is to take the objects out of the global scope so that their initialization can be scheduled. The easiest way to do this is to create a simple function containing a static object of the type required, which the function returns by reference. This is sometimes known as the Meyers Singleton after Scott Meyers, who described this approach in his book *Effective* C++.[4] The technique itself is much older than that, having been used in the 1980s. For example:

```
Manager& manager() {
  static Manager m;
  return m;
}
```

Now the function is global, rather than the object. The `Manager` object will not be created until the function is called: static data at function scope falls under different initialization rules. "But," you may ask, "what about the concurrency problem? Surely, we still have the same issue of multiple threads trying to access the object before it has been fully created?"

Fortunately, since C++11 this is also thread safe. If you look at section [stmt.dcl][5] in the standard you will see the following: "If control enters the declaration concurrently while the variable is being initialized, the concurrent execution shall wait for completion of the initialization." This is not the end of your troubles, though: you are still distributing a handle to a single mutable object, with no guarantee of thread-safe access to that object.

How to hide a singleton

You might look at that and decide that we have simply hidden a singleton behind a function. Indeed, hiding singletons is easy and the Core Guidelines remarks that enforcing their nonuse is very hard in general. The first enforcement idea offered by

3. https://eel.is/c++draft/lex.name
4. Meyers, S, 1998. *Effective* C++. Reading, MA: Addison-Wesley.
5. https://eel.is/c++draft/stmt.dcl

this specific Core Guideline I.3: "Avoid singletons," is "look for classes with names that include singleton." This might seem somewhat specious, but since Singleton is one of the Design Patterns it is remarkably common for engineers to add it to the name of a class, to identify that "this is a singleton" or "I have read the *Design Patterns* book." Of course, doing so embeds the implementation in the interface, which is A Bad Thing, but that is another topic.

The second idea offered by the guideline is "look for classes for which only a single object is created (by counting objects or by examining constructors)." This requires a complete, manual, class-by-class audit of your codebase. Sometimes singletons are created by accident. An abstraction may be inducted and a class formed from it, and all the scaffolding required to manage the life cycle of and interactions with that class may be created, such as the special functions, public interface, and so on, but only one instance of the object may ever exist at one time. It may not have been the engineer's intention to create a singleton, but that is what has happened; a count of all the instances reveals the quantity to be one.

The final idea is "If a class X has a public static function that contains a function-local static of the class type X and returns a pointer or reference to it, ban that." This is exactly the technique described above to resolve the static initialization order fiasco. The class may have a superset of the following interface:

```
class Manager
{
public:
  static Manager& instance();

private:
  Manager();
};
```

The giveaway here is the private constructor. Nothing can create this object except a static member or a friend, and we see no friend declarations. Nothing can derive from it unless another constructor is added to the nonprivate interface. The private constructor indicates that "my construction is tightly controlled by other functions in my interface" and lo! And behold! The public interface contains a static function which returns a reference to an instance. You will no doubt be able to guess the general content of this member function by looking at the `manager()` example function above.

A subtle variation of this is the reference-counted singleton. Consider a class that is a huge resource hog. Not only do you not want two instances of these to exist at once, but you also want it to be destroyed the moment it is no longer needed. This is somewhat complex to manage, since you need a shared pointer, a mutex, and a reference counter. However, this is still a singleton and falls under the "Avoid singletons" guideline.

You might be looking at that public static member function and saying to yourself "surely the guideline should say 'Avoid static storage duration objects.' They are singletons, after all." Hold that thought.

But only one of these should ever exist

Throughout the teaching of C++ there have been some popular examples to describe object orientation. Gas stations have cars, pumps, a cash desk, tankers delivering fuel, prices, and so on, yielding an ecosystem rich enough to describe many kinds of relationships. In the same vein, restaurants have tables, customers, menus, a serving hatch, wait staff, chefs, food deliveries, garbage collection, and other features. In today's textbooks they probably also have a website and a Twitter account.

Both examples have one thing in common: an abstraction that should only exist singly. The gas station has one cash desk. The restaurant has one serving hatch. Surely these are singletons? If not, what is to be done?

One solution we have seen to this problem is to create a class with an entirely static interface. All the public member functions and the private data are static. We now want to take a diversion and tell you about W. Heath Robinson. Born in 1872 in Finsbury Park, London, this English cartoonist was best known for his drawings of ludicrously elaborate machines that went to great lengths to solve simple problems. One of the automatic analysis machines built for Bletchley Park during the Second World War to assist in the decryption of German message traffic was named "Heath Robinson" in his honor. I was given a book of his cartoons as a young child and marveled at the intricacy of the operation of his devices. He had an American counterpart, Rube Goldberg, born in July 1883 in San Francisco, who also drew overly complex devices, and inspired the board game Mouse Trap. Their names have passed into common parlance in the English language to describe overengineering.

This is precisely what a class with an entirely static interface is an example of. When you create a class, you create a public interface for viewing and controlling the abstraction, and a pile of data and nonpublic functions for modeling the abstraction. However, if there is only one instance of all the data, why do you need to attach it to a class? You can simply implement all the public member functions in one source file and put the single instance of the data and all the nonpublic functions in an anonymous namespace.

In fact, why are you bothering with a class at all?

What we have arrived at, in a self-referentially convoluted way, is the correct solution to the problem of singletons (small s). They should be implemented as namespaces rather than classes. Rather than this:

```
class Manager
{
public:
  static int blimp_count();
  static void add_more_blimps(int);
  static void destroy_blimp(int);

private:
  static std::vector<Blimp> blimps;
  static void deploy_blimp();
};
```

you should declare this:

```
namespace Manager
{
  int blimp_count();
  void add_more_blimps(int);
  void destroy_blimp(int);
}
```

The implementation does not need to be exposed to the client like some Heath Robinson drawing of marvelous and fascinating complexity. It can be hidden away in the dark recesses of a private implementation file. This has the additional advantage of improving the stability of the file in which the namespace is declared, minimizing large-scale dependent recompilation. Of course, the data used to model the abstraction will not be owned by an object, so it will be static. Beware of the static initialization order fiasco as described above.

Wait a moment...

You might be looking at this namespace solution and remarking to yourself "but this is still a Singleton."

It is not a Singleton. It is a singleton. The problem that the guideline is warning about is the Singleton pattern, not the existence of single-instance abstractions. Indeed, in an interview with InformIT in 2009, Erich Gamma, one of the four authors of *Design Patterns,* remarked that he wanted to remove Singleton from the catalogue.[6]

6. https://www.informit.com/articles/article.aspx?p=1404056

There are two problems that we have with C++ advice. The first is that what was smart advice once may not remain smart advice forever.

At the moment, a new version of C++ is released every three years. The introduction of `std::unique_ptr` and `std::shared_ptr` in 2011 changed the advice on how we matched `new` and `delete` pairs ("Don't delete an object in a different module from where it was created") by making it entirely feasible to never use raw `new` and `delete`, as advised by Core Guideline R.11: "Avoid calling `new` and `delete` explicitly." Learning a set of advisories and then moving on with your life is not sufficient: you need to continually review advice as the language grows and changes.

What was smart advice once may not remain smart advice forever.

An immediate manifestation of this problem is that you may have a favorite framework that you use extensively, which may contain idiomatic use of C++ that has been deprecated. Perhaps it contains a Singleton for capturing and manipulating environment variables, or settings informed by the command-line parameters which may be subject to change. You might feel that your favorite framework can do no wrong, but that is not the case. Just as scientific opinion changes with the arrival of new information, so does best C++ practice. This book that you are reading today may contain some timeless advice, but it would be supremely arrogant and foolish of me to suggest that the entire text is wisdom for the ages, with stone-carved commandments about how you should write C++.

The second problem is that advisories are the distillation of several motivations, often hidden entirely from the snappy and memorable phrase that sits in our immediate recall. "Avoid singletons" is much easier to remember than "avoid overengineering single-instance abstractions into a class and abusing access levels to prevent multiple instantiations." Learning the advice is not enough. You must learn the motivations so that you know why you are taking a particular approach, and when it is safe not to do so.

C++ Core Guidelines is a living document with a GitHub repository on which you can make pull requests. It contains hundreds of advisories with varying amounts of motivation, and the purpose of this book is to highlight some of the deeper motivations for 30 of them.

Earlier we remarked that you may be thinking that all static objects are Singletons, so all static objects should be avoided. You should be able to see now that static objects are not Singletons, nor are they necessarily singletons. They are an instance of an object whose duration is the entire duration of the program. Nor are they necessarily globals: static data members have class scope, not global scope.

Similarly, "Globals are bad, m'kay?" is not universally the case. It is global mutable state that can hurt you, as revealed in Core Guideline I.2: "Avoid non-`const` global variables." If your global object is immutable, then it is merely a property of your program. For example, while writing a physics simulation for a space game we could quite reasonably declare an object of type `float` called `G`, which is the gravitational constant, in the global namespace like this:

```
constexpr float G = 6.674e-11; // Gravitational constant
```

After all, it is a universal constant. Nobody should be changing this. Of course, you might decide that the global namespace is not the right place for such a thing, and declare a namespace called `universe` like this:

```
namespace universe {
  constexpr float G = 6.674e-11; // Gravitational constant
}
```

There is an outside chance that you might want to experiment with a universe with a different gravitational constant; in this case you may want to use a function that simply returns a value, and then change the logic behind the interface according to your crazy experimental needs.

The point is that you know WHY globals are bad, for the reasons enumerated earlier, and you can decide when it is appropriate to bend that rule, with a full understanding of the technical debt you are taking on.

Summary

In summary:

- Avoid singletons: the pattern, not the single-instance abstraction.
- Prefer a namespace to a class to model this type of abstraction.
- Use static data carefully when implementing a singleton.
- Understand the motivations for the Core Guidelines.
- Review the Core Guidelines as the C++ language grows and evolves.

Chapter 3.3

C.90: Rely on constructors and assignment operators, not `memset` and `memcpy`

Chasing maximum performance

C++ has a proud reputation for bare metal performance. Other languages have come and gone, trying to take the performance crown from C++, but still it remains the go-to language for zero-overhead abstractions. It has inherited this pedigree from C, which offers some very efficient library functions. Some of these can be implemented as single processor instructions.

For example, consider `double floor(double arg)`. This function lives in header `<cmath>` and will return the largest integer value not greater than `arg`. There is a single x86 instruction that will do this for you, called `ROUNDSD`. A call to `floor` in the hands of a smart optimizing compiler can be replaced with an inline invocation of that instruction. This will fill a typical performance-hungry engineer with delight.

There are several surprising instructions available to this CISC processor. Perhaps you want to know the number of leading zeros in a value so that you can assess what the nearest power of 2 is. There is an instruction called LZCNT which does precisely this. Perhaps you want to know the number of set bits in a value because you are calculating Hamming distance. Step forward, POPCNT. This is such a useful instruction that Clang and GCC will spot if you are trying to write it and replace your code with a call to POPCNT. This is excellent service. Remember to tip your compiler writer.

When I first started programming, I quickly jumped from BASIC to assembly language, first Z80, then 68000. When I first learned C, I was, in the right light, able to treat it as a macro assembly programming language, which made my transition to C rather smooth. I was reasoning about my code like it was assembly language, except that it was faster to write and easier to test and debug. I was producing excellent code much more quickly than when I was using 68000 assembly.

When I started moving to C++, I was a little suspicious about certain aspects of the language. A little examination would usually alleviate my suspicions. For example, virtual functions looked like dark magic until I realized that they were function pointers at the top of my struct, although they were an additional level of indirection away from where I would expect them. Function overloads and function templates were nice, since I was able to eliminate swathes of symbols and I learned about eliminating implementation from interface, leading to much more readable code.

The things I liked most in the language were the syntactic sugar that allowed me to write clearer code. Things that slowed me down were definitely not wanted on voyage.

Constructors, though. They were the worst.

The horrendous overhead of the constructor

The moment I learned assembly language, I learned to isolate an area of memory for work, fill it with zeros with a single assembly instruction, and get on with my life. If I was feeling particularly confident I wouldn't even zero it, I would initialize it according to context, although that occasionally complicated debugging as I would lose track of which addresses I had already set and which were yet to be set.

In C, I quickly learned to declare all my `int`s, `float`s, and `struct`s at the top of a function and, in debug builds, call the `memset` library function in `<string.h>` to initialize everything to zero in one call. I was simply increasing (or decreasing) the stack pointer and backfilling the space with zeros.

With C++ I had to unlearn this habit. I had to get used to the existence of default constructors. I had to learn that they would be called no matter what, that I could not suppress them. I had to look at the generated assembly and wince slightly. Nothing was as fast as The Old Ways. The best mitigation I could come up with was to call `memset` in the body of the constructor. Initialization lists just would not do the trick: I would directly set everything to zero in one assembly instruction.

You can imagine how I felt about assignment operators and copy constructors. Why weren't they calling `memcpy`? What was it with this delicate, dainty, member-by-member stuff? I could understand in those cases where I actually had something to do during the constructor body, but when I was simply setting aside an area of memory, why was there such wastage?

I struggled through, cursing these inefficiencies, and trading them against the more intelligible code the other features were yielding. Sometimes I would write the truly performance-critical parts in C and exploit the fact that both languages were mutually intelligible to the linker.

The chimera is a mythical fire-breathing beast with the head of a lion, the body of a goat, and the tail of a dragon. I was writing these ghastly code chimeras in the 1990s. It took me a long time to realize that the error I was making was in declaring my objects too early in the function before they were ready to be used. In addition, this was prior to standardization and the introduction of the as-if rule. It took me even longer to realize the true value of that fine piece of legislation. Let's look a little closer at the rules about construction.

The standard describes initialization of classes over 12 pages of standardese, starting at [class.init],[1] referring a further eight pages at [dcl.init][2] if there is no constructor. This really isn't the place to parse all that, so we'll keep things simple and summarize, starting with aggregates.

The simplest possible class

Aggregates are classes with

- No user-declared or inherited constructors
- No nonpublic data members which are not static
- No virtual functions
- No nonpublic or virtual base classes

Here is an example:

```
struct Agg {
  int a;
  int b;
  int c;
};
```

Aggregates are useful things. You can initialize them with curly braces like so:

```
Agg t = {1, 2, 3};
```

The initialization rule is that each element is copy initialized from the corresponding element. In the above example, this looks like:

```
t.a={1};
```

1. https://eel.is/c++draft/class.init
2. https://eel.is/c++draft/dcl.init

```
t.b={2};
t.c={3};
```

If no elements are explicitly initialized, then each element is initialized with a default initializer or copy initialized from an empty initializer, in order of declaration. This will fail if one of the members is a reference since they must be bound at instantiation. For example:

```
auto t = Agg{};
```

Declaring `t` like this will result in `t.a` being initialized with `{}`, then `t.b`, then `t.c`. However, since these are all `int`s, that initialization will be a no-op: there is no constructor for built-in types. "Ah!" we hear you exclaim. "So, this is where I call `memset`, obviously. The contents of the struct are nondeterministic and that is a bad thing, so I shall simply zero them. It's clearly the right thing to do."

No, it is not. The right thing to do is to add a constructor that performs this initialization, like so:

```
struct Agg {
  Agg() : a{0}, b{0}, c{0} {};
  int a;
  int b;
  int c;
};
```

"But now it's not an aggregate anymore," you observe, correctly. "I want that brace initialization feature and `memset` please."

All right then, what you can do is use member initializers, like this:

```
struct Agg {
  int a = 0;
  int b = 0;
  int c = 0;
};
```

Now if you declare

```
auto t = Agg{};
```

`t.a` will be initialized with `= 0`, as will `t.b` and `t.c`. Even better, you can use designated initializers, new to C++20, which allow parts of the object to be initialized with different values, like this:

```
auto t = Agg{.c = 21};
```

Now, `t.a` and `t.b` will still be initialized with `0`, but `t.c` will be initialized with `21`.

"All right, yes, designated initializers are nice and it's back to being an aggregate," (I can sense a "but" forming in your consciousness) "but the members are still being initialized one at a time! I want to use `memset` to initialize them in a single instruction."

That is a really bad idea. You are separating the initialization of the object from its definition. What happens when you add members to the aggregate? Your call to `memset` will only cover part of the object. C++ allows you to collect the whole life cycle of an object into a single abstraction, the class, which is of immense value. You should not try and subvert it.

"I shall use `sizeof` to ensure that I remain independent of any changes to the class."

Still not a good idea. What if you introduce a member that does NOT default to zero initialization? You will then have to ensure that your `memset` call honors the value of that member, perhaps by splitting it into two. That is simply an accident waiting to happen.

"I do not accept this! I own the aggregate, it is defined in a private implementation file, not a header, it is NOT going to be modified in nature without my knowledge, it is TOTALLY SAFE to call `memset`! What is going on here? Why shouldn't I call `memset`?"

Well, the fact of the matter is that you do not actually need to call `memset`. Let's talk about the abstract machine.

What is the standard talking about anyway?

P.2: "Write in ISO Standard C++" is one of the first Core Guidelines. The standard dictates how a conforming implementation of C++ behaves. Any divergence from this is not standard C++. There are many implementations of C++ for many platforms, all of which behave in different ways depending on things like the machine word size and other target-specific features. Some platforms do not feature offline storage in the form of disk drives. Others do not feature a standard input. How does the standard accommodate all this variation?

The first three clauses of the standard are Scope,[3] Normative references,[4] and Terms and definitions.[5] On pages 10 to 12 the fourth clause, General principles,[6]

3. https://eel.is/c++draft/intro.scope
4. https://eel.is/c++draft/intro.refs
5. https://eel.is/c++draft/intro.defs
6. https://eel.is/c++draft/intro

precisely explains this problem. This is only one of the reasons why it is important to RTFM (Read The Front Matter).

The first four clauses that make up the front matter tell you how the document is structured, what the conventions are, what "undefined behavior" means, what an "ill-formed program" is: in fact, the entire frame of reference is described here. In the General principles clause, in particular in section [intro.abstract],[7] you will find the following text:

"The semantic descriptions in this document define a parameterized nondeterministic abstract machine. This document places no requirement on the structure of conforming implementations. In particular, they need not copy or emulate the structure of the abstract machine. Rather, conforming implementations are required to emulate (only) the observable behavior of the abstract machine as explained below."

A footnote is attached to this paragraph, which says:

"This provision is sometimes called the "as-if" rule, because an implementation is free to disregard any requirement of this document as long as the result is as if the requirement had been obeyed, as far as can be determined from the observable behavior of the program. For instance, an actual implementation need not evaluate part of an expression if it can deduce that its value is not used and that no side effects affecting the observable behavior of the program are produced."

This is a marvelous get-out clause (more correctly, get-out paragraph). All that an implementation must do is emulate the observable behavior. This means it can look at your code, examine the result of its execution, and do whatever is necessary to match that result. This is how optimization works: by looking at a result and substituting the optimal set of instructions required for achieving it.

What does this mean for our example aggregate class?

Since the member initializers are all zero, the compiler will see that a default instantiation of an `Agg` object will set three `int`s to zero. This is identical to a call to `memset`, so it will probably call `memset`. A manual call to `memset` is unnecessary.

But wait! The class consists of only three integers. On a typical 64-bit platform with 32-bit integers, this means that only 12 bytes need to be set to zero. This can be done in two instructions on an x64 platform. Why on earth would you want to call `memset`? We can check this by visiting the Compiler Explorer website and trying out some code:

```
struct Agg {
  int a = 0;
  int b = 0;
  int c = 0;
};
```

7. https://eel.is/c++draft/intro.abstract

```
void fn(Agg&);

int main() {
  auto t = Agg{}; // (1)
  fn(t);          // (2)
}
```

The function call at (2) prevents the compiler from optimizing away t.

The x86-64 gcc compiler, with the optimization flag set to -O3, yields the following:

```
main:
        sub     rsp, 24
        mov     rdi, rsp
        mov     QWORD PTR [rsp], 0    // (1)
        mov     DWORD PTR [rsp+8], 0
        call    fn(Agg&)              // (2)
        xor     eax, eax
        add     rsp, 24
        ret
```

We can see the two mov instructions doing the work of zeroing the three ints. The compiler writer knows that this is the fastest way of setting three ints to zero. If there were many more members to be set to zero, the MMX instruction set would be brought into play. The joy of the Compiler Explorer website is that you can try this out yourself very easily.

We hope this convinces you not to use memset.

But what about memcpy?

Just as I would use memset in my C programs to zero a struct, so would I use memcpy to assign it to another instance. C++ assignment is very similar to initialization: by default, it copies data member-wise in the order of declaration using the assignment operator of that member's type. You can write your own assignment operator, and, unlike the constructor, it does not start by implicitly performing a member-wise copy. You might think the argument for calling memcpy is stronger here, but for the same reasons as above, it is neither a good idea nor necessary. We can return to the Compiler Explorer website and make a modest change to the source:

```
struct Agg {
  int a = 0;
```

```
  int b = 0;
  int c = 0;
};

void fn(Agg&);

int main() {
  auto t = Agg{};  // (1)
  fn(t);           // (2)
  auto u = Agg{};  // (3)
  fn(u);           // (4)
  t = u;           // (5)
  fn(t);           // (6)
}
```

This now yields the following:

```
main:
        sub     rsp, 40
        mov     rdi, rsp
        mov     QWORD PTR [rsp], 0          // (1)
        mov     DWORD PTR [rsp+8], 0
        call    fn(Agg&)                    // (2)
        lea     rdi, [rsp+16]
        mov     QWORD PTR [rsp+16], 0       // (3)
        mov     DWORD PTR [rsp+24], 0
        call    fn(Agg&)                    // (4)
        mov     rax, QWORD PTR [rsp+16]     // (5)
        mov     rdi, rsp                    // (6)
        mov     QWORD PTR [rsp], rax        // (5)
        mov     eax, DWORD PTR [rsp+24]
        mov     DWORD PTR [rsp+8], eax
        call    fn(Agg&)                    // (6)
        xor     eax, eax
        add     rsp, 40
        ret
```

As you can see, the compiler has generated the same `QWORD`/`DWORD` trick and has emitted code to directly copy the memory from the original object in four instructions. Again, why would you call `memcpy`?

Note that if you turn down the optimization level, then the generated code will behave more explicitly like the standard dictates and will make less use of the as-if rule. This code is faster to generate and easier to step through in the general case. If you are considering using `memset` and `memcpy`, then we are going to assume that optimization is at the top of your priority list, and you would be content to generate the most optimized code. In the above assembly you can see that some unexpected reordering has taken place. The compiler author knows all about the execution characteristics of these instructions and has reordered the code appropriately: all that is required is to emulate the observable behavior.

Never underestimate the compiler

The way to get the most out of your compiler is to tell it exactly what you want it to do and at the highest available level of abstraction. As we have seen, `memset` and `memcpy` have higher levels of abstraction available to them: construction and assignment.

The way to get the most out of your compiler is to tell it exactly what you want it to do and at the highest available level of abstraction.

As a final example, consider `std::fill`. Rather than setting a range of memory with a single value, or copying a multiword object to a single piece of memory, `std::fill` solves the problem of duplicating a multiword object to a range of memory.

The naïve implementation would be to create a raw loop and iteratively construct in place or assign to the existing object:

```
#include <array>

struct Agg {
  int a = 0;
  int b = 0;
  int c = 0;
};

std::array<Agg, 100> a;

void fn(Agg&);
int main() {
  auto t = Agg{};
  fn(t);
  for (int i = 0; i < 1000; ++i) { // Fill the array
    a[i] = t;
  }
}
```

`std::fill` will do this for you, though, so there is less code to read, and you are less likely to insert a bug as happened above. (Did you see that? Check the size of the array and the iteration count of the `for` loop.)

```
int main() {
  auto t = Agg{};
  fn(t);
  std::fill(std::begin(a), std::end(a), t); // Fill the array
}
```

Compiler writers go to a lot of effort to generate the best code possible. The typical implementation of `std::fill` will include SFINAE machinery (or, more likely now, requires clauses) to enable a simple `memcpy` for trivially constructible and trivially copyable types where `memset` is safe and constructor invocation is not necessary.

The motivation behind this guideline is not simply to dissuade you from using `memset` and `memcpy`. It is to persuade you to use the facilities of the language to give the compiler the best possible information to generate the optimal code. Do not make the compiler guess: it is asking you "what would you like me to do?" and will respond best of all to the correct and fullest answer.

Summary

In summary:

- Use construction and assignment rather than `memset` and `memcpy`.
- Use the highest available level of abstraction to communicate with the compiler.
- Help the compiler to do the best job it can for you.

Chapter 3.4

ES.50: Don't cast away `const`

Story time

When asked about my favorite C++ features, besides deterministic destruction, `const` always makes the list. It allows me to divide an interface between view and control, giving users a head start in learning how to use it. This separation has come to my rescue countless times, but never more starkly than in my first big game project.

At the turn of the century, my employers started a mighty work, a computer game called *Rome: Total War.* This was a real-time strategy game set in the era of the Roman Empire. The game featured field battles with hundreds of soldiers operating in cavalry, infantry, and artillery units, along with the extensive control options necessary to navigate them around the battlefield. You could arrange individual units into formations, group units together, send them into battle against enemy forces controlled by a cunning AI opponent, and watch the entire drama unfold in beautifully rendered, glorious 3D.

It turned out to be quite a lot of work, rather more than we expected. One reason for this was the desire to make it a multiplayer game. Rather than going into battle against an AI opponent, we wanted to offer the opportunity to compete against another human player. This presented a considerable set of problems, not least of which was how to maintain the same world state on both machines.

This is a problem throughout multiplayer games. If you are playing a motor racing game, it is important that all cars appear to be in the same position on all players' machines. If two different cars cross the finish line first, the game is spoiled. One way of overcoming this is to designate one machine as the authoritative world server, ensure all the client machines send regular updates about their instance of the game to this server, have the server resolve these updates into a new world state, and then send the new state back to the client machines.

In the case of a motor race, that would mean sending, say, 20 new car positions and accelerations back to the client machines. This is no great burden: only an x and y component are needed (unless your racetrack features bridges), so that resolves to four components for 20 cars at four bytes per component for float types, which is 320 bytes per world update.

Back then, 30 frames per second was an entirely acceptable frame rate, but you did not need to update the world for every frame, merely the view of the world. Your model of the world includes the positions and accelerations of each vehicle, so you can make a reliable estimation where each one is going to be thanks to Newton's equations of motion. All you need are world updates that are faster than the human brain can recognize. Ten hertz is enough, which means the server must broadcast 3,200 bytes per second to each of its clients. Squeezing that around the internet in the last decade of the 1990s was not a problem. Everyone was on 56Kb/s modems, so approximately 26Kb/s was a manageable chunk of bandwidth.

Dealing with rather more data

Unfortunately for our game, that approach was infeasible. A car does one thing, which is move. The soldiers in the game carry out a variety of actions. Walking, trotting, running, sprinting, throwing a spear, waving a sword around, and pushing a siege engine toward city walls are just a small set of the things they could do, each with its own unique animation. This meant that there were six components rather than four components per soldier since we needed to include their action and how far through the action they were. This amounted to 18 bytes per soldier.

Worse, there were rather more than 20 soldiers. In fact, to make things meaningful, we needed to accommodate 1,000 soldiers. This made for unattractive arithmetic:

```
10 Hertz *
1,000 soldiers *
18 bytes *
8 bits =
1,440,000 bits per second
```

In the early years of this century this was a great big nope. We were just seeing ADSL networks rolling out to households, and upstream bandwidth exceeding 1Mb/s was very rare. The only solution was to send to each client the list of commands that had been applied to the soldiers in that update, and to ensure each client applied that list of commands. Since commands were only issued to a unit of a few soldiers every few seconds, this was a much easier load to bear. Of course, this relied on each client maintaining an identical copy of the world, known as synchronous state.

This was a remarkably tricky problem. To remain deterministic, everything had to be identically initialized. If a new data member was added to a struct, it had to be deterministically initialized. Random numbers had to be deterministic. Nothing could be overlooked. Weird things would crop up, like floating-point modes being changed by graphics drivers which would change calculation results on different machines. The biggest problem, though, was preventing the view of the world from interfering with the model of the world.

Each client would have a different window onto the world. The renderer would look at the world and call the `const` member functions of each thing to get the information it needed to do its work. Calling the `const` functions meant that the renderer would not interfere with the world. Unfortunately, `const` only works so far. Look at this class:

```
class unit {
public:
  animation* current_animation() const;

private:
  animation* m_animation;
};
```

The renderer may hold a unit `const*` object, call the `current_animation()` function, and make changes to the `animation` object if one is returned. The unit may not necessarily have its own animation: sometimes all the soldiers in a particular unit will share an animation, sometimes they will have their own animation, for example when they are hit by a spear while marching in formation. The `const`-qualified member function returns a constant pointer object by value, not a constant `animation` object by pointer.

The `const` firewall

There are several solutions to this, such as having pairs of functions where the `const` function returns an `animation const*` and the non-`const` function returns an `animation*`, but the point was that the abuse of `const` was subtle and catastrophic. One small change would bubble out to the rest of the world and not be noticed until it was far too late to work backward. It was the butterfly effect writ large.

The const interface, or const firewall as we called it, was of vital importance. It highlighted, in code, in the language itself, which functions were part of the view and which functions were part of the controller. Abuse of the const firewall represented a great disservice to the remainder of the team. The hours required to work out why the world was desynchronizing mounted up throughout production.

As you can imagine, the appearance of const_cast anywhere in the code would set off alarm bells. Painful, baroque interactions between objects could be resolved with a const_cast and programmers had to be reminded constantly of the terrible fate that awaited them. Advertising something as const-safe and then modifying it deceives your clients in the worst possible way.

For example, imagine this function:

```
float distance_from_primary_marker(soldier const& s);
```

Anything should be able to safely call this function for every soldier without interfering with the model of the world. It is advertised as a function that makes no change to the soldier at all. Imagine what would happen if, halfway through, this happened:

```
float distance_from_primary_marker(soldier const& s) {
  …
  const_cast<soldier&>(s).snap_to_meter_grid(); // Oh, the humanity…
  …
}
```

The calculation performance is improved by working at meter scale, but rather than cache the current value and do all the required arithmetic, the author has simply moved the soldier by a few centimeters, possibly with the intent of restoring its position later.

What a calamitous approach to take.

Implementing a dual interface

The codebase ended up being scattered throughout with a dual interface, one of which was const and one of which was non-const. Member functions would be duplicated with const qualification, like this:

```
class soldier {
public:
  commander& get_commander();
  commander const& get_commander() const;
};
```

Every soldier has a commander, but finding out who it is requires traversing quite a few objects and making a few queries. Rather than duplicating the code and the accompanying maintenance burden, it is tempting to forward to the const-qualified overload, like this:

```
commander& soldier::get_commander() {
  return const_cast<commander&>(
    static_cast<soldier const&>(*this).get_commander());
}
```

Although you are const_casting the return type, it is reasonably safe to assume that, since this is a non-const function, this is not a dangerous thing to do. It goes against the spirit of the guideline, though. Fortunately, since the introduction of trailing return types in C++11, there is a better solution:

```
class soldier {
public:
  commander& get_commander();
  commander const& get_commander() const;

private:
  template <class T>
  static auto get_commander_impl(T& t)
    -> decltype(t.get_commander) {
      // do the work
  }
};
```

The public get_commander functions simply forward to the static function template. The superior feature of this solution is that the function template knows if it is operating on a soldier const object. The const qualifier is part of the type T. If the implementation breaks const, the compiler will emit an error telling you so. No casting is required, and that is a good thing, since casting is ugly.

This is not always going to work, though. Consider the current_animation example:

```
class unit {
public:
  animation* current_animation();
  animation const* current_animation() const;

private:
  animation* m_animation;
};
```

You might look at this and think that the function simply returns a pointer to the animation. Sadly, it is not quite as simple as that, and there is a fair amount of logic to do with animation blending that we need to go through.

It is tempting to carry out the same trick. However, if the calling code expects to modify the animation, and the const-qualified member function does not expect the returned value, which it does not own, to be modified, we have a bug. In this case, though, it is safe to assume that the implementation of each function will be different.

Caching and lazy evaluation

Another example that might tempt you to reach for the const_cast keyword is the caching of expensive computations. There are plenty of these in the domain of modeling the world, even a 2km-by-2km subset of it. As we remarked, establishing the identity of the commander is a nontrivial task, so let's consider trying to preserve the value for later speedy recovery.

```
class soldier {
public:
  commander& get_commander();
  commander const& get_commander() const;

private:
  commander* m_commander;

  template <class T>
  static auto get_commander_impl(T& t)
    -> decltype(t.get_commander);
};
```

The rules are such that if the commander has died, a new commander is established. The get_commander_impl function is called many times, while the commander is only likely to die a few times in an entire game, so the trade-off of the extra pointer in exchange for many identical calculations is a good one.

The first thing the function will do is see if the current commander is still alive. If so, the function can make a quick exit, returning that cached value. If not, the function trudges through the objects representing the world, establishing who the commander is and writing the value back to the m_commander member, before dereferencing the pointer and returning a reference to the entity in question. This is a remarkably costly procedure. We use the word "trudges" advisedly: with so many objects making up the world, and with so many different relationships to maintain and monitor, it occasionally feels like walking through an outdoor festival, yelling out the name of your friend in the hope that they will respond quickly. It is an ideal candidate for caching.

Unfortunately, this function template needs to work with objects of type soldier const as well as of type soldier. Changing the pointer will not be allowed in the former situation. The only solution would seem to be to const_cast t:

```
template <class T>
auto soldier::get_commander_impl(T& t) -> decltype(t.get_commander) {
  if (!t.m_commander->is_alive()) {
    … // Find the new commander
    const_cast<soldier&>(t).m_commander = new_commander;
  }
  return *t.m_commander;
}
```

This is not pretty.

Two types of **const**

There are two ways of apprehending "constness". The benefit that const delivers is that, upon calling a const-qualified member function, there is no observable difference in the nature of the object. If the object is entirely self-contained and does not reference other objects, in the same way that a pure function references no data external to its scope, then successive calls to const-qualified member functions will always yield the same results.

This does not mean that the representation of the object will remain unchanged. That would be considering the wrong level of abstraction. The implementation is not your concern: the visible interface is what you should be caring about.

In fact, this touches on an important aspect of class design. What does your class own, what does it share ownership of, and what is it merely interested in? In the example of the unit class, part of the member data was a pointer to another object, owned by something else entirely. What does a const qualification mean to the client in that case?

All it can mean is that the function does not change the object it is bound to in any observable way. This is known as logical const. The other type of const is known as bitwise const. This is what is imposed on the function author by const-qualifying a member function. This means that no part of the representation of the object may be changed during execution of the function; this is enforced by the compiler.

The presence of const_cast inside a const-qualified member function should at the very least make you feel a little queasy. You are lying to your clients. Unfortunately, the caching example for lazy evaluation is not the only place where you might feel the need to reach for const_cast. What if you want to guarantee that your class is thread safe?

One way of achieving this is to include a mutex in your member data and lock it when your functions are executed. We cannot let that last sentence past your apprehension without remarking that you should minimize the reach of a mutex: as little data as possible should be covered by it, and it should be part of the smallest possible abstraction. This chimes with Core Guidelines ES.5: "Keep scopes small" and CP.43: "Minimize time spent in a critical section." Having said all that, using a member mutex brings with it one problem: how do you lock it in a const-qualified member function? That requires changing the mutex.

Now that we have established the difference between logical const and bitwise const, we can introduce the keyword mutable. The specific purpose of this keyword is to respect the logical const nature of an object while not respecting the bitwise const nature. It is not a modern keyword: you will find it in quite old codebases. This keyword decorates a member datum, signifying that it is amenable to modification during execution of a const-qualified member function.

Returning to the unit example, here is how it might be used:

```
class soldier {
public:
  commander& get_commander();
  commander const& get_commander() const;

private:
  mutable commander* m_commander; // Immune from const constraint

  template <class T>
  static auto get_commander_impl(T& t)
    -> decltype(t.get_commander) {
    if (!t.m_commander->is_alive()) {
      … // Find the new commander
      t.m_commander = new_commander; // Always amenable to change
    }
    return *t.m_commander;
  }
};
```

The m_commander member is now mutable. This means it is amenable to modification from a const reference.

Surprises with `const`

Obviously, `mutable` should not be scattered liberally through your class. It should decorate the data that is used for bookkeeping, rather than for modeling the abstraction. In the case of decorating a mutex member, we can see that this is a sensible policy. In the above example, though, it is not so clear. Raw pointers are confusing things that muddy the waters of ownership, as discussed in Core Guideline I.11: "Never transfer ownership by a raw pointer (`T*`) or reference (`T&`)," and they also trip up API design when it comes to separating the view from the controller.

For example, this piece of code is legal:

```
class int_holder {
public:
  void increment() const { ++ *m_i; }

private:
  std::unique_ptr<int> m_i;
};
```

`mutable` should not be scattered liberally through your class. It should decorate the data that is used for bookkeeping, rather than for modeling the abstraction.

This surprises typical users, because they expect to be unable to change the `std::unique_ptr` object and what it contains. In fact, `const` extends only as far as the `std::unique_ptr` object. Dereferencing the object is a `const` operation since it makes no change to the `std::unique_ptr`. This highlights the importance of recognizing the difference between a `const` pointer and a pointer to `const`. A pointer to `const` can be modified but the object it points to cannot. A `const` pointer cannot be modified but the object it points to can. This is somewhat similar to how references behave: they cannot be reseated, which means they cannot refer to a different object through their lifetime, but the object they refer to can be modified.

Speaking of which, the same surprise is not available for references:

```
class int_holder {
public:
  void increment() const { ++ m_i; }

private:
  int& m_i;
};
```

This will not compile. However, it is rarely a good idea to store objects by reference in classes: it entirely disables default assignment since a reference cannot be reseated.

What is needed is a form of the “pImpl” idiom, bundling up a pointer to an object inside a single class and propagating `const`ness. Such an entity has been proposed for standardization and is, at time of writing, available in library fundamentals v2 under the name `std::experimental::propagate_const`. There are other solutions pending as well: watch the skies.

Summary

In summary:

- The `const` keyword is supremely valuable to your interface design and to your clients, cleanly dividing the API between view and control.
- Do not lie about `const` by casting it away via `const_cast`.
- Understand the difference between logical `const` and bitwise `const`.
- Make use of `mutable` when appropriate, usually in bookkeeping member data rather than modeling member data.
- Be aware of how far `const` will propagate, and be mindful of the difference between a `const` pointer and a pointer to `const`.

Chapter 3.5

E.28: Avoid error handling based on global state (e.g. `errno`)

Error handling is hard

There may be some people whose code never goes wrong and is perfect in every way at all times. Sadly, for us mere mortals, sometimes things do not go according to plan. This can be for a variety of reasons: the problem was incorrectly specified, or the range of input was exceeded, or the hardware has broken down. It is not usually acceptable for the program to simply shrug its metaphorical shoulders, mumble "meh," and stop working, nor simply attempt to carry on to the best of its abilities. Programs are not people: they are machines, with moving parts and without conscience. They are supremely good at doing what they are told, although you may find this rather hard to believe at times.

Error handling has a long, varied, and checkered history. The presence of the word "varied" should alert you to the fact that there are many ways of handling errors and a universally useful facility has yet to emerge.

C and `errno`

This guideline is about avoiding signaling error in global state, so we'll start there. Two problems should immediately spring to mind when we think of global state:

1. Thread ownership
2. Error reference

The thread ownership problem is simple enough: in today's multithreaded world, a global error object would need to contain thread information about which thread signaled the error. You might try using an object with thread-local storage duration, but that would mean that errors relevant beyond a particular thread would be hidden. Alternatively, you could create a single object containing per-thread error information, which would require some careful synchronization. This is not insurmountable, but it demotes this approach down my ranking of preferred error-handling solutions.

Of course, it wasn't always like this, and legacy code will indeed contain references to an object called `errno`. This is part of the C standard and is simply an `int`. Since C++11 it is an object of thread-local storage duration; prior to that it was static. It is not necessarily a bad approach: if something goes wrong, you want to be able to invoke an error-handling function to deal with it. A single error code means that it doesn't matter where the error happens, the error-handling function can identify what went wrong. The error code can be divided up into groups of bits: some bits refer to the domain of the error, others refer to the nature of the error, and still other bits provide context.

It is not without problems, though. What happens if another error occurs while you are navigating to your error code? Your error code can only hold the most recent error, which makes recovery a tricky proposal. Also, it simply doesn't scale very well. All code needs to check the error status after a function call in case that function has signaled an error. Even if no error signaling is documented, that doesn't mean that the function won't change and start signaling errors. Finally, clients can and will ignore or forget about error codes, no matter how forcefully you exhort them not to do so in your documentation.

This is rather reminiscent of "globals are bad, m'kay?" Since `errno` has no owner, there is no way of controlling how it is managed in the case of unusual circumstances. What happens if there is an error in the error recovery? As the guideline remarks, global state is hard to manage.

Unfortunately, as remarked above, `errno` is part of the standard, and some parts of the C Standard Library use `errno` to signal failure. For example, if you try and calculate the square root of a negative number by calling `sqrt`, `errno` will be set to `EDOM`.

It has long been known, since before the advent of C++, that `errno` is problematic. Plenty of alternatives have been considered, with varying degrees of success, which permeate codebases around the world, some of which have been adopted as standard practice. Let's take a look at other approaches to error handling.

Return codes

The most common way of signaling an error is to simply tell the caller directly. You can achieve this with a return value. If your function has a well-defined domain of results, you can use values outside that domain to signal an error. For example, `scanf` returns the number of receiving arguments that have been successfully assigned to, which is a number greater than or equal to zero. However, it signals an error by returning `EOF`, which is a negative value.

This method has one obvious shortcoming, which is that the returned type must accommodate the result domain and the error domain. Consider the standard library function for finding the natural logarithm of a number:

```
double log(double);
```

Conceptually, the result domain completely exhausts the type. There is no way to signal an error. The standard has such a function and returns special values which signal that something has gone wrong; it can do this because there are a few values of `double` set aside to represent error conditions. This can be quite a surprise to the new programmer.

A more practical shortcoming is that callers can ignore return codes unless the function is marked with `[[no_discard]]`. Even then, the caller can choose to ignore the object that contains the return code. While this quietly shifts the blame to the caller, it is not in anyone's interests to permit errors to be absorbed without consequence.

Another way of returning an error code is to pass an error-reporting destination into the function. This leads to an API that looks like this:

```
double log(double, int&);
```

The caller provides somewhere to report errors and checks after calling that no error was reported. There are a few things wrong with this solution too. First, it's just ugly. Readable APIs will simply tell you what is going on: if you want a logarithm, you expect to pass in a number and get one back. The extra parameter is a little extra cognitive load.

Second, it represents additional overhead in circumstances where you are very confident of the range of numbers you are expecting to pass to the function. Such an approach will often lead to a dual-function API, where each function has a matching overload containing an additional error return parameter. This is rather inelegant.

Exceptions

With the arrival of C++ came constructors. These are special functions that do not return anything and, in some circumstances, take no arguments. No amount of signature shenanigans would help you here: unless you sacrificed your default constructor there was nothing you could do to signal error. Worse, the destructor has only one function signature, taking no arguments and returning nothing. Overloaded operators are similarly affected.

Exceptions were introduced to deal with this. They create an additional return path that can be followed in the event of error, called throwing, which bypasses the usual return path, and performs all the necessary cleanup normally required at the end of a function. Additionally, exceptions can be caught anywhere in the call stack, rather than precisely at the function's call site, enabling the programmer to deal with errors where possible or to simply ignore them, bubbling them up through the call stack otherwise.

This comes at a cost. The end of a function is very obvious: there is a return statement or a final closing brace. An exception can occur during any call which requires a lot of additional furniture to manage. Whenever you call a function an exception may be thrown, so the compiler must insert all the code required to clean up what's on the stack in that event. This extra furniture comes with not only an execution speed cost, but also a space cost. This cost is so large that all compilers provide an option to disable exception unwinding, in exchange for being unable to use `try`/`catch` blocks.

This is really quite a bad thing indeed. In a survey by the C++ Foundation in 2019,[1] results suggested that about half of all C++ projects ban exceptions in whole or in part. This means that the community is divided in two. Worse, banning exceptions shuts projects off from using those parts of the standard library that use exceptions to signal errors.

`<system_error>`

The second C++ standard, C++11, introduced `std::error_code` and `std::error_condition` which can be found in the `<system_error>` header. This is an error-signaling mechanism that provides a way of standardizing error reporting from the operating system or from low-level interfaces in the case of unhosted systems. Not only does it include an error code, but it also includes a pointer to an error category.

1. https://isocpp.org/files/papers/CppDevSurvey-2019-04-summary.pdf

This innovation allows programmers to create new families of errors by deriving from the `error_category` base class.

This solves the problem of making errors look more like one another. A large collection of error codes are defined in an enumeration called `errc` which are imported from POSIX and given more comprehensible names. For example, `ENOENT` is translated to `no_such_file_or_directory`. Predefined error categories include `generic_category`, `system_category`, `iostream_category`, and `future_category`.

Unfortunately, this is merely an upgrade to `errno`. It is still an object that needs to be returned to the caller somehow. It doesn't persist in global state or propagate through the stack unless you throw it as an exception, so while it gives you a good way to stop using `errno`, it still leaves you with many of the problems inherent to error handling.

What to do.

Boost.Outcome

Naturally, others have attempted to square the error-handling circle and proposed alternative solutions. You can find one of these at boost.org,[2] which is a rich source of helpful classes for improving your code. There are two classes in Boost of interest to the problem of error handling.

The first is `result<T, E, NoValuePolicy>`. The first parameter is the type of the object being returned. The second is the type of object containing information about the reason for failure when the function fails. An instance of `result` will contain either an instance of `T` or an instance of `E`. It's rather like a variant in this regard. The third parameter you can read about in the Boost documentation; the default value is enough for most purposes, and the documentation is rather involved.

By creating an object for returning things, you can offer a `bool` conversion that indicates whether the result was successful or whether an error was encountered, along with functions for interrogating the nature of the error. Since it is either a `T` or an `E`, in the normal error-free case it will cost nothing. You might use it like this:

```
outcome::result<double> log(double);  // function prototype

r = log(1.385);
if (r)
{
  // Proceed as normal
}
```

2. https://www.boost.org/doc/libs/develop/libs/outcome/doc/html/index.html

```
else
{
  // Handle error
}
```

This is nice: there is a consistent way to test for `error`, with error information wrapped up in the object in the case of failure. Everything is local. Unfortunately, it is still possible to forget to test.

The second class of interest is `outcome<T, EC, EP, NoValuePolicy>`. Where the `result` class signals a simple success or failure bundled with context, the `outcome` class exposes failure in two ways: expected and unexpected failure, which are specified by the second and third parameters. The expected failure can be recovered from, while the unexpected failure cannot. This unrecoverable failure is where an exception would feature in the usual run of things within the language.

This class is a way of retrofitting exception safety to a codebase. It can transport exceptions across layers of the program that were never designed with exception safety in mind.

While `boost::outcome` is a useful part of the Boost library, it has not been standardized (more on this shortly), and so is only available in codebases where use of Boost is permitted. There are a surprising number of environments where this is not the case, which leaves you with only three error-handling options: throw and catch exceptions, propagate error codes back through the call stack, or roll your own superior, solution-domain-specific error-handling mechanism. This seems less than satisfactory.

Why is error handling so hard?

The first problem is that different types of errors need handling in different ways. Let's identify three types of errors.

Consider a function for converting a string to a number. This will fail if the string does not include a number and only a number. This is a recoverable error that you should report back to the caller: there was a logic error in the calling code that meant that the input did not meet the constraints identified by the author of the function. This is the simplest kind of error: "I was expecting this, you supplied that, that's wrong, please go and think about what you have done." It is a violation of a precondition and the caller should always be told about this.

The next kind of error is the programming bug. Rather than the caller getting something wrong, the thing being called has got something wrong, for example dereferencing memory that it shouldn't. The trouble with these bugs is that they put the program in a corrupted state, and everything should stop. You can no longer reason about what is going on with the program and there is no value in reporting this to the caller. What could they possibly do about it? The program is in a corrupt state, from which there is no restoration.

The final kind of error is a little more subtle. This occurs when the program environment breaks. If you have Read The Front Matter of the standard you will have learned all about the "abstract machine" at the same place that you learned about the as-if rule. You will find it in the standard at [intro.abstract].[3] There are a few ways you can break the abstract machine: exhausting the free store, or exhausting the stack, are the two most common. Both are out-of-memory conditions. You would exhaust the free store by requesting a vector of a billion doubles on a 32-bit machine. You would exhaust the stack with infinite recursion.

You do not know how your calling code is going to respond to errors. You cannot rely on your caller handling the error.

It is only in the case of the first error, the recoverable error, that you should notify the calling code by throwing an exception or returning an error value. Otherwise, you should simply stop the program and tell the programmer via an `assert` or by writing to a log file or to `stdout`. If you have broken the abstract machine your options for telling the programmer are very limited.

The second problem is that you do not know how your calling code is going to respond to errors. You cannot rely on your caller handling the error. They might intentionally discard the error value entirely and carry on their merry way, or they may simply forget about it.

For example, your string conversion function could return a double and take a reference to an error code in addition to the string to be converted. That error code may be ignored entirely. The problem of ignoring return codes in the general case has been partially solved with the addition of the `[[no_discard]]` attribute, but this is only useful if you are exclusively using the return value for returning errors. Even then, the caller may store the return value and forget to consider it. Forcing users to check for errors is a bad idea anyway: it is for them to decide how to deal with failure, not you.

The trouble is that there are more ways for code to go wrong than to perform correctly. Much like the human body, we can identify when it is in good working order, but identifying the myriad ways in which it can fail is a tall order.

3. https://eel.is/c++draft/intro.abstract

Light at the end of the tunnel

We mentioned that the Boost solutions have not been standardized and are only available where use of Boost is permitted. The committee is considering several papers to improve matters. The first of these proposes `std::expected<T, E>`, which is a type that may contain a value of type `T`, or a value of type `E`, which represents the reason why a value of type `T` is not present. It is rather like a specialized version of `std::variant`. This was first proposed shortly after C++14 was finalized, so it has spent a long time being considered. You can check progress by examining paper P0323.[4]

Next, we have zero-overhead deterministic exceptions, which throw values rather than types. This paper addresses the divided C++ community by making exception handling much more palatable. Particularly, the values that are thrown are stack allocated and statically typed, which means no heap allocation is required and RTTI is not used. They are like a special return type. You can check progress by examining paper P0709.[5] Note that Boost.Outcome is a partial, library-only implementation of this idea. Language changes will need to be made to fully implement it.

The third paper under consideration proposes a new `status_code` and standard error object. This operates with zero-overhead deterministic exceptions. It offers some improvements over the `<system_error>` header, such as not including the `<string>` header, which brings with it a large quantity of additional machinery such as allocators and algorithms, greatly increasing build and link times.

One aspect of error handling we have yet to mention is the use of the `assert` macro. This is a way of discovering instances of the second type of error described in the previous section. It highlights what the programmer is expecting to be the state of the abstract machine at a particular instant and directs the program to stop execution if that state turns out to be different. This is different from a broken abstract machine: this is the programmer getting things wrong.

As a development of this idea, there is yet another proposal under consideration which very nearly made it into C++20. In fact, it got as far as the working draft before being pulled out at the last minute. We are talking about contracts. These define pre- and post-conditions in the language rather than as a library macro, by decorating the function definition with programmer-defined expectations.

Unfortunately, this cornucopia of upgrades to the language and library is yet to be emptied into the C++ Standard working draft at time of writing. Today, in the community of C++ users, things have remained largely unchanged for many years. Programmers are still using old C-style error-handling strategies for want of a better option. The future looks bright, but it has yet to arrive.

4. www.open-std.org/jtc1/sc22/wg21/docs/papers/2021/p0323r10.html

5. www.open-std.org/jtc1/sc22/wg21/docs/papers/2019/p0709r4.pdf

Summary

In summary:

- Global state is a bad place to handle errors. Keep error state local and pay attention to it.
- If you can throw and catch exceptions, do so.
- Differentiate between different types of error: bad input, bad logic, bad environment, and so on.
- If exception handling is not available to you, consider using Boost.Outcome, but pay attention to upcoming changes to the standard; the Core Guidelines do not cover this approach since it is outside the scope of the standard.

Chapter 3.6

SF.7: Don't write `using namespace` at global scope in a header file

Don't do this

Please, don't do this. Ever.

Never. Not ever. Not even once.

Please.

The Core Guidelines document offers the following example:

```
// bad.h
#include <iostream>
using namespace std; // bad <- "You're not kidding," says Guy

// user.cpp
#include "bad.h"

// some function that happens to be named copy
bool copy(/*... some parameters ...*/);

int main()
{
  // now overloads local ::copy and std::copy, could be ambiguous
  copy(/*...*/);
}
```

"Bad" is an understatement. We know it seems we are belaboring the point, but this example only exposes part of the horror.

Disambiguation

There is one and only one global namespace. From the standard, [basic.scope.namespace][1]:

"The outermost declarative region of a translation unit is also a namespace, called the global namespace. A name declared in the global namespace has global namespace scope (also called global scope). The potential scope of such a name begins at its point of declaration and ends at the end of the translation unit that is its declarative region. A name with global namespace scope is said to be a global name."

Do not pollute the global namespace: it is a precious resource.

Do not pollute the global namespace: it is a precious resource.

Namespaces are a useful encapsulation tool, collecting together related symbols within a single scope and enabling the reuse of names. My favorite example is `vector`. This has two meanings in my domain: there is the automatically resizing contiguous container, and there is the tuple of numbers representing a mathematical quantity. The former lives in namespace `std`, while the latter lives somewhere else. In my case, it lives in namespace `gdg::maths`. Namespace `gdg` is my personal namespace that I use in all my code, while namespace `maths` is contained within that and consists of mathematical types and functions, like `matrix`, `vector`, `normalize`, `intersect`, and all the other types you might need for geometry. I am British, so I say "maths." Ask me about it one day if you dare.

Having two classes called `vector` is not a problem, since we can simply apply namespace scope resolution to the symbol, and type `std::vector` when we want to contain things in the `maths` namespace and type `gdg::maths::vector` when we want to manipulate geometric objects outside of the `maths` namespace.

`std::` is not much to type for disambiguation purposes. On the other hand, `gdg::maths::` is a little long. It interferes with rapid apprehension of code. The excessive colons slightly disrupt reading. Fortunately, we can type

```
using gdg::maths::vector;
```

earlier in the scope and the compiler will choose that vector over `std::vector` when it tries to resolve the symbol. This is known as a using-declaration. It is distinct from typing

```
using namespace gdg::maths;
```

1. https://eel.is/c++draft/basic.scope.namespace

which is a using-directive.

The trouble with introducing a using-directive into a header file at global scope is clear for all to see: you have hidden from the user the fact that all the symbols in the namespace have been introduced into the parent scope of every function and class definition. Worse, if you introduce a different using-directive into a different header file and include both of those header files, they become order dependent. You will get subtly different compilation if you change their order.

Unfortunately, this is only the start of the madness.

Using `using`

The keyword `using` has four uses. The first is aliasing. For example:

```
using vector_of_vectors = std::vector<gdg::maths::vector>;
```

This is very specific. We are introducing a new name as an abbreviation for another name. Here, we are introducing the name `vector_of_vectors` to directly map to a standard vector of my `maths` vectors. We are using `using` in this way to reduce typing and improve clarity.

The second is for importing class members. For example:

```
struct maths_vector : std::variant<vector<float, 2>, vector<int, 2>> {
  using variant::variant;
}
```

Here, we are introducing a member of a base class into a derived class. This allows me to construct a `maths_vector` object using a `variant` constructor.

The third is for introducing names defined elsewhere into the declarative region of the using-declaration. For example:

```
namespace gdg::maths {
  using std::inner_product;
}
```

We can now call the standard version of `inner_product` from within the `gdg::maths` namespace without having to prefix it with `std`. If the name already existed in an outer scope, it is hidden by this new declaration. If we wanted to call a different `inner_product` function we would have to qualify it.

Using-declarations are more specific than using-directives. They introduce a single symbol into the current scope. Still, using-declarations should be used with care, at the narrowest comfortable scope. Making a using-declaration may also create an overload set, so make sure it is always easily visible to the client engineer. The danger of making them at file scope is less than that of making a using-directive at file scope, but risks still remain.

The fourth is for making using-directives. These are of very limited use: perhaps you are writing a slide for a presentation and you want to signal to the audience that you are using a particular namespace in some example code. For example:

```
#include <iostream>
using namespace std;

int main() {
  cout << "Hello, world!";
  return 0;
}
```

Rather than type `std::cout`, you are relying on the introduction of all symbols from the `std` namespace so far declared in the `<iostream>` header. It is very convenient.

Very, very convenient.

This is a very simple use of a using-directive, suitable for trivial code. In more complicated code surprising things happen, because a using-directive does not only introduce the new symbols into the current scope.

We'll just say that again: a using-directive does not only introduce new symbols into the current scope. It does something rather more surprising, and we need to cover a little graph theory to work out what's going on.

Where do the symbols go?

First, we need to look at the idea of a directed acyclic graph, or DAG, a term coined by Bjarne Stroustrup's office mate, Al Aho. A graph is a set of nodes with relationships between them. A directed graph is a set of nodes with relationships between them that only operate in one direction. For example, a class hierarchy is a graph with is-child-of and is-parent-of relationships between classes, which are the nodes. These relationships follow different directions. If we take out the is-child-of relationships, we have a directed graph because the relationships work in one direction only. An acyclic graph has an entry and an exit; there is no way to end up back where you started by following the relationships. A class hierarchy of parent relationships is not only directed, but also acyclic.

The same thing can be said of namespaces and containment relationships. A namespace can nest another namespace, but the graph of nesting is a DAG. For example:

```
namespace World {
  namespace Buildings {
    namespace Municipal {}
    namespace Business {}
  }
}
```

We can go from `World` to `Municipal` by examining nested namespaces, but we can't go from `Municipal` to `World` in the same way.

Second, we need to look at the lowest common ancestor (LCA). The LCA of a pair of nodes is the deepest node common to both. In the above namespace example, both namespace `World` and namespace `World::Buildings` are common ancestors of namespace `World::Buildings::Municipal` and namespace `World::Buildings::Business`, but namespace `World::Buildings` is the LCA.

You should now be comfortable with the idea of a DAG and an LCA, so let's examine exactly what a using-directive does. This is covered over three pages of the standard at [namespace.udir].[2] To summarize, a using-directive introduces its new meanings into the scope which is the LCA of the current scope and the target namespace's own scope. This can be quite surprising and becomes more surprising as a codebase grows and acquires more namespaces. Let's try out a real-world example using the above namespace hierarchy.

```
namespace Result {
  struct Victory {};
  struct DecisiveVictory : Victory {};
  struct CrushingVictory : DecisiveVictory {};
}

namespace gdg {
  int signal_result(Result::CrushingVictory);
}
namespace World {
  int signal_result(Result::CrushingVictory);
  namespace Buildings {
    namespace Municipal {
      int signal_result(Result::DecisiveVictory);
    }
    namespace Business {
      int compete() {
        using namespace Municipal;
        using namespace gdg;
        return signal_result(Result::CrushingVictory());
```

2. https://eel.is/c++draft/namespace.udir

```
        }
      }
    }
  }
```

We have added a Victory type in a new namespace called Result, and a function called signal_result that describes an outcome to a game. Let's see what happens in the compete function.

First of all, using namespace Municipal injects int signal_result (Result::DecisiveVictory) into the LCA of Municipal and Business. Remember that this hides previous meanings of signal_result. Can you identify what this has hidden?

It has hidden gdg::signal_result and World::signal_result. Keep that in mind.

The next using-directive introduces gdg::signal_result into the global namespace. This is the LCA of namespace gdg and namespace Business. However, that itself has been hidden by World::signal_result, which has itself been hidden by Municipal::signal_result. So which signal_result is invoked at the end of the test function?

Municipal::signal_result is the only available choice. Even though it takes a DecisiveVictory rather than a CrushingVictory, it is the best fit, being the only fit.

Did you follow that, answer the questions correctly and deduce the correct function?

Now, I appreciate that this might seem contrived and overly complicated. However, this is not too dissimilar from a real-world example that utterly defeated me for the best part of a week. I have taken out all the extraneous furniture that was nothing to do with the bug to aid exposition. Imagine this code spread over a few thousand lines through a handful of source files. Imagine this code manifesting by silently recording the wrong kind of victory that was not too far from the right kind of victory. Imagine thinking that this bug is unrelated to the quality of the victory, but to the way that the details of the victory are passed to the rest of the system. Why on earth would you think that CrushingVictory would not be recorded? There it is, right there in the code. The solution only came to me when I was stepping through the code and suddenly realized that I had gone to the wrong place. I blamed the debugger and spent far too long arguing about optimizers with anyone who would listen. Perhaps a COMDAT had been incorrectly folded. But no, the error was that I didn't understand how using-directives worked.

An altogether more insidious problem

Perhaps you remain unconvinced. Perhaps you work on small projects and you do not nest your namespaces. There is yet another trap you can fall into. Consider this snippet of code from 2005:

```
// numerical_maths.h
namespace maths {
  float clamp(float v, float max, float min);
}
using namespace maths;

// results.cpp
#include "numerical_maths.h"
#include <algorithm>
using namespace std;
```

`results.cpp` contained quite a lot of calls like this:

```
int x = clamp(12, 6, 4);
```

Even though there was no overload that took `int` rather than `float`, the existing function was a suitable candidate since `int` can convert to `float`, albeit with loss of precision at higher magnitudes. Technically, this was a bug, but it failed to manifest in any code since the values were always reasonably small.

Something important happened in 2017: the function `clamp` was added to the `std` namespace. As a result, `results.cpp` contained an additional overload for `clamp`. Unfortunately, being a function template, it was a superior choice to `maths::clamp()` if the parameters were all of type `int`, since it required no parameter conversions. Fortunately, it did the same thing as `maths::clamp()`. Unfortunately, it took the `max` and `min` parameters in the reverse order. Fortunately, the implementation would warn you if the `max` parameter was less than the `min` parameter. Unfortunately, we disabled all the furniture that emitted this warning because it made debugging awfully slow.

As a result, weird and subtle bugs started appearing. Incorrect clamping results would propagate to unexpected parts of the code that were not necessarily catastrophic but did not properly match with the intention. Nor was this limited to `results.cpp`: `clamp` was a widely used function. Fortunately, there was plenty of time to fix all the bugs and a huge sigh of relief was heaved by all at the end of that debacle.

Actually, that last sentence is not true.

It was not a happy time, and it wasn't until someone was browsing through cppreference.com that they learned of the introduction of `std::clamp`, noticed that the order of parameters was different, and felt a terrible realization swamping their attention. With several thousand uses of `clamp` scattered through the codebase, a frustrating, detailed search through the codebase was required to ensure that the intended `clamp` was being called, and that the engineer had got their parameters the right way round.

Simply moving the using-directive out of the header file and into each source file where it was included would not have been enough: the same problem would have arisen, although at least the presence of a namespace would have advertised another source of symbols. Nor would making a using-declaration at the top of each source file have been sufficient either, since there were some places where the engineer had written code subsequent to the C++17 upgrade, inadvertently inverted the parameters, but invoked the `std::clamp` function rather than the `maths::clamp` function. Each of those uses would have been invalidated.

The only defenses against this horror in the first instance were to make a using-declaration, not a using-directive, in the source file, ideally at the narrowest scope, or to fully qualify uses of `clamp`. When you put a using-directive in your source, you are exposing yourself to the risk of the silent introduction of new meanings to your symbols in other namespaces at inopportune moments. If you are lucky, you will get an "ambiguous symbol" compiler error. At worst, a superior overload will appear with subtle differences to the choice you were expecting.

We invite you to review the first part of this chapter.

Solving the problem of cluttered scope resolution operators

The convenience of using-directives at global scope is very hard to let go of. Without it, we have to liberally sprinkle scope resolution operators, `::`, throughout our code. This is perhaps bearable when the namespace is `std`. But when the namespace is `World::Buildings::Business`, things become rather harder to read and easily apprehend. Let's review the correct use of namespaces.

Recall the existence of one single global namespace. The things you should declare in the global namespace are strictly limited to other namespaces, the `main` function, and `extern "C"` declarations. As a result of this, you should declare all your symbols inside your own namespaces.

Namespaces encapsulate symbols but also offer abstraction capabilities. Keeping abstractions small enough to apprehend in a single glance is a commendable strategy: gathering related classes into a single namespace is a form of abstraction. However, as projects grow the number of classes will grow, as will perforce the number of namespaces if you are being smart about small abstractions. This leads to declarations as described above, such as `World::Buildings::Business`. This is a lot of typing and highlights why engineers are tempted by using-directives.

Fortunately, a more fine-grained approach exists. Aliasing is available to namespaces as well. This enables you to abbreviate `World::Buildings::Business` to something a little more palatable:

```
namespace BizBuild = World::Buildings::Business;
```

This namespace alias does not import any symbols into the current scope, or into a parent scope, or anything inconvenient and confusing like that. It simply introduces another name that aliases a namespace. From the above declaration of this namespace, it allows you to type

```
auto x = BizBuild::compete();
```

rather than

```
auto x = World::Buildings::Business::compete();
```

Before namespaces, there was a common pattern of naming which sought to embed domains into identifiers, for example:

```
int BizBuild_compete();
```

which is the `compete` function within the Business Buildings domain. It is still common to see engineers choosing to use underbars to separate domains from contextual identifiers, but there is no need if you have the facilities of namespaces and aliases. For the price of an extra character, a double colon rather than a single underbar, you get semantic separation of domain from identifier, of context from symbol. That semantic separation is visible to a C++ parser and becomes useful to editor tooling, such as automatic symbol completion, listing of namespace members, and so on.

The temptation and The Fall

We must offer one final warning. It is very hard to turn back from this path once you start to walk it.

Large codebases ideally consist of many libraries, each declaring their own namespace. It conveniently divides the solution domain; it is a useful abstraction technique. Each library will have a set of headers to expose its functionality through a well-designed API. If you decide to follow these declarations with a using-directive, clients of the code do not need to qualify any of the symbols. You may think you are doing them a favor by saving them extra typing.

This may seem like a good idea, but as the codebase increases in size and the number of symbols starts to balloon, the chances of inadvertently creating overload sets increase. Eventually common sense will prevail, and you will have to remove all your using-directives. Suddenly your compilations will fail hard and heavy, as thousands of unknown symbols announce themselves to the compiler. The only solution will be to migrate the using-directives to clients of the header files, and then further out to the implementation files, and then finally to replace them with more specific using-declarations. This will not be a pleasant, rewarding, or especially educational task.

One day, tooling will solve this problem for us. We will be able to view source files and switch full namespace qualification of symbols on and off at the flick of a UI option. Warnings will be emitted when using-directives are encountered at the broadest scope, and suitable alternatives will be suggested that can be used to modify errant source code. Until then, please, please, follow the advice of Core Guideline SF.7: "Don't write `using namespace` at global scope in a header file."

Summary

In summary:

- Using-directives at broad scopes are risky and costly, creating unexpected overload sets. Prefer using-declarations.
- Ignoring this guideline becomes more dangerous as codebases grow, and more expensive to repair.
- Make using-declarations at the narrowest comfortable scope, for example in class and function definitions.

Section 4

Use this new thing properly

Chapter 4.1

F.21: To return multiple "out" values, prefer returning a struct or tuple

The shape of a function signature

When we learn about functions, we learn about taking arguments, manipulating these inputs, and returning a value, an output. A function can take as many arguments as you like, but it can only return one thing.

This can cause problems. How do you signal an error condition? As discussed elsewhere, this problem remains without satisfactory resolution, but one historically popular approach is to take an error argument and write to that, while returning the result.

This gives us two kinds of function argument: input parameters and output parameters. The input parameters are used in the evaluation of the function, while the output parameters are used to report other values in addition to the return value.

This gives rise to the common practice of arranging parameters in a function in this order:

```
Return-value, identifier(input-parameters, output-parameters);
```

For example, a function that takes some string data and returns it, along with the amount of data added to the string, might look like this:

```
int amend_content(std::string const& format, std::string& destination);
```

The return value is an `int`, the input is the `format` parameter, while the output is the `destination` parameter. The caller must create their own string before calling the function, passing this string as the second parameter.

This gives rise to a potential pitfall. How do you know where the input parameters end and the output parameters begin? Additional documentation is required of the author to ensure that the user arranges their arguments correctly. The function declaration should look something like this:

```
int amend_content(std::string const& format,
                  /*output parameter*/ std::string& destination);
```

In this example, you might think that a non-const reference is hinting clearly to the user that this is going to be written to. However, you should assume nothing about your users, and this documentation is a maintenance burden just waiting to be overlooked. The addition of further input and output parameters, for example additional format details or an error channel, demands that the documentation be kept up to date.

There is also the matter of deciding which of the output values should be the return value rather than an output parameter. Some might want the function to return the revised string rather than the amount of data added to it. This can lead to utterly tiresome and vacuous arguing for no real benefit as use cases are presented to the programming team and decisions boil down to who is the squeakiest wheel.

A single return value, on the other hand, is self-documenting: it is, by definition, an output value.

Documenting and annotating

Back at the turn of the century, Microsoft proposed a solution to the problem of documenting the nature of function parameters. It is called the source code annotation language (SAL) and it lives in the header file `sal.h` as part of the vendor implementation.[1] It takes the form of annotations within the function signature that describe the ins and outs of the parameters. For example, you may be familiar with the function signature of `memcpy`:

```
void* memcpy(
  void* dest,
  const void* src,
  size_t count
);
```

1. https://docs.microsoft.com/en-us/cpp/code-quality/using-sal-annotations-to-reduce-c-cpp-code-defects

Applying the annotations yields:

```
void* memcpy(
  _Out_writes_bytes_all_(count) void* dest,
  _In_reads_bytes_(count) const void* src,
  size_t count
);
```

These keywords provide extra machine-readable information about the nature of the parameters. In this example, `_Out_writes_bytes_all_(count)` signals that the output writes count bytes while `_In_reads_bytes_(count)` signals that count bytes are read in. There are a lot of annotations available, making this a very rich way of disambiguating the precise nature of the parameters.

These annotations are macros that disappear during the preprocessor phase, but tooling within the Microsoft Visual Studio IDE ensured that functions were being used correctly. If you use Visual Studio you can try it out and benefit from the extra code analysis.

However, SAL does not eliminate the burden of maintaining documentation. It may enable superior reporting of errors and abuse, but it merely moves the problem of parameter description elsewhere. This problem was inherited from C, and while SAL is useful for decorating C functions, there are additional ways in C++ to make your function signatures more expressive that involve the use of the language itself. This has the advantage of being closer to the goal of self-documenting code.

Now you can return an object

A useful thing you can do is return an instance of a `struct` or `class`. All the values calculated by your function can be bundled together into a single entity and handed back to the caller, rather than scattering output parameters through your function signature. Being able to return an object is a great bonus to clarity, enabled by the introduction of copy and move constructors. However, this feature has had a checkered history.

When I first started using C++, I despaired at the cost of returning objects by value. I would typically see a copy constructor being invoked to return the object and then an assignment operator being invoked to assign the result of the call. During the years prior to standardization, different compilers would optimize this in different, unreliable ways.

One easy optimization was to pass an output parameter to the function so that rather than this:

```
BigObj create_big_obj(); // Function prototype
BigObj big_obj = create_big_obj();
```

you would do this:

```
void create_big_obj(BigObj&); // Function prototype
BigObj big_obj;
create_big_obj(big_obj);
```

Rather than return and assign a `BigObj`, you would construct and modify instead. This was a particularly big win if the class contained a container, since the copy cost would include copying the contents of that container twice.

During the 1990s, copy elision started to appear. This elided the return and assign into a single operation. Different compilers enabled different elisions under different circumstances, though, so returning objects portably was not an option. For example, one problem with eliding the return and assign is that there may be side effects for each of those operations, which would now disappear.

Look at this class:

```
class SmallObj {
public:
  SmallObj() {}
  SmallObj(SmallObj const&) {std::cout << "copying\n";}
};
```

The copy constructor has a side effect, sending text to the standard output. Look at this snippet of code:

```
SmallObj so() {
  return SmallObj(); // RVO (see below)
}
int main() {
  std::cout <<"Testing...\n";
  SmallObj s = so();
}
```

Running this would yield any one of the following outputs, depending on your compiler, and even its settings:

```
Testing...
copying
copying
```

```
Testing…
copying
Testing…
```

As you can imagine, this was fantastically annoying. There were two types of elision: return value optimization (RVO) and named return value optimization (NRVO). The first of these you saw demonstrated above. If you return a nameless temporary object, then the compiler can construct it directly where the returned value would be copied.

The second of these was a little trickier to get right. If you return a named object, then under certain conditions the compiler can construct it directly where the returned value would be copied. Divining the nature of these conditions was akin to sorcery. You could help the compiler by providing the definition of the destructor and copy constructor inline, along with those of all the members, but it was trivially easy to spoil things and introduce a massive performance spike into your code as copy elision was suddenly and unexpectedly denied.

Heroic efforts have been made to update the standard so that returning objects is as cheap as possible as often as possible.

Frustratingly, I set aside returning by value. With standardization came the as-if rule, which made very clear that you could emulate required behavior, explicitly permitting elision even if side effects were observable. Still, it was not guaranteed, and again I found it too easy to introduce performance spikes with a carelessly introduced member datum.

Things got even better with the next standard. C++11 introduced move semantics which gave elision a broader meaning. Now you could define a separate constructor specifically for moving objects rather than copying them. This made returning objects a much more attractive proposition because the move constructor would be invoked to return something, so even if elision didn't take place, at least the cost could be reduced and copying containers would be cheap.

Heroic efforts have been made to update the standard so that returning objects is as cheap as possible as often as possible. Since C++17, compilers are required to omit the copy and move construction of class objects, even if that means omitting observable side effects, in a return statement when the object being returned is a prvalue of the same type as the function return type. Before C++17 this was existing practice in most compilers, but standardizing this practice reassures the user.

This means that RVO is a safe bet, and you should always make heroic efforts to ensure that you return objects from a function as a constructor invocation, as in the

RVO example above. You may have also seen return invoked with an initialization list:

```
std::pair<int, int> f(int a, int b) {
  return {a + b, a * b};
}
```

This is also a prvalue and will enable the compiler to generate RVO-flavored code. NRVO is not required, since the object has no name. This requirement is not attached to optimizations or compiler flags: this will Just Happen, due to fundamental changes in C++17 to the specification of temporary values and prvalues.

This can trip up old coders (whistles innocently) because it means the compiler will prefer elision to side effects, so if you log things in move constructors or destructors you may be surprised by their nonappearance. However, this is the right thing for the standard to prefer and is in line with the goal of C++ to offer zero-overhead abstraction. Performance opportunities should not be avoided lightly.

You can also return a tuple

Given that you can comfortably rely on being able to return by value without loss of performance, we have not only eliminated a use case for out parameters, but we can also now look at eliminating out parameters entirely.

A very common use case for an out parameter and a return value is for signaling an error. Let's flesh out `BigObj` for this section:

```
class BigObj {
public:
  BigObj(int a, int b);

private:
  // implementation
};
```

You may have encountered a function prototype that looks like this:

```
BigObj do_stuff(int a, int b, error_code& err);
```

The function takes some input data and a reference to an error collection object and returns an object. The caller can check if the object was created correctly, or at all, by interrogating the error code. Perhaps the author is unwilling or unable to throw an exception if something goes wrong during the creation of a `BigObj`.

This is a somewhat inelegant way of doing things. Two ways of passing data back to the caller are offered, via the return object and via the `error_code` reference. There are other guidelines about error handling discussed in Chapter 3.5 which speak against this way of doing things. One suggestion is to return a variant of the `BigObj` and the `error_code`. However, perhaps you want to signal the validity of the returned object, for which you would use a special zero error code, to signify no error.

Given that you can safely return objects by value, you can also safely return a pair by value. This would lead to a function that looks like this:

```
std::pair<BigObj, error_code> do_stuff(int a, int b) {
  // validate inputs
  return { {a, b}, {error} };
}
```

The return statement constructs a prvalue, so the copy and assignment can be elided as an RVO. The standard library uses this technique in a few places. The insert member function on the associative containers returns a `std::pair<iterator, bool>` which signals whether the insertion took place and where.

Indeed, you are not limited to a `std::pair`: you can return a `std::tuple` of any size. There is a useful library facility for binding elements of the `std::tuple` to individual objects, called `std::tie`, which was introduced in C++11. It allows you to declare objects and then tie them to a `std::pair` or `std::tuple`, like this:

```
BigObj bo;
error_code ec;

std::tie(bo, ec) = do_stuff(1, 2);
```

We know what you're thinking, though. This is just declaring an object and then assigning to it; we are back to the bad old days of construct and assign rather than copy elision.

You would be absolutely right, and this is why in C++17 structured bindings were introduced. By supporting the feature in the language as well as the library you can choose to put the returned values directly into new objects, like this:

```
auto [bo, ec] = do_stuff(1, 2);
```

Here you can see how `tie` has been eliminated and replaced with some syntactic sugar in the form of `auto` and brackets.

Structured binding was my favorite C++17 feature. You can even use it to bind to an array or a struct:

```
int a[2] = {1, 2};
```

```
auto [b, c] = a; // b and c are ints, where b = 1 and c = 2

struct S {
  int a;
  int b;
};
S make_s();

auto [d, e] = make_s(); // d = the first member of the returned struct
                        // e = the second member.
```

The use cases for out parameters are few. While returning tuples is a neat trick, do not overlook returning a struct. If your return values are related in some way, you may be in the process of unearthing an abstraction. The same tricks used to return a tuple are used to return a struct. Copy elision means the values are created where they will be needed by the caller.

Always check that you are not discarding an abstraction when you merely return a tuple. A pair of `BigObj` and an error code doesn't sensibly lend itself to being composed into a new abstraction, but a tuple consisting of several related objects most likely needs names for the individual parts. Consider the string and the character count: there is a small abstraction with a name like `modified_string` waiting to be manifested.

Always check that you are not discarding an abstraction when you merely return a tuple.

Passing and returning by non-`const` reference

At the start of this chapter, we talked about input parameters and output parameters. There is a third type of parameter called an in-out parameter. Like an out parameter, this is also a reference or pointer to a non-`const` object. Typically, in-out parameters sit between in and out parameters in a function declaration, so we can expand the prototypical function described at the start thus:

```
Return-value, identifier(input-parameters, input-output parameters,
                         output-parameters);
```

The thrust of this guideline is to separate inputs from outputs so that inputs lie between the parentheses of a function declaration, while outputs are limited to the return type. Can we apply that wisdom to this style of parameter?

Consider a reporting object collecting data from a variety of sources. Each source exposes a function that takes a reporting object and some additional parameters and returns the number of items added to the object. For example:

```
class Report { … };

int report_rendering(int, int, Report&);    // input parameters…
int report_fileIO(int, int, int, Report&); // then in-out parameter

std::pair<Report, int> collect_report(const char* title) {
  auto report = Report(title);
  int item_count =  report_rendering(1, 2, report);
  item_count += report_fileIO(0, 0, 1024, report);
  return {report, item_count};
}
```

If we were to return the output values as a single object, we would have to change the file signatures to:

```
std::pair <Report, int> report_rendering(int, int, Report&);
std::pair <Report, int> report_fileIO(int, int, int, Report&);
```

This would have a slightly unpleasant effect on the code:

```
std::pair<Report, int> collect_report(const char* title) {
  auto report = Report(title);
  int item_count = report_rendering(1, 2, report).second;
  item_count += report_fileIO(0, 0, 1024, report).second;
  return {report, item_count};
}
```

The trailing `.second` is ugly, and the first item in the pair is being discarded. The caller already has the object, since they passed it in, so why return it?

In fact, if we restore the function prototype return types, and move the in-out parameter to the position before the input parameters, we get this:

```
int report_rendering(Report&, int, int);
int report_fileIO(Report&, int, int, int);
```

These functions take an object and modify it according to some input parameters. This sounds like a member function, particularly if we look at a potential member function signature:

```
int Report::report_rendering(int, int);
int Report::report_fileIO(int, int, int);
```

The technique of passing in-out parameters in addition to input parameters is in fact just a way of extending the class's API without creating a new member function. This is a valuable technique for a client of the class since it does not require you to find the original author and hound them for additional functionality. It is also a valuable technique for the author since it enables the support of Core Guideline C.4: "Make a function a member only if it needs direct access to the representation of a class."

This guideline contributes toward keeping your interfaces minimal and complete. If a function can be enabled in this way, as a nonmember function, then that is one fewer function for your class interface. Alternatively, if you have a collection of nonmember friend functions, or a collection of getters and setters which are only called by a few functions that could be friend functions, you have identified candidates for extending your interface. If you can correct this imbalance, do so.

Having said all this, it turns out that there is a use case for taking an object by non-`const` reference and returning it: the iostream library. The chevron operator for outputting a character looks like this:

```
template<class Traits>
std::basic_ostream<char, Traits>& operator<<(
   std::basic_ostream<char, Traits>& os, const char* s);
```

The `basic_ostream` is passed in and returned, which facilitates daisy-chaining successive calls into a single statement, like this:

```
std::cout << "Hello, world!" << std::endl;
```

This could be rewritten as:

```
operator <<(std::cout, "Hello, world!").operator <<(std::endl);
```

Only the first call is a nonmember function. The second call is a member function because `endl` is a function pointer and `basic_ostream` has a member `operator <<` which takes function pointers of this type. The first incantation is clearly the more pleasant and less confusing rendering. The mixed type of daisy-chaining in the second incantation takes a while to parse and introduces an unnecessary cognitive load.

It is perfectly legitimate to design an API for daisy-chaining. If you have a series of operations that you want to carry out, unless an exception is thrown, this sort of thing can look quite easy on the eye.

```
class Obj {…};

Obj object;
```

```
object.f1(a, b, c) // Each member function returns an Obj&
      .f2(d, e, f)
      .f3(g, h);
```

Finally, we would observe that if you find yourself passing multiple in-out parameters to a function, there is a good chance that you are missing an abstraction. You may be attempting a kind of double (or more) dispatch and trying to confect a way of modeling the interactions of multiple classes. Be assured, this is not the place to do that.

Summary

Advice from earlier times to arrange parameters in the order in, in-out, out is obviated by advances in C++.

- Mandatory copy elision for returning prvalues means that careful design of the constructor API can facilitate optimal return-by-value.
- Multiple values should be returned as a struct or as a tuple.
- Structured binding is preferable to `tie` as it is a language facility rather than a library facility. Additionally, it obviates the need to default-construct the object you're going to tie to the return value.
- In-out parameters can individually expand the API of a class and should be placed before the input parameters.
- Returning in-out parameters can be used to daisy-chain function calls in the style of the chevron operator, although effort is required to make this legible.
- Multiple in-out parameters require special care and may hint at a missing abstraction.

Chapter 4.2

Enum.3: Prefer class enums over "plain" enums

Constants

Constants are great. Types are great. Constants of a specific type are really great. This is why class enums are just fantastic.

Historically, and we hope you no longer feel the need to do this, constants were defined as preprocessor macros. You might have seen something like this in a geometry-related source file:

```
#define PI 3.1415926535897932385
```

If you were unfortunate, in another file you might have seen something like this:

```
#define PI 3.1415926 // fine for float, insufficient for double
```

Or this:

```
#define PI 3.1415926535987932385 // mis-transcribed
```

Or this:

```
#define Pi 3.1415926535897932385 // Slightly different name
```

They may even have been defined in header files, just to really spoil your day. These preprocessor symbols have no type, nor scope. They are simply lexically substituted during the preprocessor phase. An early win for C++ was the realization that you could declare scoped objects of `const`-qualified type (please never call them `const` variables). A single, well-placed definition of `pi` was a welcome sight. In fact, since

C++20 we have a standard definition of pi. You will find it in the <numbers> header, defined in the namespace std::numbers:

```
template <>
inline constexpr double pi_v<double> = 3.141592653589793;
inline constexpr double pi = pi_v<double>;
```

Some constants are important, but their values are arbitrary. Unlike PI, or E, or MONTHS_IN_YEAR, there are times when we need a handful of named values to represent some ideas. These have always been in the form of small integers, such as 1 for edit, 2 for browse, -1 to quit, and so on. There is still code out there with vast swathes of macros defining related integers. From WinUser.h, part of the Windows SDK:

```
#define WM_CTLCOLORSCROLLBAR            0x0137
#define WM_CTLCOLORSTATIC               0x0138
#define MN_GETHMENU                     0x01E1

#define WM_MOUSEFIRST                   0x0200
#define WM_MOUSEMOVE                    0x0200
#define WM_LBUTTONDOWN                  0x0201
```

Why is there a jump from 0x01E1 to 0x0200? Most likely, there was a change in domain after MN_GETHMENU and there was no guarantee that there would be no further additions. It would be easy to identify the domain by looking at the second nibble. Or maybe it was completely arbitrary. We can never know. We cannot capture this information with simple preprocessor definitions.

Enumerated types provide a way of gathering constants together, which make them ideal for identifying, for example, error values, thus creating a specific error abstraction. Rather than declaring:

```
#define OK = 0
#define RECORD_NOT_FOUND = 1
#define TABLE_NOT_FOUND = 2
```

you can define an enumeration instead:

```
enum DB_error {
  OK,
  RECORD_NOT_FOUND,
  TABLE_NOT_FOUND
};
```

The enumerators have the same values as the preprocessor constants since enumerations start at zero by default and increment by one for each enumerator. They are spelled using uppercase letters since they are directly replacing those preprocessor constants. This should be the exception rather than the rule and enumerators should usually be spelled using lowercase letters. This is a matter of style rather than part of the standard: following this style prevents collisions with preprocessor symbols, which are conventionally spelled using uppercase letters.

Unfortunately, the `enum` keyword does not define a scope, nor does it define an underlying type. This can lead to some interesting problems. Consider an enumeration of two-letter codes for US states. Here is a snippet:

```
enum US_state {
  …
  MP, // Great quiz question…
  OH,
  OK, // Uh-oh…
  OR,
  PA,
  …
};
```

Since the braces do not define a scope as normally expected, `OK` is now an ambiguous identifier. If the enumerations themselves are defined in unrelated scopes this is not a problem. Otherwise, we need to modify the enumerators to disambiguate them. `OK` is obviously a hugely useful identifier, so it cannot be allowed to exist unadorned. In the pre-C++11 world you would come across enumerators like `S_OK`, `R_OK`, `E_OK`, and so on, leading to somewhat illegible code. Indeed, using a single letter was a luxury afforded only to the biggest players. In the above example you would be far more likely to use `DBE_OK` or `USS_OK`. Once you had adorned one enumerator, you felt obliged to adorn all the others, with the result that your code would become scattered with TLAs and underbars prefixing all your enumerators.

Fortunately, although ugly and inconvenient, this hindrance would manifest at compile time in the form of a simple error, easily resolved by uglifying your colliding enumerators a little bit more. The other, rather more insidious problem was that of implicit conversion. Functions could cheerfully return an enumerator like `OK`, or more likely `DBE_OK`, and that value could be freely converted to an `int`. The same was true the other way around: a function could take an `int` but be passed an enumerator. This leads to interesting bugs where you pass an enumerator from one enumeration and it might be interpreted as an enumerator from another enumeration.

Scoped enumerations

C++11 expanded the `enum` keyword and added two new features. The first of these was the scoped enumeration. This introduced an amendment to the syntax by adding the keyword `struct` or `class` to the declaration:

```
enum class DB_error { // Scoped, and now lowercase identifiers…
  OK, // …except for OK which is uppercase anyway.
  record_not_found,
  table_not_found
};

enum struct US_state {
  …
  MP, // Northern Mariana Islands, since you ask…
  OH,
  OK,
  OR,
  PA,
  …
};
```

The scoped enumeration provides the enumerators with a scope, and thus a way of disambiguating them from identically named enumerators elsewhere. When you use a scoped enumerator, you explicitly resolve the scope using the scope resolution operator, which might look something like this:

```
static_assert(DB_error::OK != US_state::OK);
```

except this will not compile since the left- and right-hand sides of the `!=` sign are of different types, requiring an explicit `operator !=` overload.

There is no guidance on when to use `struct` or `class`. Personally, I use `class` when I have defined other operations on the enumeration. For example, consider a days-of-the-week enumeration:

```
enum class Day {
  monday,
  tuesday,
  wednesday,
  thursday,
  friday,
  saturday,
  sunday
};
```

Perhaps you want to be able to cycle through the days of the week, so you might decide to define a pre-increment operator:

```
constexpr Day operator++(Day& d) {
  switch (d) {
  case Day::monday:    d = Day::tuesday;   break;
  case Day::tuesday:   d = Day::wednesday; break;
  case Day::wednesday: d = Day::thursday;  break;
  case Day::thursday:  d = Day::friday;    break;
  case Day::friday:    d = Day::saturday;  break;
  case Day::saturday:  d = Day::sunday;    break;
  case Day::sunday:    d = Day::monday;    break;
  }
  return d;
}

Day today = Day::saturday;
Day tomorrow = ++today;
```

Underlying type

Enumerations have an underlying type which can be defined at the point of declaration or definition. One advantage this gives is that, since C++11, enumerations can be declared without being defined, since the size of the type can be inferred. If no underlying type is specified, then a default is used. Such an enumeration cannot be forward-declared. The default underlying type depends on whether the enumeration is scoped or unscoped.

If the enumeration is unscoped, then the underlying type is an implementation-defined integral type that can represent all the enumerator values. Looking at our days of the week, the enumerator values range from zero to six, so one might expect the underlying type to be `char`. If the enumerator is scoped, then the underlying type is `int`. This may seem a little wasteful. On a typical implementation, a `char` would be sufficient. To specify the underlying type, new syntax was added in C++11, thus:

```
enum class Day : char {
  monday,
  tuesday,
  wednesday,
  thursday,
  friday,
  saturday,
  sunday
};
```

This syntax is available to both scoped and unscoped enumerations. Specifying the underlying type should be restricted to situations where it is necessary; the three-byte saving is only going to be noticeable if you have thousands of instances of an object storing `Day` instances. The default is the easiest to read and write. However, specifying the type can also aid ABI compatibility.

Enumerations are also used to define power-of-two constants for bitwise masking. For example:

```
enum personal_quality {
  reliable    = 0x00000001,
  warm        = 0x00000002,
  punctual    = 0x00000004,
  …
  generous    = 0x40000000,
  thoughtful = 0x80000000
};
```

The underlying type could be `int` if it stopped at `generous`, but `thoughtful` requires an unsigned `int`. In the general case you should not specify the value of enumerators: it can lead to typing errors and it can degrade the performance of switch statements. However, this is an exception.

Prior to C++11 there was something of a gray area. Some implementations would permit forward declaration of enumerations by fixing their size to 32 bits unless an enumerator exceeded the maximum representable value. However, this was not guaranteed to be portable. This is the problem with implementation-defined parts of the standard: you need to be able to identify how all your target implementations define them. This is still the case: an unscoped enumeration that does not specify an underlying type defaults to an implementation-defined underlying type.

Implicit conversion

Another feature of the unscoped enumeration is that it is freely convertible to an `int`. A common bug of yore was to pass an enumerator to a function taking an `int`. This was considered perfectly acceptable and common practice, but the enumerator value may have different meanings in different scopes.

```
// territory.h
enum US_state { // unscoped enumeration
  …
  MP, // There are four other territories
  OH,
```

```
  OK,
  OR,
  PA,
  …
};
…
void submit_state_information(int); // Hmm, US state or nation state?

// US_reporting.cpp
submit_state_information(OH); // OH is from an unscoped enumeration
```

With luck, `submit_state_information` does indeed take a US state and not a nation state. Unfortunately, with that API, there is no way of being sure.

You are still able to convert scoped enumerations to their underlying type, but you have to do it explicitly with `static_cast` or with `std::underlying_type`:

```
// territory.h
enum struct US_state { // scoped enumeration
  …
  MP,
  OH,
  OK,
  OR,
  PA,
  …
};
…
void submit_state_information(int);

// US_reporting.cpp
submit_state_information(static_cast<int>(US_state::OH));
```

That explicit cast demonstrates that you are personally taking responsibility for the effects of this potentially dangerous activity. In the above invocation, you have decided that `submit_state_information` takes a US state. Casting is always a good place to start looking for weird bugs.

Alternatively, you can construct an `int` from the enumeration:

```
// US_reporting.cpp
submit_state_information(int(US_state::OH));
```

Of course, this problem is down to bad API design. The function should have been more explicit about its parameter:

```
void submit_state_information(US_state);
```

Unfortunately, occasionally it can be unwise to rely on the best efforts of your colleagues and the safest approach is to seek clarification.

Summary

Prefer class (scoped) enumerations over "plain" (unscoped) enumerations to benefit from a reliable default underlying type and to enable disambiguation of symbols.

Simply adding the keyword `class` to all your `enum` declarations is cheap and improves safety by disallowing implicit conversion, while enabling you to improve readability by removing "decoration" from enumerators that was only added to make them unique.

Postscript

Back in the last decade I arranged for some C++ training for my team to be given by Scott Meyers. This was a pretty big deal for us, and he truly delivered. One of the things that sticks in my mind was that it was the first time I heard someone say `enum` differently to me. I am English, and I've only ever heard this word pronounced to rhyme with "bee-come." He rhymed it with "resume," as if he were beginning to say "enumeration" but lost interest after the second syllable.

Chapter 4.3

ES.5: Keep scopes small

The nature of scope

"Scope" is another of those words that is overloaded with meaning. It comes from computer science, but each programming language puts its own little twist on it. In the specific case of C++, scope is a property of the declarations in your code, and it is where visibility and lifetime intersect.

All declarations in your program appear in one or more scopes. Scopes can nest, like namespaces, and most scopes are introduced with an identifier. Names are only visible in the scope they are declared in, but the lifetime of objects is not necessarily limited to the scope of their name. This fuzziness catches engineers out time and again when it comes to objects of dynamic storage duration.

Deterministic destruction is the preeminent feature of C++. When the name of an object of automatic storage class falls out of scope, the object is destroyed. Its destructor is invoked, and everything is cleaned up. There is no waiting around for a garbage collector to work its magic and sweep the floor, which is usually the case with managed languages, and which can lead to unpleasant nondeterministic side effects such as running out of resources at inopportune moments, or for cleanup to be skipped entirely. However, when the name of a raw pointer falls out of scope, it is the pointer that is destroyed, not the object it points to, leaving the object to persist without a name and thus without a means of having its destructor invoked.

The lifetime of an object of dynamic duration is only loosely bound to the scope of its name. Indeed, the pointer can be assigned to another name and survive beyond the scope of the name it was first bound to. It can be assigned to many names and cause all manner of headaches when it is to be decided when the object should be destroyed. This is why we have the `std::shared_ptr` class. When the last name bound to a `std::shared_ptr` object falls out of scope, the object it points to is destroyed. We looked at this where we discussed Core Guideline I.11: "Never transfer ownership by a raw pointer (`T*`) or reference (`T&`)." Reference counting is used to do all the bookkeeping. The reference is increased when a name is bound to the `std::shared_ptr` object, and decreased if the name falls out of scope.

It is important to remember that names have scope, not objects. Objects have lifetime, or more precisely, storage duration. There are four types of storage duration: static, dynamic, automatic, and thread-local. How many scopes can you name? More than two? In fact, there are six. They are:

- Block
- Namespace
- Class
- Function parameter
- Enumeration
- Template parameter

We shall now look at them all.

Block scope

Block scope is probably the first one you thought of, although you might not know its name. A block, or compound statement, is a sequence of statements enclosed by braces, as in the following example:

```
if (x > 15) {
  auto y = 200;
  auto z = do_work(y);
  auto gamma = do_more_work(z);
  inform_user(z, gamma);
}
```

The body of the `if` statement is a single block scope. This is a healthy example of the form. It is a small scope. It is easy to see what is going on: `y`, `z`, and `gamma` are declared, and then destroyed at the end of the scope after `inform_user` returns. Block scopes are found after function definitions, control statements, and so on.

Scopes can be nested. Block scopes can nest by simply opening another pair of braces:

```
if (x > 15) {
  auto y = 200;
  auto z = do_work(y);
  {                             // New scope
    auto y = z;                 // Scope of the next y starts here
    y += mystery_factor(8);     // Still referring to the next y
    inform_user(y, 12);         // Still referring to the next y
  }                             // Scope of the next y ends here
  y = do_more_work(z);          // Scope of first y resumes here
  inform_user(z, y);
}
```

This example demonstrates a discontiguous scope, and there are some interesting things going on here. The symbol y has been "shadowed" in a nested scope, so there are two objects called y. The first y lives in the outer scope and is no longer in scope once the scope of the next y starts. It comes back in scope at the end of the nested scope, which means its scope is broken up, or discontiguous.

This example is not as healthy as the first one. It is entirely legal, although at best unwise, to reuse names in nested scopes. This is the sort of thing that happens when you paste code from another location and is yet another reason why pasting code is a last resort. The scope and the nested scope take up fewer than a dozen lines that are readable after a fashion, but it is only a matter of time before the code is amended and expanded. Once that happens, the likelihood of the two objects named y becoming mixed up by the author increases.

Some implementations will warn you if you mask a name in this way. Indeed, my implementation of choice introduced this and interfered quite heavily with our no-warnings policy. My stubborn refusal to disable warnings meant that the largest part of the upgrade to this new version of the compiler was fixing all instances of this, uncovering a surprising number of bugs in the process.

Namespace scope

Like block scope, namespace scope begins after an opening brace. Particularly, it is the brace after the namespace identifier, thus:

```
namespace CG30 { // Scope begins here
```

Any symbol declared before the matching closing brace is visible from its point of declaration. Unlike block scope, it remains visible after the closing brace in all subsequent definitions for the same namespace, for example:

```
namespace CG30 {
  auto y = 76; // Scope of y begins here
} // Scope of y is interrupted here

…

namespace CG30 { // Scope of y resumes here
  auto x = y;
}
```

While the scope of `y` is interrupted, you can still reference it by explicitly resolving the scope. This is done by using `::`, the scope resolution operator, and prefixing with the scope you are intending to resolve to. To refer to `y` declared in the namespace `CG30`, you write `CG30::y`.

There is one occasion where namespace scope does not begin after an opening brace, and that is for the outermost scope. The start of a translation unit is the beginning of a namespace called global namespace scope. Habitually, this scope gets called file scope or global scope, but those are hangovers from C. Now that we have namespaces, we have a more accurate name.

Since global namespace scope is never interrupted, symbols declared there are visible everywhere. While this is enormously convenient, it is an equally enormously terrible idea to declare anything other than namespaces at global namespace scope, with the exception of `main()` and operator overloads whose operand types are declared in different namespaces. Globals are bad, m'kay?

There is another special namespace called the anonymous namespace. Symbols declared in an anonymous namespace are in scope until the end of the enclosing scope and have internal linkage. For example:

```
namespace {
   auto a = 17;  // private to the current translation unit.
}
```

Having mentioned linkage, we need to clearly differentiate between scope, storage duration, and linkage. We need to be clear on the difference between a name and an object. A name has a scope that determines when that name is visible without requiring scope resolution. An object has a storage duration that determines the lifetime of an object. An object binds to a name.

Objects with static or thread-local storage duration also have a linkage, which is internal or external. Internal linkage makes an object inaccessible from another translation unit. Objects with automatic storage duration have no linkage.

Objects with dynamic storage duration do not bind to a name, nor do they have linkage. They bind to a pointer that binds to a name. That indirection is what causes so many problems with memory leaks, but it is also a reason why C++ delivers superior performance: the engineer can precisely schedule the lifetime of the object rather than rely on garbage collection.

If you open an anonymous namespace at global namespace scope, then all the symbols will be in scope until the end of the translation unit. This can be particularly unpleasant if you open an anonymous namespace in a header file: the translation unit will typically end long after the end of a `#include` directive. Additionally, if you reuse the header file, you will end up with multiple instances of the same defined entity, which may not be what you intended. If you are going to open an anonymous namespace at global namespace scope, do not do it in a header file.

```
namespace CG30 {
  auto y = 76;
  namespace {
    auto x = 67;
  } // x is still in scope
  auto z = x;
} // Scope of x is interrupted here.

namespace {
  constexpr auto pi = 3.14159f;
} // pi is still in scope
```

The final namespace scope to consider is the inline namespace scope. Like the anonymous namespace, the scope of symbols declared in an inline namespace is not interrupted at the end of that namespace, but at the end of the enclosing namespace, like so:

```
namespace CG30 {
  auto y = 76;
  inline namespace version_1 {
    auto x = 67;
  } // x is still in scope
  auto z = x;
} // Scope of x is interrupted here
```

As you can see, there is a little more to namespaces than meets the eye. The global namespace scope is the largest possible scope, so keeping scopes small means not declaring any symbols in it. We can see a useful overlap of guidelines here. Also, keeping a namespace scope small makes it easier to apprehend the contents. Long, rambling namespaces lose their coherence and should be avoided.

Class scope

Class scope represents yet another variation on the block scope. The scope of a symbol declared in a class begins at the point of declaration and persists beyond the end of the class definition. It includes all default arguments for member-function parameters, exception specifications, and the member function bodies:

```
class RPM {
  static constexpr int LP = 33;
  static constexpr int Single = 45;

public:
  static constexpr int SeventyEight = 78;
  int RotorMax(int x, int y = LP);
}; // RotorMax, LP, Single and SeventyEight remain in scope
   // within member function bodies of RPM

int RPM::RotorMax(int x, int y)
{
  return LP + x + y;
}
```

While the scope of `SeventyEight` is interrupted, you can still reference it by explicitly resolving the scope since it is a public member of the class. This is done by, again, using `::`, the scope resolution operator, and writing `RPM::SeventyEight`. The scope resolution operator narrows the number of places for the compiler to search for the name.

What does keeping class scope small entail? It means keeping the interface minimal and complete. As an interface grows it loses coherence.

> *Badly named classes invite badly designed APIs.*

We have all seen the epic interface: that one class in the project that has become a home for waifs and strays, with a name like Manager or Globals or Broker, and a nickname like The Blob. Badly named classes invite badly designed APIs. Classes with broad names invite broad APIs. Manager is both a bad and broad name for a class. The increasing cost of a big API is the loss of meaning and the brake that it applies to development: whenever you are forced to interact with The Blob, you need to parse screenfuls of interface and, with luck, many pages of documentation.

There are several techniques for keeping class scopes small. In fact, some of these are expressed as Core Guidelines. Both C.45: "Don't define a default constructor that only initializes data members; use member initializers instead" and C.131: "Avoid trivial getters and setters," discussed in the first section, have the side effect of reducing class scope size. In the case of C.45, one fewer function implies smaller scope because the class definition is smaller and there is one fewer member function definition, which is also part of the scope of the class. In the case of C.131, the same reasoning applies: fewer member functions imply smaller scope.

Core Guideline C.4: "Make a function a member only if it needs direct access to the representation of a class" reduces scope by replacing member functions with nonmember nonfriend functions where possible. These functions may be declared near the class, but they do not need to be declared in the scope of the class. Of course, this increases the size of the namespace scope, but any declaration is going to have an impact on a scope somewhere.

Simply refusing to grow the interface of a class beyond a certain size will keep class scopes small. You might decide that, whenever a public interface exceeds 10 functions, it is time to examine the abstraction and see if there are two more inside, ready to be realized. Perhaps the class invariants can be partitioned into two, and a more refined pair of abstractions can be drawn out.

The same approach can be taken to shrinking The Blob. Checking the invariants (and often, a class will start off with a handful of invariants whose quantity grows slowly over time), gathering them, and partitioning them will highlight the set of abstractions that model the broad collection of concepts contained therein.

We hope that this overlap of guidelines is making it apparent that following the guideline of keeping scopes small is a golden rule that rewards you many times over.

Function parameter scope

Three scopes remain for discussion. Function parameter scope is a little like block scope but with the addition of the function signature. The scope of a function parameter starts at its point of declaration within the function signature and ends at the end of the function declaration or, if the function is being defined, at the end of the function body. For example:

```
float divide(float a, // Scope of a begins here
             float b); // Scope of a ends here

float divide(float a, // Scope of a begins here
             float b) {
  return a / b;
```

```
} // Scope of a ends here
```

There is another variation, which involves the use of a function `try` block:

```
float divide(float a, // Scope of a begins here
             float b)
try {
  std::cout << "Dividing\n";
  return a / b;
} catch (...) { // Scope of a continues beyond here
  std::cout << "Dividing failed, was the denominator zero?\n";
} // Scope of a ends here
```

Function parameter scope ends at the end of the final `catch` clause.

This is rather like the block scope, which is to be expected since a function is like a big compound statement. Here is another overlap of guidelines. Consider F.3: "Keep functions short and simple." This is served by keeping the function scope small. In fact, adhering to F.2: "A function should perform a single logical operation" will usually yield functions with small scopes.

Enumeration scope

The nature of the enumeration scope seems clear and keeping it small seems counterintuitive. After all, there are 56 two-letter US state abbreviations, 118 elements of which the news has come to Harvard, and 206 bones in the adult human body. These are constants, and they are independent of any edict to keep scopes small.

However, this is not the whole story. Look at these scopes:

```
enum US_state_abbreviation { // unscoped enumeration
  ...
  VT,
  VA,
  VI,
  WA,
  WV,
  WI,
  WY
}; // Scope of VI (Virgin Islands) does not end here.

enum class Element { // scoped enumeration
  ...
  Nh,
  Fl,
  Mc,
```

```
  Lv,
  Ts,
  Og
}; // Scope of Lv (Livermorium) ends here.

US_state_abbreviation southernmost = HI; // HI in scope
// Element lightweight = H;              // H not in scope
Element lightweight = Element::H;        // H in scope
```

While the scope of `H` is interrupted, you can still reference it by explicitly resolving the scope. This is done by, you guessed it, using `::`, the scope resolution operator, and writing `Element::H`. The scope resolution operator tells the compiler "I mean this one, over here, look!"

Perhaps the name `Element` is itself in a namespace. Indeed, we would hope that is the case, since declaring anything other than a namespace at global namespace scope is a bad idea. In that case, you direct the compiler to the name `Element` by resolving its scope, for example, `Chemistry::Element::H`. You may draw parallels between this and the global Domain Name System, where top-level domains like .com, .net, and country codes resolve the scope; for example google.ie versus google.fr.

In the above example we have yet another overlap of guidelines. Enum.3: "Prefer class enums over "plain" enums" is motivated by the readiness with which enumerators convert to `int`s, leading to alarming consequences as outlined in the prior chapter. However, preferring `enum` classes, more properly known as scoped enumerations, will minimize the scope of an enumeration to its definition. It will keep the scope small. This is particularly advantageous for single-character identifiers, like H for hydrogen.

Template parameter scope

For completeness, we shall review template parameter scope. The scope of a template parameter name begins at the point of declaration and ends at the end of the smallest template declaration in which it was introduced. For example:

```
template< typename T,           // scope of T begins
          T* p >                // T remains in scope
class X : public std::pair<T, T> // T remains in scope
{
  …
  T m_instance;                 // T remains in scope
  …
};                              // scope of T ends
```

This is another scope whose size is dependent on external factors, such as the size of the class being defined. Keeping this scope small is unachievable without keeping the class scope small, so there is little to add to this part.

Scope as context

As you can see, keeping scopes small will reward you many times over. Fundamentally, scope is how we think about parts of things. The notions of scope and relevance are closely related. You can think of your code as a story made up of chapters, each chapter being a different scope. All the declarations in your code appear in a scope, ideally not the global scope, and it is an obvious step to associate related declarations in a single scope, and to pinpoint associations in minimal scopes.

Scopes are how abstractions are identified and enclosed.

Scopes are how abstractions are identified and enclosed. They are collections of names. Be it a class scope or a function scope or a namespace scope, it is the scope that contains the declarations relevant to that abstraction. They are the fundamental building blocks of your solution domain. Keeping your scopes small keeps your abstractions small as well.

Not all scopes have names, though, nor do all abstractions need names. It is perfectly acceptable to open a block scope within another scope and use it to perform some small, self-contained task; maybe it needs to be bounded by a `std::scoped_lock`. However, keep in mind that nested scopes carry the danger of hiding names. You may unwittingly interrupt the scope of an existing name by redeclaring it in a nested scope.

Scope and duration are related but not always interchangeable. For example, names with global namespace scope are all bound to objects with static storage duration. However, names with enumeration scope are not bound to objects at all; they are merely literal constants requiring no storage.

Moving your attention from scope to scope requires a mental context switch, just as reading a book requires you to build a model of the plot and characters. Scope can be thought of as the immediate context for what is going on in your program. It partitions the solution domain, the thing that your program is achieving, into individual pieces that can be easily apprehended. By mastering the interplay of scope, context, and abstractions you can easily decompose any problem into manageable parts and make programming a joy.

Summary

In summary:

- Names have scope, not objects.
- Keep clear the distinction between scope and storage duration.
- Readability is inversely proportional to scope size.
- Keep scopes small to minimize retention of resources required by objects of automatic storage duration.
- Beware of hiding names when nesting scopes.
- Prefer scoped enumerations to keep scopes small.
- Maintain minimal and complete interfaces to keep scopes small.
- Keep scopes small to optimize abstraction.

Chapter 4.4

Con.5: Use constexpr for values that can be computed at compile time

From const to constexpr

Prior to C++11, const machinery was restricted to two things: qualifying a type as const, and thus any instance of that type as immutable, and qualifying a nonstatic member function such that *this is const in its body, like this:

```
class int_wrapper {
public:
  explicit int_wrapper(int i);
  void mutate(int i);
  int inspect() const;

private:
  int m_i;
};

auto const i = int_wrapper{7}; // i is of type int_wrapper const
// i.mutate(5); // Cannot invoke non-const qualified
                // member function on const object
auto j = i.inspect(); // Assign from inspect
```

We are sure you are familiar with this. You may also be familiar with the keyword mutable that qualifies nonstatic member data as immune from const restrictions, particularly if you have read Chapter 3.4, ES.50: "Don't cast away const." This is part of the const machinery insofar as it applies to const-qualified member functions.

New to C++11 was the keyword constexpr. The idea behind this was to improve compile-time programming by allowing a very limited set of functions to be executed at compile time. Engineers were already doing this in an unpleasant way using preprocessor macros. With the arrival of `constexpr` these macros could be eliminated and replaced with proper, type-safe functions. It was a nice feeling being able to eliminate another use case from the preprocessor.

It was not without constraints, though. You were allowed only one expression per function, which led to a resurgence in recursion and a lot of ternary operator use. The standard example, as for template metaprogramming, was generating factorials and Fibonacci numbers, but a lot of math functions were available, such as trigonometric expansions. A single expression was very limiting but sharpened everyone's thoughts about functional programming.

Here is a factorial example:

```
constexpr int factorial(int n) {
  return n <= 1 ? 1 // Base case
             : (n * factorial(n - 1)); // Recurse case
}
```

Of course, all this recursion highlighted to everyone what the limits of the compiler were; 12! is the largest factorial to fit in a 32-bit representation.

> *The `constexpr` facilities are becoming a language within the language, supplanting the preprocessor in many places with a type-safe, scope-aware variation.*

It was fantastically popular, and C++14 broadened the scope still further. The single-expression restriction was lifted and `constexpr` libraries started to appear. Particularly, decent compile-time hashing became possible. The genie was well and truly out of the bottle and nothing was going to stop the expansion of `constexpr` throughout the language, and the relaxing of constraints.

Now you could write your factorial function using plain old if-then statements:

```
constexpr int factorial(int n) {
  if (n <= 1) return 1; // Base case
  return n * factorial(n - 1); // Recurse case
}
```

C++17 brought yet more innovations. Lambdas could be `constexpr`. This might seem a little peculiar, but if you think of a lambda expression as syntactic sugar for a class with a function operator, a `constexpr` lambda has a `constexpr` function operator. Additionally, a new construct was introduced: `if constexpr`. This allowed you to eliminate some cases of `std::enable_if` and reduce the number of overloads for your function templates. It simplified code still further, and reduced compilation time and code comprehension burden by eliminating some of the cost of SFINAE.

C++20 introduced what would have seemed truly bizarre 10 years earlier: `constexpr` virtual functions, `try/catch` blocks in `constexpr` functions, `constexpr` STL algorithms, and `constexpr` dynamic allocation leading to `constexpr std::string` and `constexpr std::vector`. There is so much available to you now at compile time. You can create extensive libraries that are entirely `constexpr`. Hana Dusíková astonished the community at CppCon in 2017 with a compile-time regular expression library.[1]

The `constexpr` facilities are becoming a language within the language, supplanting the preprocessor in many places with a type-safe, scope-aware variation.[2] This guideline was first proposed back in the C++14 days but its scope could be reasonably expanded to "use `constexpr` wherever possible" or even "use `constexpr` by default."

Default C++

C++ has something of a reputation for getting its defaults wrong. For example, nonstatic member functions are mutable by default, when it would be safer to make them `const` instead. Changing state requires more thinking, reasoning, and apprehension than inspecting state, so making a nonstatic member function mutable should be an active choice: the engineer should be thinking, "I have chosen to make this a mutable function, and I'm going to signal that." As the standard stands, it is possible for a nonstatic member function to behave as if it were `const`-qualified, but if the engineer fails to apply the qualification that information is not passed to the client. Not allowing things to be changed by default is safer than allowing them to be changed.

This can be extended to types. An instance of a type is mutable by default. Only if the type is `const`-qualified does an instance of it become immutable. Again, it is safer to prevent things from being changed without explicit permission than it is to allow them to be freely changed. An object can behave as if it were `const` without being qualified, when it would be clearer if everything were `const` unless otherwise specified.

The `[[no_discard]]` attribute is another candidate for default operation. It looks like this:

```
[[no_discard]] bool is_empty(std::string const& s)
{
  return s.size() == 0;
}
```

1. https://www.youtube.com/watch?v=3WGsN_Hp9QY

2. Gabriel Dos Reis and Bjarne Stroustrup: General Constant Expressions for System Programming Languages. SAC-2010. The 25th ACM Symposium on Applied Computing. March 2010.

When return values holding error codes are discarded, that is allowing errors to be ignored. The calling code should at least acknowledge that it is discarding the error. Similarly, consider pre-increment and post-increment. The pre-increment operation will increment the object in question and return it. The post-increment operation will take a copy of the object, increment the object, and return the copy. If post-increment is used and the returned copy is discarded, then storing the copy was wasted effort. Nor can the as-if rule come to your rescue here: unless the compiler knows that there is no observable difference between the two, for example in the case of a built-in type, it is not permitted to exchange the post-increment for a pre-increment. A `[[no_discard]]` attribute would signal that wasted code was being executed. Finally, `empty()` returns a bool and is regularly confused with `clear()`. A `[[no_discard]]` attribute would signal that the return value from a function that does nothing to the object was being ignored, rendering the call redundant.

However, in the face of this criticism, one needs to think about the history of C++. It was developed on top of C, and the decision was made to ensure that C programs would still compile using a C++ compiler. If these defaults had been swapped round, all C programs would have failed. The success of C++ is due in large part to its compatibility with existing code. It is easy to introduce a new language. For some engineers it is a hobby pursuit. Getting other engineers to use it is very hard, and demanding a complete rewrite of existing code is a very high price to pay.

Using `constexpr`

As you can see from the examples, the `constexpr` keyword is simple to use. Simply decorate your function with the `constexpr` keyword and you are good to go. However, consider this function:

```
int read_number_from_stdin()
{
  int val;
  cin >> val;  // What could this possibly yield at compile time?
  return val;
}
```

Clearly, this makes no sense as a `constexpr` function since part of its evaluation can only take place at runtime: interaction with the user.

You might be asking yourself, "Why isn't the entire standard library simply `constexpr` now?"

There are two main reasons. First, the standard library is not entirely amenable to `constexpr` decoration. For example, file stream access is dependent upon the client file system, and decorating std::fopen as constexpr would be meaningless in most situations, just as a function collecting input from stdin would be. Functions like std::uninitialized_copy also suffer from the same problem. What does uninitialized memory mean in a constexpr context?

Second, in some cases it has yet to be proposed. To put forward a paper titled "Make the standard library constexpr" would require an enormous amount of wording changes to the standard. C++20 devotes 1,161 of its 1,840 pages to the standard library. Such a paper would be shot down before it reached serious consideration during committee time. Additionally, just finding out which functions could be constexpr is a mammoth task. Any function called by a constexpr function must be constexpr as well, which means you would end up chasing down constexpr until you encounter a leaf function or a function that cannot be constexpr and working your way back to where you started from. Building that tree is not a pleasant task. When const first started becoming a serious programming tool, it would not be unusual to chase const through your call graph and hit functions that could not be const. Once you start down this road, you cannot stop, because const and constexpr are both viral, spreading through all they touch, which is both their beauty and their cost.

However, there are still remaining candidate containers that could indeed be constexpr. It is entirely feasible for you to write your own constexpr map and unordered_map with identical APIs to std::map and std::unordered_map. With std::vector, std::string, and a constexpr map, ordered or unordered, you can write some very useful compile-time parsers that can be used to configure your builds.

Let's look at a simpler example. We want to calculate sin x using the Taylor series, which looks like this:

$$\sin x = \sum_{n=0}^{\infty} (-1)^n \frac{x^{2n+1}}{(2n+1)!}$$

The only functions we need to achieve this are a power function and a factorial function. Summing the terms will complete the job.

We already have a factorial function. Let's add a power function:

```
constexpr double pow(double t, unsigned int power) {
  if (power == 0) return 1.0;
  return t * pow(t, power - 1);
}
```

We can now add a sin function:

```
constexpr double sin(double theta, int term_count) {
  auto result = 0.0;
```

```
    while (term_count >= 0) {
      auto sign = pow(-1, (term_count));
      auto numerator = pow(theta, (2 * term_count) + 1);
      auto denominator = factorial((2 * term_count) + 1);
      result += (sign * numerator) / denominator;
      --term_count;
    }
    return result;
}
```

The term_count value is a precision request. Each successive term is smaller than the last, and eventually the contribution will be negligible. There is another reason for introducing this parameter, which we will come to in a moment. We can complete the example with a main function:

```
#include <numbers>

int main()
{
  return sin(std::numbers::pi / 4.0, 5) * 10000;
}
```

For exposition, we are invoking the function and then turning it into an integer so that it can be returned.

If you look at this on the Compiler Explorer page for this chapter, you will see two lines of assembly:

```
mov eax,7071
ret
```

sin $\pi/4$ in radians is $1/\sqrt{2}$, which is about 0.7071, so we can be assured of the correctness of this function. If you are interested in the accuracy of the function, you can try increasing the scalar multiplier to 1 million, or you can try increasing the term count.

Increasing the term count is where things get interesting. At the time of writing, using gcc trunk, if you increase the term count to 6, then code is generated for the pow function. The pow function is no longer amenable to compile-time evaluation and calculation is deferred to execution time. The pow function must calculate $\pi/4$ raised to the thirteenth power, which seems to be the point at which the compiler decides that we are asking too much of it. Increase the term count to 8 and code is generated for the factorial function as well.

Another useful feature of constexpr is that it forbids undefined behavior and side effects in the function it qualifies. For example, consider this dangerous piece of code:

```
int get_element(const int *p) {
  return *(p + 12);
}

int main() {
  int arr[10]{};
  int x = get_element(arr);
}
```

The problem is quite clear in this case: the function get_element reads the twelfth element of the array while the array being passed only has 10 elements. This is undefined behavior. Consider what happens when you make everything constexpr (apart from main(), which cannot be constexpr):

```
constexpr int get_element(const int *p) {
  return *(p + 12);
}

int main() {
  constexpr int a[10]{};
  constexpr int x = get_element(a);
  return x;
}
```

This yields the following compiler error:

```
example.cpp
<source>(8):
  error C2131: expression did not evaluate to a constant
<source>(2):
  note: failure was caused by out of range index 12;
        allowed range is 0 <= index < 10
Compiler returned: 2
```

Forbidding undefined behavior in constexpr functions highlights places where you are taking advantage of it. You should make this choice consciously and decide whether exploiting undefined behavior is a price you want to pay. Take care when using constexpr in this way, though. The following code compiles quite happily:

```
constexpr int get_element(const int *p) {
  return *(p + 12);
```

```
}

int main() {
  constexpr int a[10]{};
  return get_element(a);
}
```

This is worth experimenting with at the Compiler Explorer page for this chapter.

Forbidding side effects in `constexpr` functions means that they become pure functions. They are easier to test and the results can be cached, but best of all they can be invoked concurrently without synchronization. This is an excellent burden to be relieved of.

This is the point at which we should talk about `consteval`. First, though, we are going to talk about inline.

inline

The `inline` keyword is an old, old keyword. It predates C. In C++ the specifier can be applied to a function or an object. It signifies that the definition can be found in the translation unit. It also tells the compiler that the function is a suitable candidate for inline substitution rather than a function call. This makes it a target for optimization: why pay the price of a function call when you can simply substitute the code instead?

There are in fact several reasons why you might not want to do that.

When a function is called, some CPU context must be preserved so that the calling function can continue upon return. Register values are usually put on the stack, and then restored after the function finishes executing. Choices of calling convention dictate whether this is done by the caller or the callee. The execution of these instructions for context preservation incurs a cost in program size and execution speed. Ideally, an inline substitution will be cheaper than all this bookkeeping. However, if the function being substituted is particularly large, it may make the program bigger. Nonetheless, you may want the inline substitution to take place because it will yield faster code: you are exchanging a few bytes of executable size for the performance gain of not preserving registers and jumping somewhere else.

In the last century that was a quite reasonable thing to assess. However, now we have instruction caches. If we make a substitution, we are in danger of filling up the instruction cache and forcing a cache miss. If we are in a loop and the inline function is only called occasionally, it may make more sense to keep it out of the loop. The compiler knows much more about the behavioral characteristics of the processor than you do, so this is a decision best left to the compiler. In addition, the as-if rule allows the compiler to perform an inline substitution on any function that may improve performance. After all, the whole point of functions is that they are invisible and convenient chunks of code Somewhere Else. Their location is irrelevant. They could exist within the call site, or far away from it. This should lead to the realization that the inline keyword is largely redundant. It is a hint to the compiler that the function is a candidate for substitution, but it is not a requirement, nor should it be. In fact, the only place that it might need to be used is if the function it specifies is likely to appear in more than one translation unit. This is likely to be the case if it is defined in a header file.

Some implementations offer a custom specifier with a name like `__forceinline`; this means "This is my decision. I am perfectly aware that I am potentially shooting myself in the foot. I believe I have additional knowledge that you, the compiler, do not." Typically, if the function cannot be inlined, the compiler will emit an error and tell you that you are, in fact, quite mistaken.

The important thing to remember is that `inline` is a hint, and `__forceinline`, if offered by the implementation, is a command.

consteval

As you may have seen from experimenting with the `constexpr sin` function, you can place sufficient stress on the compiler for it to give up and defer calculation to runtime. Just as `inline` is a hint to the compiler to substitute the entire function body for a call to the specified function, so is `constexpr` a hint for the compiler to attempt compile-time computation. It is not a requirement, and if it fails it will do so silently. The keyword means only that it *can* be evaluated at compile time, not that it *must*. If you pass values that can only be known at runtime, then it will simply postpone evaluation to runtime.

There are reasons why you may not want this to happen. You may have something that can spiral out of control under certain circumstances; for example an iterative function system that never stabilizes. It would be safer to be able to rely on the compiler to only invoke the function when it can do so safely.

This is the purpose of `consteval`. It specifies that a function is an immediate function, which means that every call to the function must produce a value computable at compile time. This is the analog to `__forceinline`, in that the compiler will emit an error if the specified function cannot produce such a value.

`consteval` should be handled with care. It is not a guarantee to the user that the expression will be evaluated at compile time. It is a requirement placed upon the user that they must constrain their inputs such that they do not burn the compiler. This is not at all portable, nor is it necessarily obvious to the user what the actual manifestation of these constraints is likely to be. If you experimented broadly with the `sin` function in Compiler Explorer, you may have seen that some implementations never compute a result at compile time. Marking those functions as `consteval` would lead to a world of pain for your users. You might decide to start by marking your functions as constexpr; then, should you observe run-time evaluation that you would rather happen at compile time, you can modify that to consteval.

constinit

We shall complete this chapter with the constinit keyword. To do this, we need to be clear about zero initialization and constant initialization. Initialization is, sadly, a huge topic worth a book on its own, so we shall only focus on these two aspects of C++ initialization.

Zero initialization is a fine example of good naming. It means setting the initial value of an object to zero. There is a small problem with C++ in that there is no special syntax for zero initialization. It occurs in a variety of situations, for example:

```
static int j;
```

Ordinarily, if you declare an object without initializing it, then you have no guarantee of its value unless there is a default constructor. Since int has no constructor, you might expect j to be random bits. However, there is a special exception for objects of static duration: they are zero-initialized as part of static initialization, before main() is called. Particularly, the value is zero explicitly converted to the type.

If the object is of a class type, then all base classes and nonstatic data members are zero-initialized. The constructors are ignored, which is worth bearing in mind. Some implementations provide default initialization of unspecified objects as a command-line switch. This is useful for debugging because the default value is normally an unusual bit pattern, so uninitialized objects are easy to spot via memory inspection.

Constant initialization sets the initial value of static variables to a compile-time constant. If the type has a constexpr constructor and all the arguments are constant expressions, then the variable is constant-initialized. If the type does not have a constructor, or it is value-initialized, or the initializer is a constant expression, then the variable is also constant-initialized. For example:

```
const int j = 10;
```

is constant-initialized if it is declared at file scope and thus has static duration. Constant initialization takes place prior to static initialization. In practice, it takes place at compile time.

The constinit keyword asserts that an object has static initialization, causing compilation to fail if it does not. For example:

```
constinit const int j = 10;
```

This is a somewhat redundant use since that expression can never fail this assertion. A more interesting example would be:

```
// definition.h
constexpr int sample_size() {
  // function definition
}

// client.cpp
constinit const int sample_total = sample_size() * 1350;
```

This expression will emit an error if the author of `sample_size()` changes the function in such a way that it can no longer be computed at compile time. This is a valuable feature. Objects marked as `constinit` are evaluated at compile time, not at runtime. This gives us a mitigation for the static initialization order fiasco.

Summary

Using the `const` prefixed keywords gives you additional opportunities to offer computation at compile time. Prefer compile-time computation to run-time computation: it is cheaper for the client.

- Use `constexpr` to hint to the compiler that a function is amenable to compile-time computation and to detect some undefined behavior.
- Use `consteval` to insist to the compiler that a function is amenable to compile-time computation on pain of error.
- Use `constinit` to assert that an object is initialized at compile time.

Chapter 4.5

T.1: Use templates to raise the level of abstraction of code

Story time

In 2012 I facilitated a code review with a colleague, let's call her Beth, which I set aside as a useful example of the field. The purpose of the function was to take a selection of icons arranged in a row along the bottom of the screen and spin through them by an arbitrary amount. We had just migrated to C++11.

After half an hour of hacking away at it, the function looked like this, having lost about a dozen spurious lines of code:

```
UIComponent* spin_cards(UIComponent* first,
                        UIComponent* n_first,
                        UIComponent* last) {
  if (first == n_first) return last;
  if (n_first == last) return first;
  UIComponent* write = first;
  UIComponent* next_read = first;
  UIComponent* read = n_first;
  while (read != last) {
    if (write == next_read) {
      next_read = read;
    }
    std::iter_swap(write++, read++);
  }
  spin_cards(write, next_read, last);
  return write;
}
```

There were three questions I posed to Beth at this point. The first was, "Have you thought about using auto for write, next_read, and read?" She rolled her eyes and asked, "Why?" We then had a conversation about programming with interfaces rather than types. Eventually I asked her to humor me and make the change:

```
UIComponent* spin_cards(UIComponent* first,
                        UIComponent* n_first,
                        UIComponent* last) {
  if (first == n_first) return last;
  if (n_first == last) return first;
  auto write = first;
  auto next_read = first;
  auto read = n_first;
  while (read != last) {
    if (write == next_read) {
      next_read = read;
    }
    std::iter_swap(write++, read++);
  }
  spin_cards(write, next_read, last);
  return write;
}
```

Then I asked, "What part of the UIComponent interface are you using in this function?" and she regarded me carefully. Along the way we had replaced a manual swap with std::swap, and then replaced that with std::iter_swap. I was waiting for the penny to drop, and for Beth to realize that UIComponent was nothing more than a forward iterator, but I had to lead her to that point. After some umming and ahhing, she replied, "Actually, I could template this over a forward iterator. All I'm doing is assigning, comparing, dereferencing, and writing." Thirty seconds later we had:

```
template <typename T>
T* spin_cards(T* first, T* n_first, T* last) {
  if (first == n_first) return last;
  if (n_first == last) return first;
  auto write = first;
  auto next_read = first;
  auto read = n_first;
  while (read != last) {
    if (write == next_read) {
      next_read = read;
    }
    std::iter_swap(write++, read++);
  }
  spin_cards(write, next_read, last);
```

```
  return write;
}
```

I suggested she choose a less specific and more descriptive name. While she reflected on the difficulty of naming, I asked her how long it had taken her to write and test the function. "About two hours," she replied. "There were some stupid edge cases that kept biting me."

"Mmm," I said. "Perhaps you could call this function `rotate`." She looked at me incredulously and somewhat crestfallen as she realized that the brief called for an application of `std::rotate`. We compared our final incantation with the implementation's definition, and found they were very, very similar. You can of course find a description of `std::rotate` at https://en.cppreference.com/w/cpp/algorithm/rotate.

Raising the level of abstraction

My favorite part of engineering is eliminating code. Fewer lines of code lead to a smaller cognitive burden and easier apprehension of the codebase. The aim of the engineer should be to express the solution domain as simply and easily as possible. Paying engineers "by the line" is a surefire way to destroy your project.

Consider the difference between the input and output of a compiler. You will typically pass in a translation unit with hundreds of lines of code and be presented with thousands of assembly instructions wrapped up in an object file. Those assembly instructions each trigger activity of greater complexity on the CPU. The assembly is more complex, more detailed than the C++ source code. The CPU activity is yet more complex than the assembly instructions. The entire effort of software engineering and language design is the reduction of complexity and detail.

When I was learning my trade in the 1980s, I was presented with the concept of high-level languages like Sinclair BASIC and BBC BASIC, and then low-level languages like Z80 assembly and 6502 assembly. The level in question is the level of abstraction. The distance between BASIC and assembly is significant. When I first started learning C, having absorbed BASIC and assembly, it was presented as a low-level language, although not as low level as assembly. I treated it like an assembly macro programming language. I could see which assembly instructions would be generated by which C constructs. I had the immediacy of assembly available to me, with the naming clarity of BASIC. I could name variables, like in BASIC, but I could easily infer how much memory they would take up. I could create control loop structures without having to fiddle about with the correct flag testing to decide whether to jump back or continue.

Fewer lines of code lead to a smaller cognitive burden and easier apprehension of the codebase. The aim of the engineer should be to express the solution domain as simply and easily as possible. Paying engineers "by the line" is a surefire way to destroy your project.

The complexity of assembly was ameliorated by nicer identifiers and clearer structure, both helping to hide that detail. C raised the level of abstraction.

When I first came across C++, it was like a macro programming language for C. Some of the fiddly things I had been doing, like wrapping up `malloc` and `init` into a single function, were being done for me by the C++ compiler in the form of new keywords. C++ raised the level of abstraction.

In both cases, raising the level of abstraction did not come at a measurable performance cost in the general case. The compilers were not perfect, and on several occasions, I was left open-mouthed at the seeming idiocy of the compiler writer, but fortunately I could resort to a truly nonportable solution and drop back down to a lower level of abstraction by inserting hand-rolled artisanal assembly language instructions. The last time I remember outperforming the compiler was in about 1991. Since then, I have been able to rely on it to do a better job than me.

Importantly, if I were to go back to hand-rolling assembly, I would make a much worse job of it, because the complexity of CPUs has increased profoundly. When I was writing assembly, there was one core, and there were no caches and therefore no data prefetching nor branch prediction. The decision to use contiguous data structures rather than node-based data structures was a meaningful one. Memory read/write operations took about the same time as an instruction execution cycle, so big-O notation meant something.

Raising the level of abstraction improves portability. My beautifully cunning assembly language would only work on one processor family. In the early 1980s that was a significant problem because the two competing home computers that were the leading game platforms ran on Z80 and 6502 processors. By the mid-1980s matters were simplified by the 68000 processor being chosen for both the Atari ST and the Commodore Amiga, as well as the early Apple Macs.

The purpose of an API is to reduce complexity by hiding details behind an interface, raising the level of abstraction. The purpose of language is to hide the complexity of individual comprehension of meaning behind corresponding linguistic tokens. Raising the level of abstraction is fundamental to the role of software engineer.

Function templates and abstraction

I hope I have convinced you of the importance of raising the level of abstraction as part of the practice of programming. Let's look at some examples.

Reviewing the opening story, you can see that we started with a solution targeting a specific problem, that of rotating the order of a set of icons. During the code review, there was an important moment when we introduced `std::swap`. The code had looked like this:

```
UIComponent* spin_cards(UIComponent* first,
                        UIComponent* n_first,
                        UIComponent* last) {
  if (first == n_first) return last;
  if (n_first == last) return first;
  UIComponent* write = first;
  UIComponent* next_read = first;
  UIComponent* read = n_first;
  while (read != last) {
    if (write == next_read) {
      next_read = read;
    }
    UIComponent tmp = *write;
    *write++ = *read;
    *read++ = tmp;
  }
  spin_cards(write, next_read, last);
  return write;
}
```

You can see the manual swap at the end of the `while` loop. I asked Beth the question, "Did you choose not to use `std::swap`?" and she replied, "I didn't see the point. `UIComponent` is a trivial object, swapping it is trivial, why call a function?"

My immediate response was "declaration of intent." There is a Core Guideline for this, P.3: "Express intent." Yes, it is obvious what was going on; we have all manually written a swap by assigning to a temporary and so on. By replacing that with a single word, `swap`, we make it even clearer at no extra cost. The function call will be substituted for the implementation by even the simplest of compilers. Additionally, if `UIComponent` stops being a trivial object and merits its own specialization of `swap`, the code benefits from that change in detail. Eliminating that little piece of detail and replacing it with a function template reduced complexity, raised the level of abstraction, and made the code more expressive. It also added some future-proofing.

Of course, we already have a large source of useful function templates in the standard library, particularly those in the `<algorithm>` header. There is a very high chance that if you find yourself writing a loop, you will be able to replace that loop with one of the function templates defined in this header. Indeed, if you cannot do that, perhaps you have found a new algorithm. You should share it with the world.

We really are quite serious.

There are likely to be some omissions from the `<algorithm>` header. For example, C++20 saw the standardization of `std::shift_left` and `std::shift_right`. This shifts elements in a range, and it was something I found myself doing quite a lot. It never occurred to me that plenty of other people might be doing something so fundamental. When I saw the paper come before the committee, I felt quite foolish: there was a lightbulb moment as I realized how much I would use this function.

Some of the function templates in the `<algorithm>` header make use of other functions from the same header. For example, `std::minmax` will make use of `std::min` and `std::max`. Every opportunity is taken to raise the level of abstraction, resulting in reuse of code and thus as few new lines of code as possible.

Once you start replacing your loops with existing function templates, your code becomes markedly more expressive and less prone to bugs. If you are unwittingly trying to write `std::find_if`, then replacing your attempt with a tested and debugged version, written by people with a greater understanding of the compilation environment than you, is surely the right thing to do. Of course, you first must realize that you are indeed attempting to rewrite one of the `<algorithm>` functions before you can do that. The best indicator of that is the use of a loop.

There are a lot of algorithms. Look at this function:

```
bool all_matching(std::vector<int> const& v, int i) {
  for (auto it = std::begin(v); it != std::end(v); ++it){
    if (*it != i) {
      return false;
    }
  }
  return true;
}
```

It's a simple function to check whether or not all the items in a vector of `int`s have the same value. It's a rather useful function, so useful in fact that a more general version of it already exists in the `<algorithm>` header:

```
template< class InputIt, class UnaryPredicate >
constexpr bool all_of( InputIt first, InputIt last,
                       UnaryPredicate p );
```

or, if you want to be dizzyingly modern and use ranges:

```
template< ranges::input_range R, class Proj = std::identity,
          std::indirect_unary_predicate<
             std::projected<ranges::iterator_t<R>,Proj>> Pred >
constexpr bool all_of( R&& r, Pred pred, Proj proj = {} );
```

The name `all_of` is more familiar to the programming community than `all_matching`. It is also more abstract. Do not reinvent this particular wheel, and watch out for raw loops. I am not the first person to say this: Sean Parent gave a legendary talk in 2013 called Code Seasoning.[1]

Particularly, consider Core Guideline T.2: "Use templates to express algorithms that apply to many argument types." The standard algorithms are immaculate examples of this approach.

Class templates and abstraction

I rejoice when I find an abstraction. It means that I have isolated part of the problem domain and that I am in a position to name it. If I am particularly successful it will be a name that crops up in the codebase in all sorts of places.

In addition to function templates, the standard library contains some useful class templates. There are rather fewer of these than there are function templates. The most widely used are probably `std::vector`, `std::string`, and `std::unordered_map`. There are a few proposals in the pipeline that seek to add additional containers, but these are offered rather less frequently than function templates.

In any programming course you should be offered a module on data structures and algorithms. This is the bread and butter of programming. By identifying the broad range of data structures and algorithms in the vocabulary of programmers, you can learn when to create a novel structure or adapt or simply use an existing one. This is a great power, only available to you because you have names for things.

The most cursory of glances through the standard library will reveal that a lot of it is delivered as class and function templates. This is because templates allow you to name things without worrying about types. You may dislike the name "vector," I certainly do, but it contains no information about what it might contain. It is not relevant to the container. It just contains things in a particular way, guaranteeing that they will be contained contiguously in memory.

1. https://channel9.msdn.com/Events/GoingNative/2013/Cpp-Seasoning

Following the conventions of the standard library containers allows you to create data structures that both are appropriate for your solution domain and will play nicely with the existing algorithms. Define iterators as part of your container so that you will be able to delegate searching and sorting to the standard library, or offer specializations optimized for your data structure. Define the appropriate member types in the same way that `std::vector` and `std::unordered_map` do. Provide a `std::swap` specialization and, from C++20, a three-way comparison operator. This makes your containers easier to reuse and understand. It allows your clients to think about how their data is stored, rather than how to correctly operate the container, or what the details about the type of data being stored are.

This independence from types lets your code describe what it is doing rather than what it is doing it with. This support is also offered by the `auto` keyword. This removes unnecessary implementation detail from your reading of the code. In fact, the full definition of `std::string` is

```
namespace std {
  template<
    class CharT,
    class Traits = std::char_traits<CharT>,
    class Allocator = std::allocator<CharT>
  > class basic_string;
  using string = basic_string<char>;
}
```

That is quite a lot of text to hold in your head when all that you are interested in is `std::string`. `std::char_traits` is not something that you should ever have to write or worry about. Writing allocators is similarly not something you want to become involved with unless you are working closer to the metal than most people, so `std::allocator` will ordinarily be entirely sufficient.

The widespread use of `std::string` also addresses one of the reasons listed in the Core Guidelines for using templates to raise the level of abstraction of code: reuse. I rejoice when I find an abstraction. It means that I have isolated part of the problem domain and that I am in a position to name it. If I am particularly successful it will be a name that crops up in the codebase in all sorts of places.

`std::string` is a great name. There are all sorts of other things it could have been called. For example, the using declarations might have been skipped by the standardization committee, and we would be burdened with saying `std::basic_string<char>` and then applying our own using declarations, creating an alphabet soup of identical types such as `char_string`, `ch_string`, `string_char`, `string_c`, and so on. String is a widely used concept across many languages to indicate a collection of characters for representing text. There are even puns on the name available. A rope, or cord, is a data structure composed of smaller strings that is used to manipulate very long strings such as articles or books. If you have ever written a text editor you will probably have used a rope to enable rapid insertion and deletion.

`std::string` is a standout success story when it comes to naming in the standard. Sadly, there are other places where we have fallen short.

Naming is hard

It is worth talking about why I dislike the name "vector" and how raising the level of abstraction of your code with a template is a two-step process.

I come from a mathematical background, taking a mathematics degree from Sussex University. My strongest field was abstract algebra. I remember the curriculum for my first term, consisting of calculus, analysis, linear algebra, and introduction to philosophy (it was a slightly unusual British university for its time). Linear algebra was taught by Professor Martin Dunwoody, and every lecture was an utter pleasure as the scales fell away from my eyes about how everything works.

The fundamental object of linear algebra is the vector. This is an n-tuple of values with a set of arithmetic operations: addition, scalar multiplication, and vector multiplication, known as the inner product. These arithmetic operations allow you to do all sorts of things: solve simultaneous equations, model Cartesian geometry—in fact, most of modern mathematics derives from linear algebra.

This is a rather different thing from `std::vector`. This is a dynamic array of anything at all, rather than a fixed array of arithmetic values. There are no operators defined upon it, so you cannot add or multiply them. In fact, the only similarity between a `std::vector` and a vector is the containment of several things. This puts the language in an odd place, by misnaming one of the most widely used containers.

In my day job I simulate fictional worlds using linear algebra to model the physical reality of them. To be fair, I can simply define my own vector type. For example, in my codebase `gdg::vector_3f` is a vector of three floats, which is used for locating something in three-dimensional space, as well as modeling its velocity and acceleration. However, when you see `std::vector` in a codebase it doesn't mean what any mathematician might think it means, and although we have become so used to that as to be blind to it, it is a bump in the road for those coming to C++ from mathematics or other languages. Perhaps `dynarray` would have been a better name. Forming an abstraction is a two-step process. First, you identify the abstraction by examining its API, its inputs and outputs, and its relationship to your problem domain. Then you give it a name. Check the literature for prior art and be mindful of the responsibility you bear and consequences you may unleash when you name something.

Summary

In summary:

- Function and class templates hide detail, and thus complexity, behind meaningful names.
- Many function templates in the standard library can replace loops.
- Many algorithms in the standard library can inform existing data structures.
- Expressing abstractions as class templates enables wider reuse, particularly when well named.

Chapter 4.6

T.10: Specify concepts for all template arguments

How did we get here?

Concepts are one of the big-ticket items of C++20. They have taken a long, long time to make their way into the standard. The first attempt at standardizing them started after C++98 and a version of concepts nearly made it into C++11, or C++0x as it was being called at the time. However, concepts were withdrawn from the working draft at the eleventh hour and put into a Technical Specification (TS). Technical Specifications are used to gather implementation experience. The Concepts TS was published at the end of 2015 allowing compiler implementers to kick the tires and check the roadworthiness of the feature.

C++17 hit feature freeze during 2016, at which point concepts were insufficiently proven for safe addition to the language. However, at the first committee meeting of the C++20 delivery cycle, in Toronto in the summer of 2017, motion 11, "Move to apply the changes in P0734 (Wording Paper, C++ extensions for Concepts) to the C++ working paper," was passed to joyous applause.

As an aside, this was my first committee meeting. I had attended study group meetings before, and national body meetings, but this was the first time I had put myself in the same room as the people who shape the standard. Concepts were not the only thing to make significant advance. Motion 12 advanced Modules for balloting among the national bodies, motion 13 advanced the Coroutines TS and motion 22 appointed an editing committee, including me, to verify the correctness of the Ranges TS. Clearly C++20 was going to be a great leap forward. This was not what I was expecting for my first visit, but history is made by those who turn up. Should you ever find yourself at your first committee meeting, come and find me and then volunteer for everything.

Returning to concepts, let's consider the problem they are trying to solve by examining the following function template:

```
template <typename T>
T const& lesser(T const& t1, T const& t2) {
  return t1 < t2 ? t1 : t2;
}
```

With any luck, you have never written this code before and always used `std::min` from the `<algorithm>` header. We have used the name `lesser` since `min` is enormously overloaded in every implementation.

The tricky part is that this function can only be invoked with certain types: if you pass a couple of `std::unordered_map<string, string>` references to this function, the compiler will tell you in no uncertain terms that this is not going to fly. There is no match for `operator<` with these operand types. The error output is a little verbose, but we can see what is going on. Here is an edited sample of some error output from GCC:

```
<source>: In instantiation of 'const T& lesser(const T&, const T&)
          [with T = std::unordered_map<int, int>]':
<source>:14:31:   required from here
<source>:6:15: error: no match for 'operator<' (operand types are
'const std::unordered_map<int, int>' and 'const std::unordered_map<int, int>')
    6 |     return t1 < t2 ?t1 : t2;
      |            ~~~^~~~
In file included from …:
<filename>:1149:5: note: candidate:
  'template<class _IteratorL, class _IteratorR, class _Container>
    bool __gnu_cxx::operator<(
      const __gnu_cxx::__normal_iterator<_IteratorL, _Container>&,
      const __gnu_cxx::__normal_iterator<_IteratorR, _Container>&)'
 1149 |     operator<(const __normal_iterator<_IteratorL, _Container>& __lhs,
      |     ^~~~~~~~
```

This is saying that while trying to instantiate the function template `lesser`, using `std::unordered_map<int, int>` as the template parameter, the compiler could see no available `operator<`. Then it lists all the candidate operators (I stopped at one, but when I tried this in Compiler Explorer it listed quite a lot of candidates) to demonstrate that there was nothing available.

This simple error, in this four-line function, produced 122 lines of error output. As you scale up to more likely functions, this error output increases considerably, and it becomes ever harder for you to identify what the root cause of the problem is. If there is a hefty call stack of function templates between your first instantiation and the error, you may spend quite a while spelunking through the output.

This problem has always been with us, but there are ways of mitigating it. While it is infeasible to overload your function for every conceivable type, you could overload for a set of types using `std::enable_if`. You have to really hate yourself and your coworkers to do this, but it looks like this:

```
template <typename T,
          std::enable_if_t<std::is_arithmetic<T>::value, bool> = true>
T const& lesser(T const& t1, T const& t2);
```

The name `std::is_arithmetic` lives in the `<type_traits>` header, along with a selection of other traits like `std::is_const` and `std::is_trivially_constructible`. This overload will be selected for any arithmetic type (integral or floating point). This is not immediately apparent unless you are familiar with this idiom. I consider this "expert-level" programming; when I am teaching, I leave this until my students are completely familiar with default template parameters and the principle of Substitution Failure Is Not An Error, or SFINAE.

We won't go into detail about this technique here. We can do better now.

Constraining your parameters

The problem with the `std::enable_if` idiom is that it is a verbose, library-level way of constraining your function. The constraint is camouflaged inside a soup of punctuation that looks like transmission line noise. The important part of the constraint is the name `std::is_arithmetic`. The rest is simply scaffolding to overcome the shortcomings of the language.

What you really want to be able to say is something like

```
template <typename std::is_arithmetic T>
T const& lesser(T const& t1, T const& t2);
```

This syntax is clearer. The constraint is right next to the type. Unfortunately, it is not valid C++. It is ambiguous to parse and becomes cluttered if there is more than one constraint to apply. Let's try another version:

```
template <typename T>
where std::is_arithmetic<T>::value
T const& lesser(T const& t1, T const& t2);
```

The constraint gets its own line between the template introduction and the function name. Neither is this valid C++: the keyword `where` is rather too reminiscent of SQL, so we substitute `requires`, like this:

```
template <typename T>
requires std::is_arithmetic_v<T>
T const& lesser(T const& t1, T const& t2);
```

This is now valid C++20. If we want something a little more constrained, we can simply add constraints to the `requires` clause, like this:

```
template <typename T>
requires std::is_trivially_constructible_v<T>
and std::is_nothrow_move_constructible_v<T>
T f1(T t1, T t2);
```

You might pause at the use of the word "and" in that example. If it's a logical conjunction, wouldn't `&&` be more appropriate?

It's a matter of taste and style. You can use both. If you want to use punctuation rather than "and" you are entirely able so to do. However, I find unambiguous English clearer than symbols.

This syntax still looks quite busy. The template introduction is required to highlight that the declaration is a function template, but the presence of constraints also implies that the declaration is a function template. Do we really need both? Can't we have a syntax like:

```
T f2(std::is_arithmetic<T> t1, std::is_arithmetic<T> t2);
```

That looks to me like a function that takes a type that must be arithmetic. Unfortunately, again we have a parsing problem. The first instance of `T` looks like a definition, not a return type. It comes out of nowhere, but we can replace it with `auto` since this is a function template and we can safely assume the definition is visible and implies the return type. The subsequent uses of `T` also pose a problem. How do we signify that we are passing a constrained type?

C++14 introduced the notion of generic lambda expressions. Rather than specify a type for each parameter, you could specify `auto` instead and let the compiler infer the type. We can use the same form here:

```
auto f3(std::equality_comparable auto t1, std::equality_comparable auto t2);
```

There is a subtle change here: there is no longer a requirement that `t1` and `t2` are of the same type, nor that either type matches the return type, as with `f1`. The only constraint is that they both satisfy `std::equality_comparable`. If they must both be of the same type, you can advertise the type of `t2` as `decltype(t1)`:

```
auto f3(std::equality_comparable auto t1, decltype(t1) t2);
```

It is a little ungainly; however, if your function only takes one parameter, then this use of `auto` becomes a much more attractive spelling.

You will also notice that we are no longer passing `std::is_arithmetic`, but `std::equality_comparable` instead. Why is that? The answer is that `std::is_arithmetic` is a class template, while `std::equality_comparable` is a concept. This syntax is only available to concepts. We shall see how to satisfy this shortly.

This syntax gives the user more information in much less space. They can read the function signature and see that it is a function template which is constrained on equality-comparable types. Moreover, if they try and call the function using arguments that are not equality comparable, the compiler can say, quite clearly, that the supplied arguments are not equality comparable, as required by the declaration.

Unfortunately, if you want to add additional constraints to your parameters, this syntax will fail you. It would look like this:

```
auto f4(std::copyable and std::default_initializable auto t);
```

The presence of the `auto` is what signifies that a constraint is being specified. The first constraint is ambiguous. The way to solve this is by defining your own concept:

```
template <typename T>
concept cdi = std::copyable <T>
and std::default_initializable <T>;

auto f4(cdi auto t);
```

Of course, `cdi` is a dreadful name. We may have mentioned this already, but naming is hard. Concepts are particularly ticklish. A name like `is_copyable_and_default_initializable` is a poor name because it simply moves the problem somewhere else. What does that actually mean?

In this case, we know perfectly well what it means: something that is copyable and default initializable is semiregular. This is a well-known part of the taxonomy of types, and the standard library provides this concept along with a selection of others in the `<concepts>` header. You can find out a little about type taxonomy at Rainer Grimm's blog.[1]

The `<concepts>` header is worth examining because it shows you how concepts build on one another. The concept `std::semiregular` is composed from the concepts `std::copyable` and `std::default_initializable`. The concept `std::copyable` is composed from `std::copy_constructible`, `std::movable`, and `std::assignable_from`.

It is important to get a grasp of the taxonomy of types, to understand, for example, the difference between regular and semiregular. These terms were introduced

1. https://www.modernescpp.com/index.php/c-20-define-the-concept-regular-and-semiregular

by Alex Stepanov, the prime mover behind the Standard Template Library, and he discusses them in his book *Elements of Programming*.[2]

How to abstract your concepts

What we have here is a problem of abstraction. The name `is_copyable_and_default_initializable` simply restated the question, "What should I call this concept?" That is not abstraction. Raising the level of abstraction means traversing the taxonomy of types and identifying what the name of the thing is that is formed from the intersection of these concepts.

This is a fundamental part of abstraction. Earlier, in Chapter 2.1, "P.11: Encapsulate messy constructs, rather than spreading through the code" we described the difference between encapsulation, data hiding, and abstraction. Naming a concept after the pieces that make it up is merely encapsulation, it is not abstraction. It is not a scalable naming method either. You should expect to compose concepts in the same way that those defined in the `<concepts>` header are composed. This mechanism of composition of concepts will reveal the level of abstraction at which you are working and will reflect how you have factored your solution domain.

When writing function templates, you are attempting to encapsulate a generic algorithm. The concepts that are appropriate for your function are abstracted from that algorithm. This may mean that some concept names simply reflect the function name. Let's develop a trivial and naïve `sort` function:

```
template <typename InIt>
void sort(InIt begin, InIt end)
{
  while (begin != end)              // (1)
  {
    auto src = begin;               // (2)
    auto next = std::next(begin);   // (3)
    while (next != end)
    {
      if (*next < *src) {           // (4)
        std::iter_swap(src++, next++);
      }
    }
    --end;
  }
}
```

2. Stepanov, A, and McJones, P, 2009. *Elements of Programming*. Boston: Addison-Wesley.

This is a bubble sort, which takes quadratic time, so we wouldn't expect to see this in production code, but it serves our purposes. What do we know about the required capabilities of the template parameter?

At (1), there is an equality comparison between two instances of `InIt`. That means they need to be equality comparable. At (2), there is a copy construction, so they need to be copy constructible. At (3), we call `std::next` which means that they need to be incrementable. At (4), we require dereferencing and comparison of the iterated type. Let's see what we have available to us from the standard and try and name this set of type requirements.

As it turns out, we have an embarrassment of riches. The standard library has been sprinkled with concepts, and there is an entire header devoted to some fundamental concepts. For example, at point (1) we need to be able to compare the iterators. This means we need `std::equality_comparable` from the `<concepts>` header. At point (2) the assignment is supported with the concept `std::copy_constructible`, while (3) is supported by `std::incrementable`, which lives in the `<iterator>` header.

Things get interesting at (4). We need to dereference and compare the values indicated by the iterator, then we need to be able to dereference the iterator and swap the indicated values. This indirect behavior is supported by `std::indirectly_readable` from `<iterator>` and `std::swappable` from `<concepts>`. Comparing the values is slightly more work: we need to invoke a comparison predicate relating two operands. And again `<concepts>` comes to the rescue with `std::invocable`, which is required by `std::predicate`, which is required by `std::relation`, which is required by `std::strict_weak_order`.

This gives us a great starting point for our concept for the parameters of this function template.

```
template <typename R, typename T , typename U>
concept sort_concept = std::equality_comparable<T, U>
and std::copy_constructible<T>
and std::incrementable<T>
and std::indirectly_readable<T>
and std::swappable<T>
and std::strict_weak_order<R, T, U>;

void sort(sort_concept auto begin, sort_concept auto end);
```

We hope you agree that `sort_concept` is a terrible name.

How about `sortable`?

Performing that substitution, our function signature looks like:

```
void sort(sortable auto begin, sortable auto end);
```

We have eliminated the angle brackets, which is a relief to my eyes. We know it's a function template because of the name-auto-name parameter list. If we pass something that does not satisfy the sortable concept, the compiler will be able to say "this type is not sortable: it does not satisfy `std::swappable`," for example.

It should not surprise you to learn that `std::sortable` is already a concept, housed in the `<iterator>` header. You can go to the documentation for `std::sortable` at cppreference.com[3] and look up precisely how it is composed. My decomposition of `sortable` from the primitive `sort` function was a first step rather than a complete solution. You will find that there are rather more components to the `sortable` concept. For example, we omitted `std::assignable_from`. However, eventually someone would attempt to instantiate the function with a type that didn't satisfy that concept and compilation would fail. After deciphering the error message, you could improve the definition of `sortable` by adding that concept.

By specifying a concept for your template arguments, you reduce the punctuation and verbiage, and crystalize the meaning at the point where it is relevant. It highlights the level of abstraction at which you are operating. This makes your API clearer, more expressive, and more usable, with better documentation, better error messages, and more precise overloading.[4]

Factoring via concepts

Note that the concept name in the above example came from the algorithm, not the type. Concepts are found in algorithms, not types. This is further highlighted by the answer to the question, "How do I make domain-specific concepts?"

For example, if you have a bunch of handy function templates for doing interesting things with payroll, they may all require that an instance of the template type parameter can perform the appropriate payroll queries. The keyword `requires` is used to define fundamental concepts like this:

```
template <typename T>
concept payroll_queryable =
requires (T p) { p.query_payroll(); };

void current_salary(payroll_queryable auto employee);
```

3. https://en.cppreference.com/w/cpp/iterator/sortable

4. Bjarne Stroustrup: Thriving in a crowded and changing world: C++ 2006-2020. ACM/SIGPLAN History of Programming Languages conference, HOPL-IV. London. June 2020. https://www.stroustrup.com/hopl20main-p5-p-bfc9cd4--final.pdf

The concept is abstracted from a thing that can be done, not a property of the type. It describes a behavior, not a property. Beware of overconstraint, though. Consider if the function were implemented like this:

```
void current_salary(payroll_queryable auto employee)
{
  std::cout << "unimplemented\n";
}
```

This invocation would generate a compiler error:

```
current_salary("Beth");
```

Even though the function template implementation makes no use of the satisfactions offered by the concept, the compiler will still tell you the associated constraints are not satisfied.

Concepts are found in algorithms, not types.

As you implement your solution and find abstractions, you can describe them not just in terms of types and functions, but types and behaviors. The beauty of concepts is that they allow you to build a taxonomy for your solution domain. Just as you aren't limited by types defined by the standard, nor are you limited to the concepts defined by the standard. You can define your own concepts, just as you can define your own types, and use them to clarify the design of your library, conveying its full meaning and utility. The process of breaking down your solution domain into manageable pieces, of finding the factors, is greatly aided by having a mechanism by which you can identify behaviors as well as types.

The only thing harder than naming is taxonomy, which is finding the names of names. Concepts allow you to bring identifiers for the behaviors of your solution domain to the surface. Of course, you don't need to go mad and identify everything, nor should you. Concepts constrain template parameters, so unless your program consisted entirely of function templates you would not be able to make use of them all. This is reminiscent of the argument against object-oriented programming that speaks about modeling every last detail. However, for optimal clarity, specify constraints in the form of concepts for all your template arguments.

Summary

Whenever I start teaching about C++, one of the first things I say is that there are two things to worry about: state and execution. Behind all the syntactic noise of class declarations and access levels and function template specializations and `const` qualification, C++ source files define objects and functions. Linkers link objects and functions into a single binary. Operating systems bind together files and processes. CS courses teach you data structures and algorithms. Now there is another pairing to think about: types and concepts.

As you write function templates, examine what you are doing with your parameters and abstract your constraints from them. Identify the requirements and reuse a concept, or form a new one, to describe them at the point at which you take the argument.

Use concepts to advertise to your users what types can be passed, and to aid the compiler in providing appropriate diagnostic messages.

Use standard concepts where possible, reverting to domain-specific concepts where necessary. Standard concepts are interoperable and generate less friction when it comes to understanding what they imply.

The Core Guidelines has several things to say about concepts, including

- T.10: "Specify concepts for all template arguments"
- T.11: "Whenever possible use standard concepts"
- T.26: "Prefer to define concepts in terms of use-patterns rather than simple syntax"
- T.121: "Use template metaprogramming primarily to emulate concepts"

They are one of the big features of C++20 and the process of their development has already generated some insights into their correct use. As usage spreads through the C++ community, keep an eye on blogs and the Core Guidelines for updates.

Section 5

Write code well by default

Chapter 5.1

P.4: Ideally, a program should be statically type safe

Type safety is a security feature of C++

I rank type safety close to deterministic destruction among my favorite features of C++. Type safety tells different parts of your program what a bit pattern means. For example, here is the bit pattern for 1,729 as a 32-bit integer:

```
std::int32_t Ramanujan_i = 0b0000'0000'0000'0000'0000'0110'1100'0001;
```

Here is the bit pattern for 1,729 as a 32-bit unsigned integer:

```
std::uint32_t Ramanujan_u = 0b0000'0000'0000'0000'0000'0110'1100'0001;
```

As you can see, it is identical. However, consider the bit pattern for 1,729 as a `float`:

```
float Ramanujan_f = 0b0100'0100'1101'1000'0010'0000'0000'0000;
```

If this bit pattern were interpreted as a 32-bit integer, it would yield the value 1,155,014,656. Conversely, if `Ramanujan_i` were interpreted as a `float`, it would yield the value $2.423 * 10^{-42}$.

Other languages use what is known as duck typing. This starts with the premise that the programmer knows exactly what they are doing at all times. Given this fact, if they want to multiply a string by a color, they should be able to do that, and the interpreter will try its very best to satisfy that request, emitting an error at runtime if it fails. Compile-time errors are preferable to run-time errors since they do not require code coverage testing to expose them. Enforcing type safety eliminates an entire class of errors.

Enforcing type safety eliminates an entire class of errors.

The C++ standard goes to extraordinary lengths to help you write type-safe and yet readable code. If you call a function that takes a `long` argument and pass a `short` argument instead, the compiler knows how to generate code to accommodate that without generating errors. If you pass a `float` argument, the compiler will silently insert a run-time function call that will round the number to the nearest integer and convert the bit pattern to the appropriate integer representation. However, this is a time-consuming function. There was a point in my career where I would grep my compiler output for the vendor implementation of this function, `_ftol`, to ensure that it was never implicitly called.

Even better, function overloading enables you to create versions of functions for different types, and function templates allow you to specify algorithms independent of types. As we saw in Chapter 1.2, overload resolution is particularly nuanced, going so far as allowing certain conversions between types to ensure correct arguments are passed to function parameters. The `_ftol` function is an example of this behavior.

The `auto` keyword eliminates type concerns by inferring types from the code you are writing. If you write

```
auto Ramanujan = 1729;
```

the compiler will treat `Ramanujan` as an integer, populating the memory consumed by the definition with the correct bit pattern. Similarly, if you write

```
auto Ramanujan = 1729u;
```

or

```
auto Ramanujan = 1729.f;
```

the compiler will infer the type from the assignment (`unsigned int` and `float`, respectively) and correctly populate the memory.

All this machinery exists so that you do not need to worry about representation. The less time you spend programming with types and the more time you spend programming with interfaces, the safer your code will be.

Union

There are several ways of subverting type safety, most of which are legacies from C. Consider the `union` keyword.

```
union converter {
  float f;
  std::uint32_t ui;
};
```

This declares a type whose contents may be interpreted as either a `float` or an `unsigned integer`. As demonstrated above, this is a road to regret and a pathway to perdition. The programmer is required to know, at all times, which type is being represented. They are entirely entitled to write code such as:

```
void f1(int);
void f2(float);

void bad_things_happen() {
  converter c;
  c.ui = 1729;
  f1(c.ui);
  f2(c.f);
}
```

The call to `f2` will pass the value $2.423 * 10^{-42}$ which MAY be what was intended but seems highly unlikely.

The correct way to contain one of many types in a single object is to use the C++17 Standard Library type `std::variant`. This is a discriminated `union`, which means that the `variant` object knows which type it is holding. This follows the advice of Core Guideline C.181: "Avoid 'naked' unions." Use it like this:

```
#include <variant>

std::variant<int, float> v;
v = 12;
float f = std::get<float>(v); // Will throw std::bad_variant_access
```

You might consider this a peculiar example, but I used such a `union` many years ago to quickly calculate an inverse square root. It looked like this:

```
float reciprocal_square_root(float val) {
  union converter {
    float f;
```

```
    std::uint32_t i;
  };
  converter c  = {.f = val};
  c.i = 0x5f3759df - (c.i >> 1);
  c.f *= 1.5f - (0.5f * val * c.f * c.f);
  return c.f;
}
```

This abomination uses type punning, which is undefined behavior in C++, to exploit the characteristics of floating-point representation and the superior speed of multiplication and bit shifting. The SSE instruction set has thankfully rendered this redundant thanks to the addition of the instruction `rsqrtss`, but since C++20 it has been possible to do this correctly using `std::bit_cast`, thus:

```
float Q_rsqrt(float val)
{
  auto half_val = val * 0.5f;
  auto i = std::bit_cast<std::uint32_t>(val);
  i = 0x5f3759df - (i >> 1);
  val = std::bit_cast<float>(i);
  val *= 1.5f - (half_val * val * val);
  return val;
}
```

This use of casting still fights type-safe programming, which allows us to segue nicely into the next section.

Casting

Casting is the act of changing the type of an object. It is a general computer science term and has a rather more precise set of meanings in C++. Changing the type of an object can hurt static type safety. Sometimes it is perfectly safe, as in this example:

```
short f2();

long result = f2();
```

Here, the result of the call to `f2` has been converted from a `short` to a `long` using an implicit conversion. This is an integral promotion, where the representation is simply widened. Every value that can be represented by an object of type `short` can also be represented by an object of type `long`. The same is true when promoting from `float` to `double`.

Not all conversions are as safe as that. Consider this:

```
long f2();

short result = (short)f2();
```

This is an explicit conversion where the destination type is named. If you know that the return value of `f2` lies within the representation range of a `short` object, then this is conditionally safe. However, it is not entirely safe: the function may change specification and start returning larger numbers. There is no requirement for the compiler to emit a diagnostic telling you that you are performing a risky conversion, although most will warn you.

This style of conversion is often known as C-style casting. The syntax comes straight from the C programming language. Conversion was important to the C programming language. Consider this function signature:

```
long max(long, long);
```

If we call this function with an object of type `long` and an object of type `short` and we don't have conversion available to us, then we will be presented with an error and we will need to write a different function:

```
long max_ls(long, short);
```

(Since C doesn't have overloading, when you write a version of the function that takes different parameter types, you need to use a different name.) Fortunately, we were saved from this excessive verbiage. In today's C++, though, we have even less reason to worry. With function overloading and function templates we can afford to be more particular about casting.

Casting really can be quite risky. It's so dangerous in fact that cumbersome new keywords were introduced to highlight that dangerous things are happening. They are:

```
static_cast<T>(expr)      // Behaves like a C-style cast
dynamic_cast<T>(expr)     // Casts to a type inherited from the expression
const_cast<T>(expr)       // Eliminates the const qualification
reinterpret_cast<T>(expr) // Reinterprets the bit pattern
```

Core Guideline ES.48: "Avoid casts" warns you against it. The sight of these should strike fear into your heart. Some compilers offer a command-line switch that warns you of an explicit C-style cast so that you can quickly spot when something nasty is going on. Often, this will happen when you are calling a function from another library that is not so well written as yours. Replacing all your C-style casts with `static_cast` invocations will highlight where everything is getting messy. Your compiler will tell you when a `static_cast` makes no sense, for example casting from an int to a std::pair<std::string, char>. Just as with the C-style cast, you are saying, "I know what the range of values is, this will be fine."

Things get more dangerous as you proceed down the list. dynamic_cast will allow you to cast through an inheritance hierarchy to a subclass. Just the sound of that description should worry you. When you type dynamic_cast you are that person who says during an argument, "I just know, I don't need evidence." A dynamic_cast can of course fail, particularly if the author's certainty was misplaced. In such a case either a null pointer is returned or, in the case of applying dynamic_cast to a reference, an exception is thrown and you will have to sheepishly catch that exception and clean up the mess. It's a design smell: you are asking, "Are you an object of type X?" but this is the purview of the type system. If you are explicitly inquiring, you are implicitly subverting it.

With const_cast, we are moving into "downright evil" territory. const_cast allows you to cast away constness or, more rarely, cast to const volatile. We covered this in Chapter 3.4, so you already know this is a bad idea. If you are eliminating const qualification, having been passed, for example, a const-qualified reference to something, you are pulling the rug out from under the caller's feet. You have advertised in your API that "you can safely pass objects to this function by reference rather than by value, foregoing the overhead of copying, and it will remain unchanged." This is a lie: if you need to cast away constness, then that suggests that you are going to change the object in some way, contradicting your advertised promise. You will win no friends proceeding like this. Again, the only time you should use this is when you are calling into a library that is poorly written, in this case one that is not const-correct. const_cast is also used to eliminate volatile qualification; there are several deprecations lining up regarding the volatile keyword, so this may become an acceptable use case.

Finally, with reinterpret_cast, we are well into footgun territory. A footgun is for shooting yourself in the foot, and this is a common outcome that accompanies the use of the keyword reinterpret_cast. It converts between types by simply declaring that the bit pattern should now be interpreted as something else. It costs no CPU cycles (unlike static_cast or dynamic_cast, which can insert a run-time function to perform the conversion) and simply says, "This is my show now. I don't need type safety for this part." Some things are unavailable for change: you cannot cast away const or volatile using reinterpret_cast. For that you need to perform two consecutive casts, which would look like:

```
int c = reinterpret_cast<int>(const_cast<MyType&>(f3()));
```

The sight of all this punctuation should give you pause for reflection. You might call something like this to create a handle to arbitrary types, but honestly, there are safer ways of doing that.

We have already encountered `std::bit_cast` earlier in the chapter. This is even nastier, but it is not a language-level operation; rather, it is a library facility. One thing that `reinterpret_cast` cannot be used for is to cast between pointer or reference types. You need to use `std::bit_cast` for that. This is the final level of depravity, as far away from statically type-safe as you can get.

Type safety is a security feature. Casting can break type safety. Highlight casting where it happens and avoid it where possible.

Unsigned

The `unsigned` keyword is a strange fish. It modifies integral types to signal that they will have unsigned representation. Particularly, it signals that the type does not use two's complement representation. This variation in representation should be making you slightly queasy now after reading about casting.

In my experience, the most common incorrect application of `unsigned` derives from a misunderstanding of class invariants. An engineer might need to represent a value that can never be less than zero, and so will choose an unsigned type to do so. However, how do they assert that invariant? This will never fail:

```
void f1(unsigned int positive)
{
  … assert(positive >= 0);
}
```

There is no representation available for any number less than zero, so it will always be greater than or equal to zero. This also informs one of my (least) favorite code review bugs:

```
for (unsigned int index = my_collection.size(); index >= 0; --index)
{
  … // your program will never leave this loop
}
```

While it may seem like a good idea to represent kelvin temperature, mass, or screen coordinates with an unsigned type, the problem comes when you want to do some arithmetic. The output of this program is counterintuitive:

```
#include <iostream>
int main() {
  unsigned int five = 5;
  int negative_five = -5;
  if (negative_five < five) // signed/unsigned mismatch
```

```
    std::cout << "true";
  else
    std::cout << "false";
  return 0;
}
```

This will print `false`. You have fallen victim to the silent cast. During the comparison operation, `negative_five` is implicitly converted to an `unsigned int`. It is an integer promotion, widening representation. Unfortunately, that two's complement bit pattern represents a huge number which is of course considerably greater than five. Core Guideline ES.100: "Don't mix signed and unsigned arithmetic" is very clear about this.

You will notice that we used explicit types rather than `auto`. If we had instead used `auto`, the type of `five` would have been `int`. To make it an `unsigned int` we would have had to type:

```
auto five = 5u;
```

The default is `signed`. This is a default that C++ got right.

If you tried compiling this yourself, you will have almost certainly encountered a warning at line 5, noting that there is a signed/unsigned mismatch. You are perfectly entitled to write this code (it is not an error), but there may be trouble. This is why you should pay attention to all warnings and eliminate each one.

If you are doing any arithmetic, including comparison, use a signed type. If you are using an unsigned type to get an extra bit of representation, you are using the wrong type and you should go wider or recognize that you are performing a very risky optimization.

The problem is that if you try mixing signed and unsigned arithmetic, unwanted and entirely predictable things will happen. Your signed values will be promoted to unsigned values, and any comparison may yield the incorrect result. In larger codebases, one of your libraries may export unsigned results, and this will infect libraries that deal purely with signed values. Disaster looms.

Even worse, some code shops obscure the use of `unsigned` by creating shorter aliases, for example:

```
using u32 = unsigned int;
```

Sight of the keyword `unsigned` should be the equivalent of neon flashing lights telling you to apply the brakes and navigate the hazardous roads ahead with extreme care.

There are some situations where `unsigned` is the correct choice. Core Guideline ES.101: "Use unsigned types for bit manipulation" highlights one of them. They are very limited, though:

- If you are modeling hardware registers that hold unsigned values
- If you are dealing with sizes rather than quantities; for example values returned by `sizeof`
- If you are doing bit manipulation with masks, since you will be doing no arithmetic with these values

Here is the rule: if you are doing any arithmetic, including comparison, use a signed type. If you are using an unsigned type to get an extra bit of representation, you are using the wrong type and you should go wider or recognize that you are performing a very risky optimization. It would not surprise me if a bitfield type makes its way into the language sooner or later, making even that case redundant.

Unfortunately, there is a rather large error in the standard library. All the size member functions on the containers return `size_t`, which is an unsigned type. This is a misunderstanding of the difference between quantity and amount. The size of a container is the quantity of elements it contains. The size of an object is the amount of memory it occupies.

Fortunately, since C++20, we have been blessed with the arrival of the function `std::ssize`, short for signed size. It returns a signed value. Disavow all use of the `size` member function, and instead use this nonmember function thus:

```
auto collection = std::vector<int>{1, 3, 5, 7, 9};
auto element_count = std::ssize(collection);
```

Buffers and sizes

Staying with sizes, consider buffers. There are two important things to keep in mind when dealing with buffers: the address of the buffer and the length of the buffer. If you do not overflow the buffer, everything is fine. Buffer overflow is a class of runtime error that can be fiendishly hard to discover.

For example, look at this code fragment:

```
void fill_buffer(char* text, int length)
{
  char buf[256];
```

```
  strncpy(buf, text, length);
  …
}
```

The obvious error is that `length` may be greater than 256. If you do not assert that the `char` array is big enough, you are open to risk.

Note that `buf` is of type `char[256]` which is a different type to, for example, `char[128]`. The size is important but can be easily lost by passing the address of the beginning of the array to a function that simply takes a pointer. Consider this pair of functions:

```
void fill_n_buffer(char*);

void src(std::ifstream& file)
{
  char source[256] = {0};
  … // populate source from file
  fill_n_buffer(source);
}
```

`fill_n_buffer` is expecting a `char*` yet it is being passed a `char[256]`. This is called array decay, and it is well named because the type is decaying into something less useful. The information about the size of the array is lost: the type `char[256]` has decayed to a `char*`. You must hope that `fill_n_buffer` is able to deal with this reduced information. The presence of the `n` in the name may suggest that it is expecting a null-terminated string, in the style of the C Standard Library, but we hope you can see that this is a risky proposition that could fail easily.

The code is working at a dangerous level of abstraction. The chance of overwriting memory is high, so the code is unsafe. The correct approach is to use a buffer abstraction rather than directly write to or read from memory. There are several available: `std::string` is a somewhat heavyweight approach for handling mutating strings of characters, but this is what we have in the standard, and this is not the place to dwell on its nature. However, if you are simply reading a buffer, there is a lighter abstraction called `std::string_view`. This marvel is a lightweight version of `std::string` consisting only of `const` member functions, aside from the special functions (the default constructor, the move and copy constructors, the move and copy assignment operators, and the destructor). It is usually implemented as a pointer and a size. You can construct it with a pointer and a size, or just a pointer, or a pair of iterators. This makes it very flexible and the first choice for working with read-only strings.

If your buffer contains something other than a character type, there are still options. In C++20 `std::span` was introduced to the library. This is a lightweight version of `vector`, also consisting only of `const` member functions. These two types mean that you should never be authoring functions with parameters that are pointer/size pairs. Wrap them into a buffer abstraction, using `std::span` or `std::string_view`.

Summary

It is easier than ever to write secure C++. This should not be a surprise: one of the goals of C++ is safety, and through that, security. You can prioritize type safety and make use of abstractions like `span` that militate against buffer overflows. You can avoid representation clashes by avoiding unsigned types when using arithmetic, casting only when interfacing with old or poorly written libraries, and preferring discriminated unions to C-style unions. All of these things are easy replacements that lead to safer, easier, and more intelligible code by ensuring that your program makes full use of the type of safety C++ provides.

Chapter 5.2

P.10: Prefer immutable data to mutable data

The wrong defaults

C++ is the language with the "wrong" defaults. Among other things, objects are created mutable unless they are qualified with `const`. But why is this the wrong default?

There are two things you can do to data: read from it and write to it. In assembly languages this is also known as loading and storing. You load values from memory into registers and store values from registers into memory. It is very unusual to store a value to memory without loading from it first. Similarly, it is very unusual to write to an object without reading from it first. However, it is much more common to read from an object without subsequently writing to it.

Read-only objects are much more common than read-write objects, which are themselves much more common than write-only objects. The default should be the most common option, so we contend that objects should be immutable by default.

This would have some interesting side effects. Imagine that C++ did not have a `const` keyword, and that the `mutable` keyword was more extensively deployed. You might write functions like this:

```
void f1(std::string id)
{
  auto write = id_destination(); // write is immutable
  …
}
```

As you develop your function, there will come a point where you will need to qualify `write` as mutable, because you are writing to it and that would violate immutability.

Imagine what would happen if you finished the function and noticed that `write` was still immutable. Immediately, this would demonstrate evidence of a bug. Why would you give something a name like `write` and never mutate it?

This bug-finding trick can be yours by simply declaring everything `const` and modifying that qualification only when you need to mutate the object. You can periodically requalify all the objects as `const` and check that everything that should indeed be written to causes the compiler to complain about its `const` qualification. It is a nice win for code clarity.

However, that is not the primary reason to prefer immutable data.

I have a car, and I have sunglasses that I keep in the car. They never leave the car. I have additional sunglasses for when I am not in the car. Driving into the sun without sunglasses is enough of a danger for me to avoid it where possible. This means the sunglasses are in one of two places: on my face, or in the special pocket I have for them in the car door. I have habituated myself to simply check that they are where they should be when I open the car door. I really do not need to think about it.

My car is sadly not an electric vehicle. I hope it will be my last gas-guzzler. When I start a journey, I must decide whether I have enough fuel for the journey. The manufacturers have gone to some lengths to make this as simple as possible. There is a fuel gauge on the dashboard, with an estimated range telling me how far I can go before I need to refuel. There is a safety margin built in, so in the normal case I do not run out of fuel because I can do the arithmetic required. Sometimes things have gone wrong, though. There are long stretches of road in the UK where there are no filling stations, for example across moors. Getting stuck in a traffic jam in that sort of situation can be a tense occasion for everyone in the car if I have allowed the fuel tank to drain a little too far.

It is much easier for me to think about my sunglasses than it is to think about my fuel tank. My sunglasses live in one place, and I can get to them without thinking about it. The volume of fuel in my fuel tank is an ever-changing quantity, and it introduces cognitive load to my driving experience. It is much easier for me to reason about the consistently located sunglasses than it is for me to reason about the varyingly filled fuel tank.

Consider this function:

```
double gomez_radius(double cr, double x1, double x2,
                    double y1, double y2, double rh)
{
  assert(rh > 1.0f);
  auto lt1 = lovage_trychter_number(cr, x1, y1);
  auto lt2 = lovage_trychter_number(cr, x2, y2);
  auto exp = 1;
  while (lt1 > lt2) {
```

```
    lt2 *= rh;
    ++exp;
  }
  auto hc = haldwell_correction(cr, lt1, lt2);
  auto gr = (lt1 * lt2 * sqrt(hc)) / rh * exp;
  return gr;
}
```

You can imagine this function being copied directly from a textbook. Apprehending this function is simplified by a sprinkling of const:

```
double gomez_radius(double cr, double x1, double x2,
                    double y1, double y2, double rh)
{
  assert(rh > 1.0f);
  auto const lt1 = lovage_trychter_number(cr, x1, y1);
  auto lt2 = lovage_trychter_number(cr, x2, y2);
  auto exp = 1;
  while (lt1 > lt2) {
    lt2 *= rh;
    ++exp;
  }
  auto const hc = haldwell_correction(cr, lt1, lt2);
  auto const gr = (lt1 * lt2 * sqrt(hc)) / rh * exp;
  return gr;
}
```

The number of moving parts has been reduced to two: the second Lovage-Trychter number and the exponent.

Imagine how complicated architecture would become if the acceleration due to the earth's gravity varied significantly around the planet. Consider the advances in twentieth-century science that emerged once the speed of light was exposed as a constant. Constants are good! Their invariant nature provides us with one less thing to think about. Where you can fix the value of something, you should do so.

`const`ness in function declarations

Although we cannot implicitly make objects `const` by default, we can qualify them whenever they are created. Member functions are also mutable by default. Again, do the smart thing and qualify them as `const` until they need to mutate something.

Things are a little more subtle here, though. As discussed in Chapter 3.4, there are two kinds of `const`, logical and bitwise. When you decide that a `const` function needs to mutate something, you need to ask yourself whether it is the function that should not be const-qualified, or the member data that should be mutable, exempting it from the rule that member data cannot be changed in a const member function.

This is a matter of API design. The purpose of const qualification is to tell the user, "There will be no observable difference in the state of the object between consecutive calls to const functions." If your function is in fact changing the state of the abstraction rather than the state of private implementation details, then your function should not be const-qualified.

For example, you may want to design a thread-safe queue for message passing. This is a common exercise when you learn about thread safety: rather than synchronizing thread progress by sharing memory, it is safer to synchronize by communicating between threads. This leads to the maxim referred to earlier: "Don't communicate by sharing memory, share memory by communicating." You can argue among yourselves about whether passing messages counts as sharing memory.

A message-passing queue might have this public interface:

```
template <typename T>
class message_queue {
public:
  … // definitions for iterator &c.
  void push(T);
  T pop();
  const_iterator find(const T&) const;

private:
  mutable std::mutex m_lock;
  … // other implementation details
};
```

Typically, you would have two threads: a producer and a consumer. The producer pushes messages and the consumer pops messages. The push and pop functions are of course going to mutate the object, but the find function, which searches for a particular object in the queue, should not. While this function is executing it will need to lock the mutex, which is a non-const operation. If find were not a const function, it could change any member data at all. Because it is const, the only value it can change is the mutex, which has been marked mutable. Simply reading the class declaration tells you this. Indeed, the only context where a mutex member datum does not need to be mutable is if there are no const member functions. Even then, it is a good habit to make mutexes mutable.

Function parameters are also, by default, mutable. They behave like local variables. It is unusual for a function to mutate its arguments: they are used to inform its operation. Of course, the functions in <algorithm> which take input iterators are a notable exception to this. However, given that function parameters are also rarely declared const anyway, you may consider avoiding the const qualification of function parameters. For example:

```
void f(char const* const p);
void g(int const i);
```

might seem pedantic rather than correct. This is a matter of style and taste. There is another related matter of style and taste regarding const, and that is where to put it.

- References cannot be const-qualified.
- Pointers are const-qualified to the right.
- Member functions are const-qualified to the right.
- Types can be const-qualified to the right or to the left of the type. This is known as East const and const West.

References cannot be const-qualified, because a reference cannot be reseated; that is, its referent cannot be changed. Qualifying a reference with const would add no further information.

Pointers sit to the right of a type name. If pointers could be const-qualified to the left, then there would be potential for ambiguity:

```
int const * j; // is the int being qualified, or the pointer?
```

The same is true for member functions:

```
int const my_type::f1(); // is the return type const-qualified
                         // or the member function?
```

It is only types whose const qualification offers a choice of position. It is possibly unwise to be dogmatic about on which side const should appear; however, I favor East const, as you may have inferred from reading this text. I like the consistency, and I also find additional clarity in declaring my objects like this:

```
int const& a = …; // a is an int const-reference
int const* b;     // b is a pointer-to-const int
int & c = …;      // c is a reference to an int
int const d;      // d is a const-int
```

English offers little help here sadly, since it places adjectives to the left of the thing being qualified, so there is a certain dissonance in writing const to the right. Having said that, consistency can improve readability, but this is not a hard-and-fast rule. My editor remarks that she is successfully training her brain to treat int as an adjective, as well as const, which describes the nature of the name. Adjective ordering is an interesting digression (why do we say "big friendly dog" rather than "friendly big dog"?) but out of scope for this text. Ultimately, always prefer readability to consistency and, more broadly, prefer pragmatism to dogmatism, especially in engineering.

In addition to parameters, it is worth thinking about return values. When a function returns a value, it is an rvalue. Qualifying it as const is irrelevant because it is about to be assigned from, constructed from, or destroyed. This being the case, is there ever any reason to const-qualify a return type?

This leading question should tell you that, in fact, there is. Although the returned object is an rvalue, it is not destroyed immediately, and it is possible to invoke functions on it. Look at this class:

```
template <typename T>
class my_container {
public:
  …
  T operator[](size_t);
  T const operator[](size_t) const;
};
```

The subscript operator, or more precisely the bracket operator, is being used to return an object by value rather than by reference, which would be more usual. It may be the case that this container has very unstable iterators; perhaps they become invalidated by operations on another thread. In this case, returning by value is the only way of safely exporting values. There are two overloads of this operator so that the correct one will be used for [] on const and non-const objects. Consider this piece of code:

```
my_container<Proxies> const p = {a, b, c, d, e};
p[2].do_stuff();
```

If the member function Proxies::do_stuff() is overloaded by const qualification, then the correct function will be called on the rvalue returned by invoking c[2].

We hope you are thinking to yourself that this is a rather contrived example, and we agree that this is the case. This very contrivance should convey to you that const-qualifying return types should be a deliberate and unusual step.

Finally, there is an exception to qualifying function parameters as const, and that is when they are passed by pointer or by reference. By default, you should take such arguments by reference-to-const or by pointer-to-const. This signals to your callers that you will not be changing the objects that are being passed in. This reinforces the idea of input and input-output parameters, as discussed in Chapter 4.1, The separation of type from `const`, reference, and pointer qualification becomes more useful here. For example:

```
int f1(std::vector<int> const& a, int b, std::vector<int> & c);
```

It is immediately clear here that the function is using two inputs, `a` and `b`, to modify another input, `c` (consider which values can be mutated and propagated back to the call site). The return value is likely an error code. The separation of `const&` from type and identifier highlights the qualification that gives us a flavor of what part we expect the object to play in the function.

Summary

It is tempting to respond to this guideline by simply sprinkling `const` wherever you can and murmuring "job done" to yourself. A little more subtlety than that is required, though. There is no correct default for `const` qualification. It is certainly true that in most cases you will want to create your objects as `const`-qualified and then update them as development continues, but it is not simply a case of dropping a `const` next to the type: there are some places where `const` is not appropriate. Having said that, the guideline's direction of preference is absolutely true.

- Immutable data is easier to reason about than mutable data.
- Make objects and member functions `const` wherever you can.
- Consider whether to use East `const` or `const` West to assist readability.
- Function parameters passed by value and returned by value do not benefit from being `const`-qualified, except to correctly propagate `const`ness in some specific situations.

Chapter 5.3

I.30: Encapsulate rule violations

Hiding the unsightly things in life

I have a room in my house that nobody may enter. It is too small to be a bedroom and too large to be a closet, but not quite large enough to be a useful office. I have no idea what the architect was thinking, but I have found a use for this room.

I like things to be neat and tidy. I like a place for everything and everything in its place. It means I can find things when I need them, rather than spending time trying to search for things that have not been correctly put away.

Unfortunately, the universe does not always support me in my aims. I carefully categorize things so that similar items are stored together, but I may have a surplus of, for example, staplers or hole punchers or staple removers because I am old and still live in a world of pens and staples and A4 ring binders.

The surplus goes into The Room.

The trouble with this approach is that there is no sensible way of storing surplus staplers. You simply put them all together in one place and hope for the best. I am not going to go into detail about why I might have surplus staplers and why I retain rather than discard them. It suffices to say that I have a small room, hidden from outside observers, filled with clutter. Some might say "tightly packed."

The point is that sometimes, despite your best intentions, things do not go according to plan.

Engineering is practiced in real life. It is messy, especially when it encounters living things with big bundles of conflicting desires and choices. The finest guidelines and the best of intentions can crumble about you when faced with an unavoidable intrusion from a lower level of abstraction. This guideline exhorts you to minimize the visibility of such horrors.

Recall the code example in Chapter 2.1 where the problem of parsing an options file demonstrated how things could get out of hand through scope creep. The solution was careful separation of concerns and abstraction behind well-designed interfaces. As an afterthought, the solution was able to parse from any source that could be presented as a stream. However, what if that facility had been an upfront requirement?

The example presented with this item in the Core Guidelines is similar in nature. Here, the program is told where to get its input from and must capture an appropriate stream. Typically, the program would be run from the command line and take up to two command-line parameters. There are three possible input sources: standard input, the command line, and an external file. Therefore, the first parameter would be an identifier for the input source, perhaps 0, 1, or 2, while the second parameter would be a command or a filename. This would lead to command lines like these:

```
sample.exe 0                Read commands from standard input
sample.exe 1 help           Run the help command
sample.exe 2 setup.txt      Run the commands in setup.txt
```

We reproduce the example code from Chapter 2.1, slightly modified, here:

```
enum class input_source { std_in, command_line, file };

bool owned;
std::istream* input;

switch (source) {
case input_source::std_in:
  owned = false;
  input = &std::cin;
  break;
case input_source::command_line:
  owned = true;
  input = new std::istringstream{argv[2]};
  break;
case input_source::file:
  owned = true;
  input = new std::ifstream{&argv[2]};
  break;
}
std::istream& in = *input;
```

From the top, we have an enumeration called `input_source` describing our three options, a `bool` called owned, and a `std::istream` called `input`. Assume that `source` is initialized from the first command-line parameter: the `case` statements compare it with the input_source enumerations. The std::istream object is set to point to either an existing std::istream object, std::cin, or a new std::ifstream or std::istringstream object. This presents us with a problem: sometimes we are going to have to destroy our stream, and sometimes we are not. We cannot statically identify which case applies, so a flag is needed to signal dynamically what should happen. If the flag is set to true, then the stream must be destroyed.

This code does not respect the Core Guidelines. For example, ES.20: "Always initialize an object" is quite unambiguous because it is so often violated with undesirable results. Here, owned and input are not initialized. Their values are not ready yet, and the author is reluctant to assign a value to them only to immediately change them before they are used.

How do we encapsulate this rule violation?

Keeping up appearances

We have already looked at the Immediately Invoked Lambda Expression (IILE) pattern, so let's try that:

```
auto input = [&]() -> std::pair<bool, std::istream*> {
  auto source = input_source_from_ptr(argv[1]);
  switch (source) {
  case input_source::std_in:
    return {false, &std::cin};
  case input_source::command_line:
    return {true, new std::istringstream{argv[2]}};
  case input_source::file:
    return {true, new std::ifstream{argv[2]}};
  }
}();
```

This is an improvement, provided you are comfortable with the idiom.

However, there is another guideline being ignored here, and that is I.11: "Never transfer ownership by a raw pointer (T*) or reference (T&)." The problem is quite clear: the author must remember whether the function owns the stream. They should certainly not try and destroy the standard input. The raw pointer doesn't provide enough information about ownership, so the owned object has to provide additional context. Then the author must ensure that they write

```
if (input.first) delete input.second;
```

and that it is executed in every code path. This sounds like a job for Resource Acquisition Is Initialization[1] (RAII), which we can model using a class.

We'll call the class `command_stream`. It needs to optionally own a `std::istream`, so we can start with this:

```
class command_stream {
private:
  bool owned;          // Possibly owns the std::istream
  std::istream* inp;  // Here is the std::istream
};
```

There's not much in there. The destructor is trivial:

```
class command_stream {
public:
  ~command_stream() {
    if (owned) delete inp;
  }

private:
  bool owned;          // Possibly owns the std::istream
  std::istream* inp;  // Here is the std::istream
};
```

The constructor should take a parameter to indicate which input stream it should be forwarding to, and an optional filename or command. Fortunately, we already have an enumeration we can use, so our class now looks like this:

```
class command_stream {
public:
  command_stream(input_source source, std::string token) {
    switch (source) {
    case input_source::std_in:
      owned = false;
      inp = &std::cin;
      return;
    case input_source::command_line:
      owned = true;
      inp = new std::istringstream{ token };
      return;
    case input_source::file:
      owned = true;
      inp = new std::ifstream{ token };
      return;
```

1. RAII is discussed in Chapter 5.6.

```
  }
  ~command_stream() {
    if (owned) delete inp;
  }

private:
  bool owned;          // Possibly owns the std::istream
  std::istream* inp;  // Here is the std::istream
};
```

However, we seem to have coupled the enumeration to the `command_stream` class. Do we really need to do that? It's always worth spending a little time decoupling early.

Of course, we don't need to import the `input_source` enumeration into the class. We can simply create three constructors instead. The simplest case is that the `std::istream` is `std::cin`, in which case nothing needs to be created and there are no ownership issues. We can make that the default constructor:

```
class command_stream {
public:
  command_stream()
    : owned(false)
    , inp(&std::cin) {}
  ~command_stream() {
    if (owned) delete inp;
  }

private:
  bool owned;          // Possibly owns the std::istream
  std::istream* inp;  // Here is the std::istream
};
```

In fact, we can do better than that and use default member initialization:

```
class command_stream {
public:
  command_stream() = default;
  ~command_stream() {
    if (owned) delete inp;
  }

private:
  bool owned = false;              // Possibly owns the std::istream
  std::istream* inp = &std::cin;  // Here is the std::istream
};
```

The other two construction methods both need to take a `std::string` and nothing else, so we need to differentiate between them. There are several ways to do this, but we're going to use a tag.

A tag is a struct with no members. It's a way of enabling the overload of a function, since overloading takes place by parameter type. Let's define a tag called `from_command_line` to differentiate the two remaining constructors:

```
class command_stream {
public:
  struct from_command_line {};
  command_stream() = default;
  command_stream(std::string filename)
    : owned(true)
    , inp(new std::ifstream(filename))
  {}
  command_stream(std::string command_list, from_command_line)
    : owned(true)
    , inp(new std::istringstream(command_list))
  {}
  ~command_stream() {
    if (owned) delete inp;
  }

private:
  bool owned = false;               // Possibly owns the std::istream
  std::istream* inp = &std::cin;    // Here is the std::istream
};
```

Finally, we need it to behave like a `std::istream`, which means supplying a conversion operator:

```
class command_stream {
public:
  struct from_command_line {};
  command_stream() = default;
  command_stream(std::string filename)
    : owned(true)
    , inp(new std::ifstream(filename))
  {}
  command_stream(std::string command_list, from_command_line)
    : owned(true)
    , inp(new std::istringstream(command_list))
  {}
  ~command_stream() {
    if (owned) delete inp;
  }
```

```
  operator std::istream&() { return *inp; }

private:
  bool owned = false;             // Possibly owns the std::istream
  std::istream* inp = &std::cin;  // Here is the std::istream
};
```

There we have it. Everything is tidily hidden away behind the public interface. The default values of `owned` and `inp` are `false` and `std::cin`. These remain unchanged when an instance is initialized with the default constructor. Other constructors are used for initializing from a string stream or a file stream. We can now rewrite our code fragment thus:

```
auto input = [&]() -> command_stream {
  auto source = input_source_from_ptr(argv[1]);
  switch (source) {
  case input_source::std_in:
    return {};
  case input_source::command_line:
    return {{argv[2]}, command_stream::from_command_line{}};
  case input_source::file:
    return {argv[2]};
  }
}();
```

This is rather clearer. The conversion operator allows us to treat this object as if it were of type `std::istream&`, so we can use the overloaded chevron operators (operator >> and operator <<) for comfortable and familiar syntax. When the name falls out of scope, the `command_stream` object will be destroyed, and the ownership flag will ensure appropriate destruction of the `std::istream` object. This is a somewhat complex piece of implementation, but it is abstracted away behind a simple interface.

Summary

We hope you will have noticed that abstraction is a running theme throughout this book: abstraction localizes and minimizes complexity. In Chapter 2.1 we looked at how abstraction is more than merely encapsulating and data hiding: it allows us to create levels of complexity and expose only the bare minimum required to interact with an object.

In Chapter 2.2 we looked at how arguments increase in number, and observed that this could be down to a missing abstraction. The complexity of comprehending

Abstraction localizes and minimizes complexity.

many parameters is hidden behind the abstraction that describes the role those parameters play.

In Chapter 4.1 we carried out a similar transformation and collected together a messy bunch of data into a single abstraction, returning that rather than taking multiple `out` parameters.

The Core Guidelines are explicitly motivated by abstraction in some cases. In C.8: "Use `class` rather than `struct` if any member is non-public," the reason for so doing is to make it clear that something is being abstracted. Since class members are private by default, a class signals to you that there are things that you do not need to see.

In Core Guideline ES.1: "Prefer the standard library to other libraries and to 'handcrafted code,'" it is observed that library code tends to be of a higher level of abstraction. As I remarked earlier, I have participated in code reviews where the engineer simply rewrote `std::rotate` or `std::mismatch` without realizing it, and did a worse job.

In Core Guideline ES.2: "Prefer suitable abstractions to direct use of language features," the use of abstraction is explicit in the title. This guideline demonstrates that application concepts are further from the bare language than they are from appropriate combinations of library features.

Even the term "abstract base class" describes an entity that hides complexity by only exposing a public API, insulating the client from the implementation details. Abstraction is fundamental to developing software in C++.

When a guideline violation seems unavoidable, facilities exist to minimize and hide the violation. One of the driving principles of C++ is zero-cost abstraction, so make use of that to maximize the clarity and comprehensibility of your code.

Chapter 5.4

ES.22: Don't declare a variable until you have a value to initialize it with

The importance of expressions and statements

This is the fourth guideline from the ES section of the Core Guidelines, Expressions and Statements, to which we have devoted a chapter. One reason for that is the size of this section (over sixty items), but more importantly it gets to the heart of C++. The section opens with the following:

"Expressions and statements are the lowest and most direct way of expressing actions and computation."

This guideline binds together with ES.5: "Keep scopes small" and ES.10: "Declare one name (only) per declaration." As you saw in ES.5, keeping scopes small is a great improvement to readability, since scope creates context. Small scopes also improve resource management, since their release is supported by deterministic destruction, minimizing their retention. In ES.10 you saw the importance of separating declarations into individual objects rather than grouping them together C-style. The facility to group declarations behind a single type is a feature of backward compatibility, no more than that. It offers no advantage to the C++ programmer, and in fact can serve to confuse and complicate.

Another way of improving readability is to delay the declaration of objects until the last possible moment. Functions grow and change. They just do. Often, we do not quite spot their rampant expansion in a timely fashion and we are left with a somewhat unwieldy collection of objects and logic. When we realize what has happened, we seek to partition the function into useful parts, to abstract it into smaller functions, hiding the complexity and restoring order to our source file. This process is hampered if declaration and initialization are spread over multiple lines, especially if they are not near to each other in the source. Let's take a quick journey through three programming styles.

C-style declaration

C used to require you to declare all your variables at the top of a function before any code was executed. It was quite normal to inadvertently declare more variables than were in use in the function. As the function changed algorithm, changed purpose, mutated in any number of ways in fact, the context required to execute it would change, and inevitably some variables would no longer be needed. For example:

```
int analyze_scatter_data(scatter_context* sc) {
  int range_floor;
  int range_ceiling;
  float discriminator;
  int distribution_median;
  int distribution_lambda;
  int poisson_fudge;
  int range_average;
  int range_max;
  unsigned short noise_correction;
  char chart_name[100];
  int distribution_mode;
  … // and on we go
}
```

This function was first written 10 years ago and has been through a lot of revisions. Five years ago, `distribution_median` was exchanged for `distribution_mode` as a summary value, but both were calculated without consideration for whether the median was needed. Nobody withdrew the state declared to support an unused part of the algorithm. Out of sight, out of mind. Additionally, it is the engineer's habit to append to a list rather than find the proper location, so `range_average` and `range_max` are separated from `range_floor` and `range_ceiling`.

If the programmer were dedicated, keen, and not in a hurry, those variables would be withdrawn from the function, improving its clarity, and the remainder appropriately collected together to highlight how pieces of state are related. If the programmer had Lint to hand, a static code analysis tool released to the public in 1979, it would warn about unused objects, making this task easier. Otherwise, the function would consume a few extra unnecessary bytes on the stack. Today this would not even be noticed as compilers would eliminate the unused variables anyway thanks to the as-if rule, but in the constrained environments of the 1970s, where the size of offline files could exceed the RAM in your machine, this might be significant.

Another problem this introduced was variable reuse. The function may reuse an `int` for a loop counter, or for storing the result of a function call. Again, as the function mutated, reused variables might take on unexpected new meanings, and their reuse might be inappropriate. The trade-off being made was readability over resource constraint.

A further impact of early declaration was that initialization was somewhat haphazard. It was easy to introduce dependencies between variables and to use them before they had been initialized. Every function had to be closely examined for variable coupling. Whenever a line of code was moved, it was important to ensure that any dependencies were honored.

This is not a pleasant way to write code. Declaring a batch of variables, and then carefully initializing them one by one, is painful, error prone, and makes your gums ache. C++ introduced late declaration, and the first thing that happened was that `struct`s and built-in types were declared and then initialized in a safe order. This was a significant leap forward. Rather than worrying about whether a `struct` was ready for initialization, you could declare all its dependent data first, initialize it, and then safely initialize the `struct`, without a care in the world.

Declare-then-initialize

When I came to C++, code still looked like C, although it was a new style of programming. I would see things like:

```
class Big_type {
  int m_acc;
  int m_bell;
  int m_length;

public:
  Big_type();
  void set_acc(int);
  void set_bell(int);
  void set_length(int);
  int get_acc() const;
  int get_bell() const;
  int get_length() const;
};

void fn(int a, int b, char* c)
{
  Big_type bt1;
  bt1.set_acc(a);
```

```
  bt1.set_bell(b);
  bt1.set_length(strlen(c));
 ...
  Big_type bt2;
  bt2.set_acc(bt1.get_bell() * bt1.get_acc());
  bt1.set_bell(bt2.get_acc() * 12);
 ...
}
```

There are some good things about this code. The data is in the `private` interface, the function variables were declared as they were needed, but the `get` and `set` functions grated on me. Why go to all the trouble of putting your implementation details in the `private` interface only to expose them through `get` and `set` functions? Also, why put the `private` interface at the top of the definition, when most clients should only want to see the `public` interface?

We looked at this in C.131: "Avoid trivial getters and setters": this was a hangover from the days of declare-then-initialize. The constructor would most likely set all the values to zero if it existed at all. I encountered local coding rules such as "ensure every data member has a getter and a setter" put in place to support this programming style. Even in the early 2000s I would encounter reluctance to declare constructors because of the associated overhead of initializing everything to zero only to subsequently overwrite the values. It was only when strict determinism was required that I could persuade my colleagues to write and use constructors.

We are of course talking about default constructors, where the class designer would dictate what the initial value would be (typically 0 throughout). The great shift was when programmers would start to use nondefault constructors and even eliminate default constructors altogether. This is the third programming style.

Maximally delayed declaration

Default constructors have their place, but they presume the existence of a default value. Some early implementations of C++ would require classes to have default constructors if they were to be contained in a `std::vector`. This requirement would propagate through the member data, requiring those types to also have default values, or for the default constructor of the containing class to be able to construct them with a meaningful value. Happily, this is no longer the case and we always advise that default constructors be added deliberately and carefully.

You might be wondering how this relates to the title of this guideline. Simply put, if a constructor demands a full set of initial conditions, you cannot create an instance of the class until you are ready to use it. As you can see from the preceding styles of initialization, declare-then-initialize, in whatever form, is an accident waiting to happen, since there is no indication that an object is ready for use. Additional instructions can be inserted during the initialization which only serves to further confuse the development of the state in your function. Reasoning about which objects are ready for use is an unnecessary burden, relieved by insisting on full initialization at the point of declaration. Let's modify class `Big_type`:

```
class Big_type {
  int m_acc;
  int m_bell;
  int m_length;

public:
  Big_type(int acc, int bell, int length);
  void set_acc(int);
  void set_bell(int);
  void set_length(int);
  int get_acc() const;
  int get_bell() const;
  int get_length() const;
};

void fn(int a, int b, char* c)
{
  Big_type bt1(a, b, strlen(c));
 …
  Big_type bt2(bt1.get_bell() * bt1.get_acc(), bt2.get_acc() * 12, 0);
 …
}
```

Both `bt1` and `bt2` can now be declared `const`, which is preferable to mutable state. The setters have been kept but it is entirely likely that they will now be unnecessary. This code is immediately more apprehensible.

There is another reason for delaying declaration until immediately prior to first use, which is eliminating redundancy. Look at this code:

```
class my_special_type {
public:
  my_special_type(int, int);
  int magical_invocation(float);
…
};

int f1(int a, int b, float c) {
  my_special_type m{a, b};
```

```
  if (a > b) return a;
  prepare_for_invocation();
  return m.magical_invocation(c);
}
```

Clearly, `m` does not need to be declared until the `prepare_for_invocation()` function call has returned. In fact, there is no need to declare a named value at all. If we rewrite this function while observing ES.5: "Keep scopes small," we might arrive at this:

```
int f2(int a, int b, float c) {
  if (a > b) return;
  prepare_for_invocation();
  return my_special_type{a, b}.magical_invocation(c);
}
```

The assembly generated by the compiler will likely be identical, in accordance with the as-if rule, assuming no side effects to construction, so there is no performance optimization going on here. However, there is one less line of code to read, as well as no possibility of introducing confusing code between declaration and use of the `my_special_type` instance.

Observe how far we have delayed the instantiation of the object. It started off as an lvalue named `m` at the top of the function and has ended up as an rvalue at the bottom. This function now has no state other than that which is passed in. Again, this is easier to apprehend since there is nothing to keep track of other than the execution order of the function calls.

Localization of context-specific functionality

Delaying instantiation has other benefits. Look at this function:

```
my_special_type f2(int a, int b) {
  int const x = perform_f2_related_checks(a, b);
  int const y = perform_boundary_checks(a, x);
  int const z = perform_initialization_checks(b, y);
  return {y, z};
}
```

Not only is the object instantiated at the end of the function, but it also benefits from copy elision via return value optimization.

In that last example, you will have seen attention being paid to P.10: "Prefer immutable data to mutable data"; `x`, `y`, and `z` were declared `const`. While this is a trivially easy guideline to follow for built-in types, more complex considerations can require more involved initialization. Look at this fragment of code:

```
int const_var;

if (first_check()) {
  const_var = simple_init();
} else {
  const_var = complex_init();
}
```

We would like to make `const_var` a constant value, but if we assign it within a conditional statement the name falls out of scope. This example could be resolved with:

```
int const var = first_check() ? simple_init() : complex_init();
```

but clearly this is not going to scale well.

Also, consider this class:

```
class special_cases {
public:
  special_cases(int, int);
…
private:
  my_special_type m_mst;
};
```

As you may be able to infer from the function `f2` above, construction of `my_special_type` includes some rather particular conditions being satisfied. How are we to construct the member datum `m_mst`? You might immediately suggest:

```
special_cases::special_cases(int a, int b)
  : m_mst(f2(a, b))
{}
```

but unless `f2` has other uses, you have created a special function solely for invocation by the constructor. That is not a nice thing to do for your maintainers, who are most likely to be future you. This is a use case for an Immediately Invoked Lambda Expression, or IILE. The IILE is a simple idiom that looks like this:

```
special_cases::special_cases(int a, int b)
  : m_mst([=](){ // Capture by value, taking no parameters
    int const x = perform_f2_related_checks(a, b);
    int const y = perform_boundary_checks(a, x);
    int const z = perform_initialization_checks(b, y);
```

```
    return my_special_type{y, z}; }
  ())            // Immediately invoke the lambda expression
{}
```

We declare the lambda expression, and then we immediately invoke it. Naming is hard, and sometimes you just have to say what you are doing, convert it into an acronym, and live with it (see also RAII). Now we have our initialization function in one place.

We can also apply this to the other example:

```
int const var = [](){
  if (first_check()) return simple_init();
  return complex_init();
}();
```

Single pieces of functionality used to initialize objects often result in the creation of temporary state whose utility expires after the declaration of the object in question. Since the temporary state is a dependency of the object, it must be declared at the same scope. Bundling it into a lambda expression creates a local scope which can export a value.

Eliminating state

Late declaration is even applicable to containers. Consider this function:

```
void accumulate_mst(std::vector<my_special_type>& vec_mst,
                    std::vector<int> const& source) {
  auto source_it = source.begin();
  while (source_it != source.end()) {
    auto s_it = source_it++;
    my_special_type mst{*s_it, *s_it};
    vec_mst.push_back(mst);
  }
}
```

Within the `while` loop, an instance of `my_special_type` is constructed and pushed onto the vector. You might consider avoiding the construction entirely and push back an rvalue instance instead:

```
void accumulate_mst(std::vector<my_special_type>& vec_mst,
                  std::vector<int> const& source) {
  auto source_it = source.begin();
  while (source_it != source.end()) {
    auto s_it = source_it++;
```

```
    vec_mst.push_back(my_special_type{*s_it, *s_it});
  }
}
```

In an unoptimized build this will create a temporary object and invoke `push_back(my_special_type&&)`, allowing the move constructor to be used rather than the copy constructor. But we can go even further by using `emplace_back`:

```
void accumulate_mst(std::vector<my_special_type>& vec_mst,
                    std::vector<int> const& source) {
  auto source_it = source.begin();
  while (source_it != source.end()) {
    auto s_it = source_it++;
    vec_mst.emplace_back(*s_it, *s_it);
  }
}
```

Declaring at point of use improves readability of code, and not declaring state at all improves things even further. Reasoning about state requires a comprehensive memory, which is a diminishing asset as codebases expand.

We have eliminated some state from the function. Now, you may think that you have improved the performance of your program by doing this. However, each of those functions does the same thing, and the compiler will probably generate the same assembly for each. In the first example the compiler can see that the instance of `my_special_type` does not persist beyond the `while` loop, and so is able to invoke `push_back(my_special_type&&)` rather than `push_back(my_special_type const&)`. In the third function we are delaying the construction still further, but this is simply a case of moving the location of the copy elision. The object will be constructed once, in the correct place, thanks to copy elision. In fact, `emplace_back` is more expensive to compile than `push_back`: it is a class template member function template rather than a class template member function. This may have an impact on your decision to use it.

These examples assume that the move constructor and the copy constructor have been defaulted and are trivial. If there is no move constructor, or it is costly to execute, then you might consider using `emplace_back`. By default, though, use `push_back` and construct in place.

Summary

You might be asking yourself, "Well, if they all generate the same code, what's the difference? Why should I choose one of these over another?" The answer is that this guideline is not about performance, but about maintenance. Declaring at point of use improves readability of code, and not declaring state at all improves things even further. Reasoning about state requires a comprehensive memory, which is a diminishing asset as codebases expand.

Delaying declaration as late as possible carries several benefits. Unnecessary state can be reduced or even eliminated. Scope is minimized. Objects are not used prior to initialization. Readability is improved. All of this adds up to improved safety and, occasionally, improved performance characteristics. I think this is a golden rule to be followed as far as possible.

Chapter 5.5

Per.7: Design to enable optimization

Maximizing the frame rate

I make games for a living. More precisely, nowadays I help to make games for a living, as I work on a team of several hundred people, all with different areas of expertise. Besides the animators, artists, audio engineers, QA, and production folk, there is a large team of engineers.

It was not always like this. I used to make games single-handed in the 1980s, and games would live or die by their frame rate. In the UK, home computers would use the family PAL TV set for display, attached to a 50Hz electricity supply. CRT displays produced an interlaced image on alternate frames, so you would aim to run your entire game loop in 40 milliseconds, producing 25 frames each second.

This was an immovable number, bound by the laws of physics, or at least by domestic electricity supply. I developed for the Sinclair ZX Spectrum, which ran on a Z80 processor. I knew how many microseconds each instruction would take to execute. Through careful bookkeeping I knew how many scan lines would be swept during each chunk (I hesitate to use the word "function"). When I got to 625, I knew my time was up.

Of course, any notion of selling to the US market was impossible. Electricity was supplied at 60Hz, but the processor ran at the same speed. There was less time to do things, and I would have to cut features to achieve the higher frame rate. One advantage of the rise of high-definition TV was the consistency of resolution and frame rate: 1920 x 1080 pixels at 60Hz. Unfortunately, with the market fractured again between 4KTV and HDTV this period of consistency has ended. It is to be hoped that the hardware arms race will settle at 4K.

Returning to video game development in the 1980s, the process of optimization meant one thing, and one thing only: faster execution in less space. There was no optimizing just for speed: a fixed amount of RAM meant that loop unrolling was robbing Peter to pay Paul. Similarly, optimizing just for size would mean increasing the amount of time it took to display a frame.

Frequent tricks included hand-specified inlining. Once a function had been written and debugged, you could decide yourself whether to make the function call or to insert the code into the call site instead. Armed with the knowledge of how long each instruction would take to execute, and how much RAM this substitution would cost, this could be a very precise way of finding speed gains.

This substitution differs from loop unrolling. With unrolling, the body of the loop is duplicated one or more times to reduce the number of jumps back to the start of the loop. This carries costs in space of course. However, substituting a function body for a function call could sometimes save space, since the effort required to call a function in terms of preserving registers could be eliminated by simply duplicating the function.

Stack manipulation was a particular favorite. When the processor encounters a call instruction rather than a jump instruction, it stores the program counter on the stack and changes the program counter to the call operand. When the processor encounters a return instruction, it pops the stack contents into the program counter. While this perfectly supports the idea of single point of entry, single point of return, it can be beautifully subverted to create jump tables. If you know a selection of functions must execute in a particular order, you could push their addresses onto the stack in reverse order of desired execution and then return. Each function would execute, and "return" to the next function in the stack. It was a valuable space saver, but fiendishly hard to debug and completely nonportable.

I found optimization to be the funnest part of making games. You could chip away at it until you decided that you had simply reached the end of the line, and you would declare your function optimal. Optimization relied upon a deep and intimate knowledge of the platform. When I was working with the Z80 processor I had to know that the register-loading instructions lay between 0x40 and 0x7f, and that the conditional return instructions started 0xc, 0xd, 0xe, or 0xf and ended 0x0 or 0x8, and that the xor instructions ran from 0xA8 to 0xAF, in the order b, c, d, e, h, l, (hl), a.

Working further from the metal

Things are different for me now. C++ takes me very close to the metal, but not on the metal. The compiler bridges that gap and embodies all the detailed knowledge that I used to have about the Z80 processor. In my current case that knowledge concerns the x86-64 architecture, which encompasses multiple processors. I cannot hope to acquire the necessary detail on my own. This is one of the reasons for moving to C++.

There is an art to optimization, but there is also an art to developing code that can be optimized well. You cannot optimize code that is utterly inflexible, and optimized code will often end up in this state. Optimizable code leaves options for the optimizer, be that a human or a compiler. Code that can be optimized is code with options to change things. Indeed, the words "optimize" and "option" both have the same Latin root, *optare*, "to choose."

Engineers tend to optimize code in two ways, either by improving the design or by improving the performance. Improving the design means improving the comprehensibility and reusability of the code or responding to refinements to the requirements. Improving the performance means giving the compiler the greatest amount of information about what it is that you want to do and the greatest range of options to improve the performance.

The Core Guidelines page offers a good example from the C standard, which we reproduce here:

```
void qsort(void* base, size_t num, size_t size,
           int(*comp)(const void*, const void*));
```

This function takes a pointer to some memory, the number of things you want to sort, the size of the things you want to sort, and a function for ordering the things you want to sort.

Let's start with optimizing the design of this function. The first problem is that we seem to be sorting memory rather than sorting things. This is the wrong level of abstraction. If you're going to name a function "sort," then the implication is that you will be sorting things. The idea of sorting memory is meaningless. Also, by taking a `void*`, the function is discarding information known at the call site: the type of object.

We can fix this immediately by jumping to C++ and exchanging the `void*` for a template parameter:

```
template <typename T>
void sort(T* base, size_t num, size_t size,
            int(*comp)(const T*, const T*));
```

This optimization improves the design by catching a typical error at compile time rather than runtime: passing a nonsensical comparison function. A `void*` can point to anything at all, while a `T*` must point to an instance of `T`. If you had a set of floating-point values that you wanted to sort, and your comparison function sorted characters, a call to `sort` may yield the wrong result.

Next, consider the two size_t parameters. First, they are an accident waiting to happen. The client must take care to pass these parameters in the correct order; they will get no warning from the compiler if they get this wrong. However, the size parameter is now redundant. Since the type being sorted is now part of the function signature, the size is known at compile time. The signature now looks like this:

```
template <typename T>
void sort(T* base, size_t num, int(*comp)(const T*, const T*));
```

Specializing the function over the type gives the compiler more information. There may be optimizations available if the total volume of memory occupied by the objects being sorted is less than, for example, the size of the L1 cache.

The final parameter is a function pointer. This is a callback function. The sort function will invoke this when it needs to decide the order of two objects. Optimizations are hard to come by here, but since sort is now a function template, it is reasonable to hope that the function will be instantiated at compile time. If the callback function definition is visible to the sort function, it may be inlined into the function template specialization.

There is a better solution, which is to make the callback function a template parameter. Consider this signature:

```
template <typename T, typename F>
void sort(T* base, size_t num, F fn);
```

There are going to be some restrictions on F. It needs to be invocable, taking two T*s and returning a negative integer value if the first argument precedes the second, zero if they are equal, and a positive integer value otherwise. After all, this is what the original function pointer did. However, we can now pass a lambda function rather than a function pointer, which makes inlining much more likely. We can also pass a std::function object, or even a member function pointer.

Of course, since we know that values will be passed to this function, we can usefully constrain the function still further and take a pair of T const&s, allowing a broader range of functions to be passed and eliminating the need to test for null pointers. This is yet more information for the compiler to work with, and yet more opportunity for optimization.

What next? Well, the first two parameters are now a little suspicious. The qsort function requires that the items being sorted lie in contiguous memory. This gives us a few advantages. First, we can simply pass a pair of iterators. In all probability, you are starting off with a pair of iterators anyway, and using std::distance to calculate the number of elements. Working at the correct level of abstraction, you should pass in the range of values you want to sort:

```
template <typename InIt, typename F>
void sort(InIt first, InIt last, F fn);
```

This is a safer spelling because you do not have to concern yourself with any arithmetic. You only need to tell the function what the ends of the range are. This provides a design optimization by reducing the opportunity for error, as well as a compilation optimization by announcing the addresses of the first and last elements, rather than requiring the compiler to emit code to calculate them. We can further improve the design by adding `requires` clauses now that we are in the brave new world of C++20. In fact, we can do even better than that and exchange the iterator pair for a range:

```
template <typename R, typename F>
void sort(R&& r, F fn);
```

Now we can add meaningful constraints, simplifying the design still further and giving the compiler yet more information, by using the `random_access_range` concept:

```
template <std::ranges::random_access_range R, typename F>
void sort(R&&, F fn);
```

As we are sure you have guessed by now, what we have done here is followed the evolution of `sort` from its pre-C++ incarnation to its C++20 incarnation. You can still find `qsort` in the standard library, but there is very little reason to use it outside of legacy environments. The function signature quoted above is not from the standard; ranges work with projections, which are beyond the scope of this chapter. For completeness, this is what one of the overloads looks like:

```
template <std::ranges::random_access_range R,
          typename Comp = std::ranges::less, typename Proj = std::identity>
requires std::sortable<std::ranges::iterator_t<R>, Comp, Proj>
constexpr std::ranges::borrowed_iterator_t<R>
sort(R&& r, Comp comp={}, Proj proj={});
```

This function:

- Takes a range, a comparison function, and a projection
- Requires that the range can be sorted with instances of the supplied types
- Is a `constexpr` function
- Returns an iterator to the final element

This function also gives the compiler much more information than `qsort` and enables a clearer call site.

However, you may look at that fistful of characters and contemplate the considerable increase in the size of the declaration. You will, unfortunately, also experience an increase in compilation time. Rather than, as with `qsort`, simply inserting a function call at the call site, the compiler will first infer the template parameters, ratify the constraints, instantiate then optimize the function template, and consider the value of inlining. You are exchanging run-time execution for compile-time execution.

Making things faster takes time. Spend that time: it is a wise investment. Be prepared to change your designs to facilitate performance improvements. However, don't dive in with the virtual stopwatch combing through every function. Let's first establish if you need to make that investment.

Optimization through abstraction

Recall the title of this chapter: "Design to enable optimization." The set of steps just taken could just as well have been included in a chapter on abstraction. Not only did we potentially improve the performance characteristics of the function, but we also improved the abstraction of the function, and these two phenomena will often appear together. But the question must be asked: was this optimization premature?

During the 1990s, "premature optimization is the root of all evil" was a warning I heard very often. Usually, it was uttered when someone spent time hand-optimizing a function before the requirements had stabilized. The phrase itself is attributed to either Donald Knuth or Tony Hoare: one may have been quoting the other. Both are remarkable computer scientists; we would go so far as to say legendary, the giants on whose shoulders we stand. Hoare invented quicksort. Knuth invented TeX. We need to pay attention to what they say, but we also need to understand what they say, and know when the phrase is being misapplied.

In "Structured Programming with `go to` Statements," published in *Computing Surveys,* Volume 6, Number 4, December 1974, Donald Knuth writes:

"There is no doubt that the grail of efficiency leads to abuse. Programmers waste enormous amounts of time thinking about, or worrying about, the speed of noncritical parts of their programs, and these attempts at efficiency actually have a strong negative impact when debugging and maintenance are considered. We should forget about small efficiencies, say about 97% of the time: premature optimization is the root of all evil.

"Yet we should not pass up our opportunities in that critical 3%. A good programmer will not be lulled into complacency by such reasoning, he will be wise to look carefully at the critical code; but only after that code has been identified. It is often a mistake to make a priori judgments about what parts of a program are really critical, since the universal experience of programmers who have been using measurement tools has been that their intuitive guesses fail. After working with such tools for seven years, I've become convinced that all compilers written from now on should be designed to provide all programmers with feedback indicating what parts of their programs are costing the most; indeed, this feedback should be supplied automatically unless it has been specifically turned off."

A common misapplication derives from the Pareto Principle, which suggests that 80 percent of execution time will occur in 20 percent of the code. This being the case, the time to optimize is at the end of development, when that 20 percent can be identified. However, if that 20 percent is diffused throughout the source, then safe modification is going to be all but impossible. Additionally, as Knuth suggests, it is extremely hard to look at a program and estimate the location of the performance hot spots. This demotivates an engineer from improving sections of code because they cannot tell that spending time on a particular section will have an impact on performance.

Optimization should take place along with refactoring as requirements stabilize. Program-wide optimization is a fool's errand. Choosing the right algorithm will impact performance to the greatest degree and making your code amenable to algorithm substitution will enable optimization. There was a time when you could simply wait for the CPU to get faster, but that time has long gone.

Consider what the "3%" figure means: that is three lines of code in each one hundred. How long are your functions? There is a good chance that your short five-line functions are in good order, but it is the longer functions that benefit from closer inspection. The best optimizations you can make are those that improve the clarity of what you are doing and maximize the information you give to the compiler, such as swapping your hand-rolled loops for existing algorithms.

Returning to the `sort` example, one difference between `qsort` and `std::ranges::sort` is the return type. Rather than returning `void` as `qsort` does, `std::ranges::sort` returns an iterator equal to the end of the range. It is not necessary, but it is useful in some cases. One way of designing to enable optimization is to provide a family of functions with different amounts of information being returned, all implemented using the same fundamental algorithm.

The standard algorithms support this. The function `std::is_sorted` takes a range and a comparison function, and returns a `bool` telling you whether or not the elements are sorted. `std::is_sorted_until` returns the iterator at which point a range stops being sorted. `std::is_sorted` could be implemented as a call to `std::is_sorted_until` and a check on whether the return value is the end of the range.

Similarly, `std::mismatch` compares two ranges, searching for the first corresponding pair of elements that don't satisfy a predicate. `std::equal` is a specialization of this: the predicate is the equality operator, and if `std::mismatch` returns the end of the range, then the ranges are equal.

What this demonstrates is a pair of functions that support a single idea, but which operate at different levels of abstraction. You can choose the correct function for the level at which you are working, and by doing so you are offering the compiler neither more nor less than what it needs to know about the task at hand to generate optimal code.

Summary

Optimization is something that the compiler is best placed to do. You may have an idea about the sort of code that will be generated from your source, but it is the compiler that will actually do the job. Signaling your intentions to the compiler, as fully and precisely as possible, is the key to getting the most out of it.

Focus on designing your interfaces for composition. As you develop a function, ask yourself if the parts that make it up could be expressed as individual functions that may have some subsidiary use. Hand optimization is not the only way to improve your code and is most likely premature optimization. Careful composition of functions and correct generalization will support superior optimization opportunities.

Everything has a cost. You may be aware of how many nanoseconds a CPU instruction takes, how many microseconds a thread context switch takes, how many milliseconds it takes to send a 1KB buffer halfway around the world, and so on. Comparison between magnitudes will serve you better than comparison across magnitudes. Leave the intra-magnitude work to the compiler.

Chapter 5.6

E.6: Use RAII to prevent leaks

Deterministic destruction

We have waxed lyrical about deterministic destruction already in this text, but it bears repeating that it is the single greatest feature of C++. Unfortunately, we have a small problem with object storage duration.

There are four classes of storage duration. An object with static storage duration will be created prior to execution of `main()` and be destroyed after `main()` returns. An object with automatic storage duration will be created as soon as it is declared and be destroyed the moment its name falls out of scope. An object with thread-local storage duration will be created when a thread begins and be destroyed when the thread ends.

Dynamic storage duration implies user-specified behavior. An object with dynamic storage duration will be created using the `new` operator and destroyed using the `delete` operator. These operators are part of the source code, written by the user. This means it is vulnerable to error. There are two types of error: using an object after it has been destroyed and losing an object entirely (by forgetting to use `delete`). It is the latter error that concerns us here. Losing an object is known as leaking.

Here is the simplest possible leak:

```
#include <vector>
int main() {
  new std::vector<int>;
}
```

This is perfectly legal code. I've just tried it on Compiler Explorer with several compilers and they all compile without warning. On execution, the `new` operator will call `std::operator new`, requesting the amount of memory required to create an instance of `std::vector<int>`, usually three words. This memory will be allocated and returned to the `new` operator, which will then call the `std::vector<int>` default constructor to populate those three words. Then `main()` will exit.

The object was not bound to a name. It did not need to be. The `new` operator did its work as instructed. By not binding the result of the `new` operator to a name, it could not be deleted, so the leak was immediate. The memory was not freed automatically when `main()` exited, although it is most likely that the operating system performed appropriate cleanup when the process ended. It will not have invoked any destructors, but it will have reclaimed the memory.

Here is the next simplest leak:

```
#include <vector>
int main() {
  auto vi = new std::vector<int>;
}
```

As you can see, we bound the result of the `new` operator to a name. Unfortunately, the name fell out of scope before we deleted the object. The thing that was destroyed when that name fell out of scope was not the `std::vector<int>` object, but a pointer to it. The type of `vi` is `std::vector<int>*` and when such an object falls out of scope, the object pointed to is not destroyed, only the pointer itself.

This was a remarkably common problem prior to C++11 when smart pointers were introduced. Now we could say:

```
#include <vector>
#include <memory>
int main() {
  auto vi = std::unique_ptr<std::vector<int>>(new std::vector<int>);
}
```

This is rather a mouthful. Since the introduction of `std::make_unique` in C++14 we have been able to say:

```
#include <vector>
#include <memory>
int main() {
  auto vi = std::make_unique<std::vector<int>>();
}
```

Rather clearer, we hope you agree. The type of `vi` is no longer `std::vector<int>*`. It is now an object of type `std::unique_ptr<std::vector<int>>`.

The life cycle of `vi` is rather different now. Rather than being initialized with a memory address at creation and simply ceasing to be when the name falls out of scope, it is initialized not only with the memory address but also instructions on how to destroy the object. When `vi` falls out of scope, it invokes the destructor of the object it is bound to, which in turn destroys the `std::vector<int>` object.

This idiom, where the creation of an object also includes details of how to destroy it, is known as Resource Acquisition Is Initialization, or RAII. The life cycle of the memory is bound to the lifetime of an object. This phrase was coined by Bjarne Stroustrup and first appeared in his book *The C++ Programming Language*.

The concept of RAII is an extremely useful benefit of the destructor. It is not only applicable to memory, but also to any resource that has a life cycle that needs to be explicitly managed. We shall spend the rest of this chapter looking at an example.

We should remark that the earlier examples were manufactured to demonstrate memory leaks. All those examples could have been fixed by creating the vector on the stack, giving the object automatic storage duration.

You should always prefer automatic storage duration to dynamic storage duration. You only need to use dynamic storage duration when you are creating objects whose lifetime must persist beyond the current scope. If you are reasonably new to C++ it is to be hoped that this is a little startling and somewhat curious. You may never have been introduced to the `new` operator and will always have used smart pointers to create large objects which can be cheaply passed around. You might have been told that you avoid memory leaks by avoiding the use of raw pointers. However, a memory leak is not the only kind of leak.

Leaking away files

Windows programmers will be familiar with the function `CreateFile`. This function creates or opens a file or I/O device and returns a handle to that object. That handle is of type `HANDLE` which is an alias to a `void*`. The handle is used with all function calls involving the file: `ReadFile`, `WriteFile`, `SetFilePointer`, and so on. When the object is no longer needed, a call to `CloseHandle` will release the resource back to the operating system.

The same is true for file handling in the standard library. If you choose to avoid the streams library, the function `std::fopen` creates or opens a file or I/O device and returns a pointer to an implementation-defined type called `FILE`. This pointer is used with all function calls involving the file: `std::fread`, `std::fwrite`, `std::fseek`, and so on. When the object is no longer needed, a call to `std::fclose` will release the resource back to the operating system.

You can see a very similar set of operations here. `std::fread` takes the `FILE` pointer as the final argument while `ReadFile` takes it as the first argument, and `std::fread` reads a number of objects of a given size while `ReadFile` reads a number of bytes, but the principle is the same: here is a handle, given by the operating system, for you to use while you engage in file manipulation.

These handles can leak, just as memory does. Returning to our example, here is the simplest possible leak:

```
#include <cstdio>
int main() {
  std::fopen("output.txt", "r");
}
```

`std::fopen` returns a `FILE*` which is not bound to a name and simply leaks away. We can repeat the second example too:

```
#include <cstdio>
int main() {
  auto file = std::fopen("output.txt", "r");
}
```

The `FILE` still leaks away. In this example it was bound to a name but `std::fclose` wasn't called to release the resource back to the operating system.

Fortunately, the C++ Standard Library comes to the rescue with the iostreams library. This library offers a selection of objects with correctly managed life cycles. Just as `std::unique_ptr` releases the memory resource when it falls out of scope, so do the iostream library objects. For example:

```
#include <fstream>
int main()
{
  auto file = std::fstream{ "output.txt" };
}
```

To open a file, you pass a filename to a `std::fstream` object constructor. This will open the file, allow you to invoke member functions such as `read`, `write`, `seekp`, and `seekg`, and close the file when the destructor is invoked.

The iostreams library is not everyone's cup of tea. It is designed with abstract base classes, burdening it with performance inefficiencies. It is a library of its time, that time being the early 1990s. We have learned many things about C++ library design since then, such as the value of composition, and were we to start again I imagine we would take a different approach. It is still a perfectly good library that delivers what it promises, but many programmers are tempted to take their own approach and write their own file-handling library from scratch.

There are easier ways to solve the problem of leaking files. One is to create an object like a `std::unique_ptr`, but rather than holding a pointer to memory, it holds the file instead. For example:

```
#include <cstdio>
class FILE_holder {
public:
  FILE_holder(std::FILE* f) : m_f(f) {}
  ~FILE_holder() { std::fclose(m_f); }
  operator std::FILE*() { return m_f; }

private:
  std::FILE* m_f;
};

int main()
{
  auto file = FILE_holder(std::fopen("output.txt", "r"));
}
```

No leaks here. There is another problem of course: assigning away from this object may result in the object being closed prematurely. In fact, what we want is something exactly like `std::unique_ptr`, but for objects created via `std::fopen` rather than via the `new` operator.

Fortunately, the committee thought of that. `std::unique_ptr` is a class template with not one but two parameters. The first parameter is the type of the object being contained, while the second parameter is the deleter. The second parameter defaults to `std::default_delete`, a very simple object, with a constructor and a parenthesis operator. A naïve implementation might look like this:

```
template<class T>
struct default_delete {
  constexpr default_delete() noexcept = default;
  template<class U>
  default_delete(const default_delete<U>&) noexcept {}
  void operator()(T* p) const { delete p; }
};
```

Rather than writing your own delete and using it when making std::unique_ptr instances, you can specialize the template for std::FILE. It is simple, as demonstrated below:

```
#include <memory>
#include <cstdio>

template <>
struct std::default_delete<std::FILE> {
  void operator()(std::FILE* f) { std::fclose(f); }
};

int main()
{
  auto file = std::unique_ptr<std::FILE>(std::fopen("output.txt", "r"));
}
```

The specialization simply replaces the parenthesis operator with a call to std::fclose, rather than calling the delete operator. When file falls out of scope, the std::unique_ptr object containing the std::FILE* is destroyed, closing the std::FILE* object on its way to oblivion.

Why are we bothering?

Ideally, all your classes that are associated with any resources should have constructors and destructors that correctly manage the life cycle of those resources. As we saw with std::FILE* we have an escape hatch for nonconforming objects, but what do we do when our resource is not exposed as a pointer?

It might have occurred to you that we seem to be going to a lot of trouble here to clean up after ourselves when surely the operating system does all that for us. When a process terminates, all the handles associated with that process are closed, all the memory is released, and everything is left ready for reuse. Why do we care about resource leaks when the environment is going to take care of that for us anyway?

There are a few reasons. The first is that if you leak resources fast enough there will come a point where you will request a resource and the operating system will decline your request, warning you that there are none left of whatever it is you are requesting. This is especially likely if your program is long lived, designed to run for the entire uptime of the computer on which it is deployed.

Second, it is a good habit to get into. If you decide that cleaning up after yourself is optional, that means you have put a decision point into your development cycle. Every time you create something that may leak, you will need to spend time deciding whether to spend time working out how to prevent it from leaking. Be in the habit of always cleaning up after yourself.

Third, in the case of files specifically, on some operating systems if a running application keeps a file open, the user is prevented from modifying, moving, or deleting the file until the program ends. This can be a cause of significant irritation—sometimes even causing users to reboot their machines to delete an unwanted file.

Finally, it is not necessarily safe to presume that the operating system will do all the cleanup. If you are using a legacy third-party library, leaking resources may have long-term consequences. Consider this fragment:

```
int open_database(const char*);
void close_database(int);

int main()
{
  auto db = open_database("//network/customer.db");
}
```

There exists a database somewhere remote from your machine. This code opens a connection and then leaks it. The operating system knows nothing about how to clean up after this leak. With any luck, the database server is a well-written piece of software that will hand out a connection and close the connection if it remains unused within a timeout period. That is not a safe assumption to hold, though.

However, we cannot specialize `std::default_delete` since `open_database` does not return a pointer. You may be tempted to use `reinterpret_cast` to turn the `int` into a pointer, but that would earn you a hard stare at code review time since you are flat-out lying to the compiler. The correct solution is to create a proxy, like this:

```
#include <memory>

int open_database(const char*);
void close_database(int);

struct DATABASE_PROXY {
  DATABASE_PROXY(int db_) : db(db_) {}
  operator int() { return db; }
  int db;
};

template <>
struct std::default_delete<DATABASE_PROXY> {
  void operator()(DATABASE_PROXY* p) { close_database(*p); }
};
```

```
int main()
{
  auto db = std::unique_ptr<DATABASE_PROXY>
              (new DATABASE_PROXY(open_database("//network/customer.db")));
}
```

The DATABASE_PROXY class wraps the returned value, allowing you to allocate a copy from the free store and pass it to the std::unique_ptr constructor. This also works for objects larger than an int, although one would hope that if a struct is being returned from a function, appropriate resource management will be taking place as part of its design.

This all seems a bit much: Future possibilities

Creating a struct just to specialize std::default_delete seems like a disproportionately large chunk of work. However, this comes in the category of "dealing with legacy code." We have learned many things as a programming community over the past 40 years of C++ development, many of which we have carefully encoded into revisions of the language standard. There will always be a cost to accommodating code that seemed well written at the time, but which did not benefit from the discovery of subsequent idioms and practices.

For example, casting was a perfectly normal, acceptable way of dealing with conflicting types when writing C code. C++ strengthened the type system philosophically and practically with the introduction of casting keywords such as static_cast and reinterpret_cast, both of which are quite ugly and both of which serve to draw attention to the fact that you are subverting an important part of the language, to wit, type safety.

The contemporary way of modeling RAII is through correct use of the constructor and destructor. All resources should be acquired in the constructors, released in the destructor, and managed correctly in the assignment operators. The resources should be abstracted in their own class with their own correct special functions so that client classes are spared the burden of managing them. This promotes the rule of five or zero.

Looking to the future, though, there is more explicit support available in C++ Extensions for Library Fundamentals, Version 3,[1] at the section named [scopeguard]. This describes a header named <experimental/scope>, a name that will be modified should this feature be adopted into the standard, which offers four classes:

```
template <class EF> class scope_exit;
template <class EF> class scope_fail;
```

1. www.open-std.org/jtc1/sc22/wg21/docs/papers/2020/n4873.html

```
template <class EF> class scope_success;
template <class R, class D> class unique_resource;
```

The first three classes wrap a function object `EF` and invoke it on exiting the scope, while `std::experimental::unique_resource` is a universal RAII wrapper for resource handle `R` that owns and manages a resource, disposing of it via the deleter `D` when the `std::experimental::unique_resource` is destroyed.

The first three classes are useful for RAII within a single scope. There can be many ways to exit a scope if a function is egregiously long, and these classes ensure that however a scope is exited, cleanup can take place. If you want to differentiate between exceptional exit and successful exit, that option is available with `std::experimental::scope_fail` and `std::experimental::scope_success`. For example:

```
void grow(vector<int>& v) {
  std::experimental::scope_success guard([]{
    std::cout << "Good!" << std::endl; });
  v.resize(1024);
}
```

There are two ways out of this function: either `v.resize(1024)` is successful or it throws. The `std::experimental::scope_success` object will write to the standard output only if the resize is successful.

`std::experimental::unique_resource`[2] is very similar to `std::unique_ptr`. However, unlike `std::unique_ptr`, `std::experimental::unique_resource` does not require the resource to be a pointer.

Revisiting the `std::fopen` example:

```
#include <experimental/scope>
#include <cstdio>

int main()
{

  using std::experimental::unique_resource;
  auto file = unique_resource(
      std::fopen("output.txt", "r"),
      [](auto fp){ std::fclose(fp); });
}
```

2. The `std::experimental` namespace is used to keep experimental features approved by the C++ Standards Committee. Entities that start life here may end up in the `std` namespace if there is enough positive feedback.

There is a problem, though: what if `std::fopen` failed? We need a way of signaling an invalid value for the result of `std::fopen`, or indeed for any resource we want to wrap in this way.

There is also an analogue to the `std::make_unique` function template, with a somewhat verbose function signature:

```
template <class R, class D, class S=decay_t<R>>
std::experimental::unique_resource<decay_t<R>, decay_t<D>>
  std::experimental::make_unique_resource_checked
      (R&& resource, const S& invalid, D&& d)
  noexcept(std::is_nothrow_constructible_v<decay_t<R>, R> &&
           std::is_nothrow_constructible_v<decay_t<D>, D>);
```

This is a function template which takes a resource type, an invalid value for the resource type, and a deleter function object, returning a `std::experimental::unique_resource` object. If the resource matches the invalid value, then the deleter function object will not be invoked.

Here is how we would rewrite the `std::fopen` example:

```
#include <experimental/scope>
#include <cstdio>

int main()
{
  auto file = std::experimental::make_unique_resource_checked(
      std::fopen("potentially_nonexistent_file.txt", "r"),
      nullptr,
      [](auto fptr){ std::fclose(fptr); });
}
```

Walking through this example, we call `std::experimental::make_unique_resource_checked` with the result from `std::fopen`, with the intent of calling `std::fclose` if the file opens successfully. If the value returned by `std::fopen` is `nullptr`, then the call to `std::fclose` is avoided.

Where can I get this?

These are very useful tools for your toolbox. Unfortunately, they are not necessarily provided by your implementation vendor. My preferred vendor does not ship `<experimental/scope>`, although there are some entries in the experimental directory.

This does not stop you from implementing it yourself, though. The full specification is provided in the Technical Specification, linked to in an earlier footnote. Search for [scopeguard]; the tag in brackets is known as the stable index. There you will find a complete specification of how these four classes and the nonmember function should work. It should take you less than 15 minutes to read. It will take you less time than you think to implement.

There are three benefits to implementing it yourself. The primary benefit is that you can start using the objects, and if they are adopted into the standard, which is quite likely, you will need to make minimal changes to your source code. The secondary benefit is that you will start to learn how the standard is specified, and how to implement library features. The tertiary benefit is that if you encounter any mistakes or ambiguities in the Technical Specification, you can pass this information back to the editors and enable them to make fixes before it gets adopted into the standard. Once something is in the standard, fixing it is quite hard. It is, of course, preferable to spot all errors ahead of time, prior to deployment.

Finally, if you think this is a useful addition to the language, you should let the committee know and ask them to prioritize it for inclusion. Alternatively, if you think this is overengineered, overly elaborate, unnecessary, or not deserving of a place within the standard, you can also let the committee know by writing a paper presenting your arguments. The committee is made up of representatives from many nations and companies who volunteer their time to improve the C++ standard. They do what the rest of the world asks them to do, within the bounds of reasonable debate on desirability, feasibility, and achievement of consensus, to deliver the C++ standard that supports the needs of the C++ community. Be advised that progress can be glacial: getting agreement from over a hundred people from dozens of companies, industries, and countries is a slow process.

It is important to stress the voluntary nature of this work. There is no membership test, no private invitation, no secret handshake: participation is achieved simply by turning up to committee meetings and helping the process along. A code of conduct moderates all behavior and keeps proceedings open and transparent.

There are several routes to participation. In my case, as a UK resident, I contacted the British Standards Institute and requested details about joining the BSI C++ panel. (In Canada, where Kate lives, it's the Standards Council of Canada you contact. In the US it is INCITS.) Each country has its own name for its National Standards Development Organization (SDO), as well as its own cost structure with some being free to participate and others charging a membership fee. You may be able to contact your own standards institute and make inquiries. Even if you don't want to participate in full, you should be able to make your views known to your national body.

Not every country in the world is represented in the C++ committee, but new countries are always welcome, and formal participation can be initiated and undertaken by anyone who is prepared to engage with their own nation's standards body.

Sometimes one person can simply bring a national body into being. In 2017 Hana Dusíková visited CppCon and gave a lightning talk about a Compile Time Regular Expression parser she had developed. She caught the attention of several committee regulars, went on to form and convene the Czech national body, and now chairs Study Group 7, Reflection.

You can find out more about the standardization process by visiting http://isocpp.org/std. There, you can find out how to contact your national body, how to participate in standards development and in committee meetings, how to report defects, and how to submit proposals. You can also find the standing documents that describe How Things Are Done. You can see this page for the ISO Programming Language committee: https://www.iso.org/committee/45202.html. Under the link for Participating Members on this page, you will see which country has participation, the SDO names of each country, and their participation status. In particular, P-members have voting rights and O-members do not. If your country is not on the list, then either your country has no SDO, or the SDO did not join this ISO Standards Committee. Now you will know how much work you have in front of you.

Engaging with the committee and shaping the standard will help C++ continue to be the language you reach for to solve your software engineering problems.

Envoi

When Kate and I started to develop this book, I did not know what would be revealed to me along the way. Part of the fun of writing is discovering what it is you don't quite know. In my day job as Head of Engineering Practice at Creative Assembly I frequently write short posts about how to use a language or library feature, and the process of clarifying it in writing forces a greater clarification in my mind.

Writing ninety thousand words rather than a thousand has magnified this experience greatly. The one thing I will take away from this book is the primary importance of abstraction and of working at the correct level of abstraction. Many of the guidelines can be viewed as advisories in the service of improving abstraction. At the end of Chapter 5.3 I listed a few.

Another part of my day job is interviewing fresh university graduates who seek to join our graduate programmer initiative. In the early days of learning C++, the student will typically focus on writing functions that conditionally read and write state from objects in the program. They will treat classes as vessels for storing state, rather than abstractions formed from invariants.

It is my fervent hope that, having read this book, you will focus more on the idea of a program being a set of small abstractions that model the problem at hand, and less on the idea of a program being a scripted sequence of actions. C++ is characterized as a blend of zero-overhead abstraction facilities and bare-metal performance opportunities. If you only take advantage of the performance opportunities and discard the abstraction facilities, your code will be hard to maintain and difficult to incorporate into other codebases.

I also hope that your interest has been piqued regarding the remaining Core Guidelines. As the language grows, so must the guidelines, and the authors welcome pull requests with improvements and evidence. Similarly, I hope you are motivated to look more closely at the development of the C++ standard, perhaps even to participate in language or library development.

With the creation of the C++ Foundation, the C++ community has burst into life over the past decade, culminating in the delivery of C++20, the biggest update to the language in its history. This would not have happened without the steady growth of the community via conferences, meetups, and blogs. I love this language and greatly enjoy solving problems with it. Therefore, my final hope is that you will increase your participation in this community and share what you have learned with all of us, for this is how communities sustain and grow.

Cheers,
G

Afterword

"Beautiful C++" is not only a catchy title, but my own personal goal and what I appreciate (and hope for) the most in C++'s evolution. While it's true that C++ is complex, writing C++ in a modern style already yields much cleaner—and yes, more beautiful—code than writing it in older C++98 or "C with Classes" styles.

But what does it mean to write C++ in a modern style? Documenting the answer to that question in one authoritative place was one of the major reasons Bjarne Stroustrup and I created the C++ Core Guidelines—including designing them with Enforcements so that you can optionally ask static analysis tools to help you stay in the "modern style" of C++ code. The guidelines are necessarily organized like an encyclopedia—a reference work you can use to look up the reasons for any of a comprehensive set of things. What makes a good encyclopedia, however, makes a terrible textbook or novel that can be easily read front to back.

Beautiful C++ shines in distilling an essence of key guidelines, and presenting that essence in a way that tells the modern C++ story. Kate and Guy have delivered a delightfully readable narrative where each chapter builds the plot further and takes us, the readers, on an enjoyable, illuminating, and satisfying journey. Now that you've enjoyed reading this book, you likely appreciate as much as I do how they have infused this set of guidelines with their own deep expertise and experience. They understand how, as C++ has evolved and grown, many of the added features really do let us make our C++ code simpler to read, write, and maintain because they let us directly express what we intend to do. That leads to code that's beautiful—and it's readable, maintainable, robust, and professional too.

As Bjarne Stroustrup has said for decades, inside C++ is a small, elegant language struggling to get out. Using C++ in a modern way is today's major step toward experiencing writing in that small, elegant language. As C++ continues to evolve in the future, I hope it will continue to grow in ways that make "C++ as she is spoke" in modern code ever more beautiful still.

—Herb Sutter
June 2021

Index

A

B

C

D

E

F

G

M

Q

R

S

T